My Other Body

a memoir of love, fat, life, and death

ANN PAI

Sunspot Press ❖ Overland Park, Kansas

Author's Note: This is a work of memory. It includes accounts of the unfailing care and compassion shown to my family by a number of doctors and nurses. To the medical and administrative staff who provided care to my sister, I and my family are eternally grateful. These accounts of their work are from memory by a writer untrained in medicine, and as such should not be read as professional assessments. This work is not intended and should not be used as a medical reference. Many names and personal characteristics have been changed.

Sunspot Press
Visit the web site at www.sunspotpress.com

10 9 8 7 6 5 4 3 2 1

Pai, Ann, 1967-
    My other body : a memoir of love, fat, life, and
death / Ann Pai. -- 1st ed.
        p. cm.
    LCCN 2005908790
    ISBN-13: 978-0-9772045-0-2
    ISBN-10: 0-9772045-0-2

    1. Pai, Ann, 1967- 2. Vandiver, Joyce M., 1962-2001.
    3. Overweight women--United States--Biography.
    4. Sisters--Death. 5. Sisters--Family relationships.
    6. Compulsive eating. 7. Obesity--Psychological aspects.
    I. Title.

RC552.O25P34 2006   362.196'398'0092
                    QBI05-600188

For Adrian Thompson,
  with love

PART ONE: THE CALL

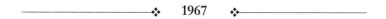

————————————— ❖ 1967 ❖ —————————————

Joyce is four and a half years old, in short play dresses and a pixie cut but already commander of her blue-gray gaze, its sternness and amusement, when I am born in springtime. Though my infant bed is moved into her room, the room remains her room until I have learned both her name and that our parents sleep elsewhere. Then the mantle of secrecy is spread over me, and the bedroom becomes, through eighteen years, four moves, and four small bedrooms, until she leaves for college, our shared skin.

Joyce saves the stories of my babyhood the way Mama hides linen company napkins. Safe in dark cedar, they require purposeful retrieval. On a sunny afternoon when we have been sent to nap but instead sit on my quilted bedspread, dressing our largest dolls, Joyce will tell me the first of the tales from when she was the only child.

She tells me that before I was born, I was all that Mama and Daddy talked about. "Every night, 'What do we name the baby? What do we name the baby?' All the time. Arrrrr! Finally I jumped up and yelled, 'Who cares! Name her Hippopotamus! Big Hippopotamus!'"

She tells me that Mama caught her standing over my crib with the billy club that our Uncle Harold gave her. Mama took the club away and went to see Uncle Harold with it. "Were you going to hit me?" I ask.

"Probably," she says, and shrugs. "Yes, I was."

My belly feels light. When she tells this story, I'm light as a sparrow, and not the sparrow hampered under God's humongous, platelike eye, but one buoyed in first flight. For Joyce is a pincher as well as a slugger. She never tips her hand, never forewarns. She sneaks up and pops you on the shoulder blade, pow! Or grabs and twists your tricep between her thumb and forefinger. So when she tells this story, I conclude she's my protectress. She can be none other than a vigilant force with sympathetic recognition of the sorts of people who might want to brain me with a club. If she meant to be one of those people, she never would have let me see it coming. "Tell it again," I ask her sometimes when we're going to sleep.

And Joyce tells me, "We had another brother."

I flail on the edge of a stopped breath; I try not to move, not to stir the hem of my dress.

"His name was Robert. He died in the hospital. I was already born."

"Was I born?" I ask.

"You weren't born," she says. "You came after Robert."

"Where is he now?"

"He died," she says. "But don't tell Mama and Daddy you know. It makes them sad to think about him."

"Okay," I say.

"If I ever know any more about that I'll tell you," she says. She arranges her walking doll's arms in an upturned V, a hurrah.

September 11, 2001, and the news fireworked, cubicle to cubicle. Software development, technical documentation, hardware production, accounting, middle management—ridiculous to name our jobs in the face of it—all shrank from consequence. Comfortable life receded and popped like the power-off blip of television light. We, in the affluent Kansas City suburbs, were helplessly far from dust and blood but only as far from the unfolding sickness as our eyes from our 19-inch monitors. We rode close to other Americans in shock and fear, in our suddenly denuded ignorance of danger.

It was only just becoming real. A plane into one tower. A plane into the second tower. The first tower crumbled. A plane into the Pentagon. The second tower crumbled. I turned to Kerri, who was typing with angry athleticism as though wrestling a door closed, blocking out pitches of alarm. I talked to the back of her blonde head, to her casual ponytail. "All the people," I said, "all those people." Crushed and dead. Clearly, thousands. A plane into the Pentagon?

"Oh, sweet Lord," I said. I grabbed at the phone and dialed for a long distance line, my parents' home number. Rural Oklahoma. Did they know?

"Are you okay?" Kerri asked. We shared a tiny office. If we backed our chairs up at the same time, we collided. Dissimilar at first glance—me, soft-faced, serious, slow to move, and Kerri, fidgety, bubbly, with a runner's strength and compact looseness—we finished one another's sentences, shared hoarded chocolate, bickered over our profession's trivia as though attempting rescue of each other's hapless souls. Our conversations were a rambling, companionable egg-hunt for common oddities.

"My brother might be at the Pentagon," I said. Hunter was processing his discharge papers this week, leaving Fort Meade and his security assignment. He could be there.

Kerri nodded. She reprised her assault on the keyboard, but occasionally turned her head in profile, listening without fingerprinting our dignity, as though it were possible she merely glanced at hallway passersby.

My parents' phone rang and kept ringing. The answering machine kicked on. I hung up and began to dial again. Between abortive calls, I babysat my pulse, tried to pacify its howling. I sifted my task list and sorted papers, discarding early project drafts. Fruitlessly, yet grateful for the fruitlessness, I tried to find more slow-downloading news. And the phone kept ringing. Danger, oddness—in the mornings my parents and sister always were home. At ten-thirty, Mama answered the phone.

"Where's Hunter?" I asked. It was no time for preludes.

"They're fine," she said. "They left Fort Meade. They're already on their way here. But I need to go now. We're taking Joyce to the hospital."

"Mama? What's happened?"

"We have to go." Her voice bent on the words, as when a child lied to her, as when she had a migraine, as when her father died. She hung up.

"All right," I said into the closed connection. Behind me, the typing ceased. Kerri swiveled her chair. She leaned forward with a veterinary, competitive care, gauging my posture, clearing her face of distracted expression, readying for response.

"They're taking my sister to the hospital," I said. I rattled the receiver back into its cradle.

"Oh, my God," she said. "What happened?"

"My mother didn't say," I said. Hypnotic logic marched out, in the mouth more like a recitation than thought, like a psalm that must be said to the end if one's to get the gold sticker. "So here," I said. "Here's how it is. If they came home and found she couldn't move, they wouldn't be able to lift her. So either she was out with them or she was home and mobile. If she were home, able to move, and sick enough to go to the hospital, she would have answered the phone to ask for help. So she was out with them, in town, in Muskogee. If she needed trauma care they wouldn't have come home. They would have taken her to the emergency room in Muskogee. So they're taking her to the hospital in Tulsa. An hour away. That's right. They would have called my aunt before they left."

The probable truth snapped into place, along with a horror of having wasted time in finding it. "I have to go. Call my aunt. I think—I might have to get there fast."

"Do you want me to tell Dean?"

"Yeah. Could you?"

"Just go," she said. "Wrap it up and get out of here. I'll let people know."

"If I'm right," I said, "it's really serious. You know."

"I know," said Kerri. "Go."

And planes were falling and buildings collapsing and people jumping, on fire. I grabbed notebooks and documents to edit, thinking of waiting rooms and of long nights outside the veil of visiting hours.

She wakes from her dream into her fat, the way yeast wakes inside dough. Dreaming, she had no gravity, no hesitancy. Awake, she rolls herself upright. The pads of her feet flatten on the hardwood, and the flabby zones of her body—the fat wing under her chin, the fat clots under her arms—sway and settle. The downward cascade of her abdominal fat is as much a part of every morning as the toothbrush or the weather check, as much and as little acknowledged.

Strange to be home in mid-morning. The cats circled round, mewling and rubbing my ankles. I called Aunt LaNita, my father's younger sister, the family's hypersensile antenna. LaNita claimed never to have aged past twenty-four. She understood the importance of an immaculately clean house, an ice-cream cake, a returned phone call. She kept, through the motherhood of four children, through the decline and atrophy of a husband who had once managed all life's practical details and into her artlessly denied age, a girl's giggle, a girl's breadth of possibility, an eager conversation. She constantly juggled in her throaty soprano a naughty, gleeful laugh and a trimly girdled practicality.

"Have you talked to your parents?" she asked.

"Mm. They didn't tell me anything."

"Huh," she said. She sighed, short and sharp, and I pictured her shaking her brushy brown curls. "Joyce is in St. John hospital in Tulsa," she said. "Ann, they took her to the doctor this morning. The doctor didn't look at her very long at all, evidently, and he told your mom and dad that she was really, really sick. Her color's yellow, and she says she hasn't been able to eat anything for days. Ann, she said that when she tried to eat, her food tasted like urine. That's not good."

"Can I call her at the hospital?" I asked. LaNita's husband, my uncle Troy, had stayed at St. John that year, in the late stages of the merciless wasting disease ALS. In the even later stages of ALS he was now at home, but LaNita still knew the St. John numbers by heart.

With the phone wedged between shoulder and ear, I tipped my paisley-print, leather-trimmed bag off the top closet shelf, then pilfered the dresser drawers for knit clothing. St. John's emergency connected me with Joyce. She sounded as though she were surrounded by people, by doors opening and closing, by rustling movements as of sheets being folded, plastic trays being stacked.

"Joyce," I said. "Are you okay?"

"No," she said, her glassine voice clear of the phlegm of sleep or tears. "Ann, something's really wrong."

"It's going to be okay," I told her. "Are Mama and Daddy there?"

"No," she said.

"Do you know where they are?"

"No," she said.

Her voice drew in on itself, like a child hiding under blankets. Her words crept out slowly. "Ann, I can't eat," she said. "I knew last week something was wrong with me, but I wanted to wait. Ann—I can't eat anything." Her voice quavered. "And you know I never pass up a meal."

Her breath, thick and sobless, registered the force with which she wasn't crying. She repulsed crying as though defending a barricade. A flood of words roared through brain canals and logjammed in the alcove of my mouth. (My baby, my baby is scared, she is so scared. My arms around you, let me. I love you. Don't blame yourself. Even if you're right don't let your heart break. Please hang on.) The words rushed onward into oblivion, unspoken.

"Joyce," I said. "Listen to me. I'm coming there."

"When?" she asked. A single, verbless half-note of trust reverberated down a tunnel of time, of typical, cynical replies.

"It'll take me about five hours," I said. "I'll be there tonight."

"Okay," she said.

"I love you," I said.

"I love you too," she said.

"I'll see you soon."

"Okay," she said, "goodbye." Her voice drifted into its habitual peevish shades as though into a fog. She hadn't wanted to hang up the phone. Whatever the straits, she had maintained her capacity for minor irritation. Perhaps this comforted her as it did me.

She's never really done eating. She eats until interrupted. The phone rings, or the garage door opens and her husband is home, or she must leave for work.

She eats so that she can't be caught, eats only enough so she can't be detected—only enough cookies so the remainder can't be counted at a glance, only enough corn chips so that the bag isn't flattened. She eats in her car, where no one knows. She eats when others have left the office. She eats when others have gone to sleep.

She eats one of everything, then a second of everything. She once finished a carton of ice cream and then raced out to purchase another, dumping scoops down the sink until the new brick resembled the original. She has retrieved dinner scraps from the trash. She has eaten full meals in secret, then full meals again with family, because she can't confess she isn't hungry.

She wasn't hungry when she did these things. Want leaves no room for hunger. She doesn't eat because the food tastes good. She eats because eating feels better than the way she feels. She eats because wanting to eat feels terrible. And she can't stop, because she hasn't killed the want.

I looked around the bedroom and made a mental list of things to pack. I looked at the cat and the cat blinked back at me. Shoes, I thought. I'll need to pack black shoes. Black hose. Black skirt. And time stopped whistling by, but glopped over my wrists like molasses, and though I was still walking, packing, I was no longer sure how fast I was moving, only that soon I would be completely enrobed and unable to tell whether or not I was moving at all. I worked one arm free of the bubble and picked up the phone again. I called my husband; I called Nitin.

"Are you watching the news?" His voice was hard, his Bombay-high-rise, cultured-black-pearl accent sharp.

"I'm home," I said. "Joyce is in the hospital. I'm leaving for Tulsa."

"Oh, no," he said. "What is it?"

"She's sick," I said. "It's bad. She went in through emergency. I talked to her. She's lucid. But she hasn't been eating and she's in pain. I don't think they've done any tests."

A silence passed, as though he were making a note to himself. "Do you want me to come home?" he asked quietly.

Should I disrupt his day for this? Do I need him? It's not what he'd asked. "Yes," I said. "Please."

"I'll be there in fifteen minutes," he said.

I called my Aunt LaNita back. "I'm coming to Tulsa," I said.

"Good," she said. (Good for you. Good girl.)

"Do you know where my parents are?"

"They're not at the hospital?"

"No," I said. "No."

"Oh, Ann."

"Do they understand what's going on?" I asked.

"No, I don't think so," she said. "If they knew it might be serious, they wouldn't have left."

"I have to go now," I said.

"Get there soon," said Aunt LaNita, a coach's benediction.

I thought of Mama, her angular, restless inquisitiveness squeezed round and harmless in the casing of routine and rest; of Daddy, placid and masterful within the fences and roadways that he knew. If they didn't already see the grim possibilities, what might be happening in Joyce's body, if they were waiting to be told . . . The scene could unfold horribly on them. I shut my eyes. I'd never thought to brace myself to help them.

She never thinks a binge is starting. She thinks the want might be stifled quickly.

Want is a physical sensation, like hunger. No one would confuse want with hunger, though food treats both. Hunger's a deep pinch in the belly, empty, sharp, fresh, healthy—the organs and tissues taut, a stretched balloon, a drought.

Want: it feels like smothered breathing. It feels like fluid in the lungs, a clot of bone in the palate. Want is in the chest, the throat, the sinus, unbearable tension. It feels like dirt left in a bandaged wound. It feels like haste. It feels like blurred equilibrium, like a pocket of sudden deafness. It feels like not being able to swallow. It feels like a bruise high in the ribcage, like heartburn.

She does not binge because she wants the food. She hates herself with every bite. She eats to numb the feeling of want, even for a moment, even though by now she knows enough to be afraid of want. When she feeds herself, it stops snarling and gashing, but only for a moment. Feed it and it grows.

Want is a swamp, a quagmire. If she feeds it enough, she thinks, maybe she can lift herself and walk across the food out of its muck. She tries to kill want by feeding it. Dimly, she's aware that this is what she's doing to herself as well.

"Is Harry there, please?" He'd been my parents' minister for years. He was fond of them and they of him. They'd want him to know the ground was rumbling under the family's feet.

"Harry," I said. "This is Ann, Norman and Toppy Vandiver's daughter." The adrenaline of decision had dissipated, and now my voice was shaking. I pictured Harry's brown eyes piercing, reading the unseen from behind the mid-weight glasses. His Midwestern farm-raised posture, unassuming wave of hair, average height and build and average Caucasian coloring somehow summed in his eyes as more than average, as a powerful presence, a man who need not assume anything about himself or the world to be nonetheless thoroughly prepared for you.

"Ann," he said. "What can we do for you?"

"I called to ask for the prayers of the church," I said. "My sister's gone into the hospital."

"Yes, I know," he said, his kind voice puzzled. "Your folks stopped by here with her on their way home and your dad came in and told me."

"They stopped?"

"Stay calm," said Harry. "Ann, be calm, now. I saw Joyce in the car. She wasn't bleeding; she didn't appear to be seriously hurt."

Like ice cubes run over my arms, like ice water on numb feet. "Harry," I said. "You know that my sister is not a well person."

"I know," he said, "but really, it doesn't seem to be that serious. I believe the doctor recommended St. John only because it's a teaching hospital and she can get better care there at a lower cost."

Of course. How could he know? Why would he think of it? And he had likely calmed my parents. Stopping at the church had likely calmed them. After family, hadn't it been my first call as well, and me a conscience-clear, backslid deist?

"Thank you, Harry," I said, measuring timbre and pace. Calm. Is this calm? This is calm. "I do think it might be serious. But we'll see." Mature. Is this mature? "I'm leaving for Tulsa in a few minutes. I just wanted to know we were in your prayers."

"Of course," Harry said, a low voice of safe bedtimes and unquestioned heaven at hard story's end. He gave me his cell phone number. "Call me," he said, "if you or your parents need anything at all. Don't worry about the time. Just call if you need to." I stared at the penciled digits and felt blot through my chest a familiar, inarticulate defiance toward the fashionable derision of churches. No need to jeer what doesn't harm you; you can find room to be grateful for goodness within it. I folded the paper and tucked it in my purse.

I waited for Nitin and thought of packing but instead stared at the news channel. Plumes of smoke poured across the screen. They could play it over and over again. (Show me something more, something new. Help me.) I hoped they would.

Who is this woman? She lives inside the body she and I have made together. She's not my sister. She's me. But I sit writing about her, and you and I reading over these words watch her—we clap our minds on her like a thrown switch—a spark jumps through her and she jolts and gasps.

She is, among so many other things, an overeater, a binge eater, and obese. She'll harbor these traits as long as she lives. Her choices, confined within her illiteracy of her genetics and psychology, have bound her to a lifelong struggle. Forever, she'll control with both hands the writhing serpent of her want for food. Whatever slender size she wears, however many miles she can run, however many acquaintances have never seen her puffy and trundling, she will always be managing her obesity. It's in her heart, in her memory, like a key not removed from a keychain. She can't escape who she has been, who she can with one false move become. The tendency to obesity is not cured, only managed. Lose weight as she might, she will never be cured.

She knows this. Watch her. Watch how her knowledge twists her. I want her not to snap and die. I want her to resist and reach toward life. None of us knows what she will do. Watch with me.

Nitin hugged me hard against his lean frame, cradled me between granite shoulders. I shrugged in his arms. "I really don't know why," I said, "but you're here. Thank you. I don't trust—I'm not sure I'm thinking clearly. Can I just tell you what I packed? Tell you the roads I'm taking?"

He nodded and listened to the manifest, the contents of my bag. He found a long distance calling card and watched me until I put it in my wallet. He filled water bottles and pulled the road atlas from the study shelf. "Pack an alarm clock," he said.

I scribbled the hospital number. "I'll call you as soon as I know what's going on," I said. He held and kissed me. There was no need to say what we feared, nor what we hoped—that when her infirmities overtook her, they wouldn't be slow and cruel in consuming. We'd said all that long ago.

Now, somewhere, Joyce lay frightened, humiliated, and alone. The love that my sister had refused, had held in abeyance, hammered at me and at a thin wall of time: five hours of her pain lay between me and her bedside. I pictured her as I had last seen her, a short woman, morose and pasty, whose face had nearly disappeared into a quicksand of fat, whose body had been lost in an avalanche of fat.

And on the drive to Tulsa, through the empty prairie and through the evening and into the night, I pressed the button from station to station, searching for planes falling and people crushed and people burning, falling, and people crying and analysis and woe and I said whenever I found these things, thank you thank you thank you don't let me think of it yet don't let me think of it don't let me think.

1968

Joyce is five and a half years old when I turn one. That fall she begins kindergarten, and in December, Joyce turns six. The fundamentals of marking time are fixed for her as they will remain throughout her life. The year begins three times. Its paramount beginning is the school year's, with the purchase of pencil box and paste jar, with new clothes and shoes, with a fresh fount of events to report and the promise of cheers and scrapes along education's blind obstacle course. It's the annual miracle, how this year one is the same person as before, but expected and able to sum fractions and read chapter books when last year no teacher or parent dreamed of demanding such a thing.

She prizes the school year. She carefully covers her books with paper shells and thumbs each glossy page, previewing the adventure of pictures and questions. She saves her mile markers in her scrapbook: report cards, field day ribbons, a kindergarten diploma, classmates' pictures the size of postage stamps. When the school year ends, her morning enthusiasm retreats into summer's fluid hibernation, an expanse of days eddying around music and swimming lessons but not, as was the school year, punctuated by rapid-fire lessons, grades, drills, crafts, comics, bullies, games, praise.

The year's secondary beginning is Christmas, when treats and shining ornaments reappear, when the household buzzes with mysteries and old, elegant carols newly learned; Christmas, when one is encouraged to say, "This is what I want this year; this is who I am this year;" when one defines herself by choosing gifts for others, and when one's parents with their gifts tell you who they think you are. Christmas is the beginning. New Year's, a nonentity to a sleeping daughter, folds seamlessly into the snowy quilt of after-holiday boredom before the school weeks start again.

Finally, last in importance, the year begins at Joyce's birthday. Because her birthday falls near Christmas, it will diminish through her childhood from a festooned, white-cake-and-candlewax celebration until it is a day quietly noted, subsumed in evergreen and hollyberry and twinkling lights.

"What's wrong? Why are you crying?"

In our bedroom, with the door closed, Joyce shakes her head. Beneath the drape of her long, brown hair, she knuckles globed teardrops from the sides of her nose.

"Are you mad at me?"

She shakes her head again.

"Mama would just say I'm being a baby. So I'm fourteen. It's stupid to be mad, I know, but Ann, I can't help it. Why do I get pajamas and underwear? Every year. I know we can't afford big stuff except at Christmas, but it's like my birthday isn't anything. I get stuff I need, that they would have bought me anyway, at my birthday." She sniffles. "They knew I wanted music. I needed pajamas."

I stand at her bedside, complicit in both the injustice and her rage, both of us knowing and not saying we expect the knock at the door; it's been closed long enough. For my last birthday, I got a book about horses and an Appaloosa pony figurine with removable bridle and saddle.

"Joyce?"

"What."

"Do you like the pajamas?"

She looks at the flannel set, yellow with white piping, still folded in the plastic sleeve. "No," she admits.

"You didn't have to try them on so everybody could see," I said.

She registers this, and blinks. Into her repertoire of shrugs she delves for the shrug of apathy, but unbidden it forms as the shrug of absurdity, her shoulders turtlenecked toward her ears and her hands splayed outward. She looks at me. Disappointment slides from her expression like window cleaner down a shower wall. In its wake, a blank severity glows faintly with uninvited humor. "Good grief," she says. "That's something." She wipes her face dry with her palms, her juniper-berry eyes shining behind stubborn salt layers.

"Come on," she says. "We'd better open the door."

When you travel somewhere alone, knowing you must react as quickly and surely as if in your own kitchen, knowing that dangers attend your neophytism, you want to leap ahead into familiarity. Your mind seizes details, for instance, locations of gas stations that might stay open late, restaurants that can serve you quickly. You time the distances between them. You pick out landmarks and thumbtack their snapshots to your mind. When you need this reference later, you may not be fit to remember it or to ask for it from strangers or to piece it out from blurred bits of spoken advice. You may be injured, or crying, or in haste to your dying sister's side. You may need to know without thinking the world in which you are foreign. So you stare hard at exit numbers, street names, relations of one building to another. You drive and walk as though you know where you are going, and it forces you to recognize wrong paths as mistakes, not mere diversions.

I missed the turn to the hospital. I began to worry that I wouldn't arrive before nine, when visiting hours ended. I found my way to St. John through twisting roads, deserted and dimly lit, weirdly rural so close to the manicured Tulsa street grid. I'd forgotten now about the terrorist attacks, which would muffle traffic and commerce in the coming day. I was racing; my heart was racing. I would still need to learn the correct route and had cost myself time. I found the hospital parking garage entrance and accelerated up ramp after ramp, as though I'd somehow know when to stop. I saw an entrance door to a breezeway, swung the car into a parking space, slammed the door behind me, and ran for the stairs.

The glass breezeway at St. John, long and jointed like a Chinese dragon dance costume, connected a separate doctor's office building to the hospital. Entering the breezeway at its midsection from the parking garage, you turn right and pace past hinged angles and passageway doors. You might pass nurses leaving a shift or patients' visitors in varied states of disgorged emotion. At night you pass the man who erases scuffs from the linoleum floor, steering a heavy polisher like a humming plow down the long, silent walk.

A set of automated sliding doors zips closed behind you. The breezeway ends. A revolving door deposits you at the elbow of two hallways, before an unmanned desk, atop which sits a phone. You have arrived late at night. You walk down the left-hand corridor, past the closed coffee shop and the closed snack bar, toward the hospital lobby with its islands of low upholstery. The lobby is empty. You try the right-hand hallway. It's strangely adrift in plastic, duct tape, and construction warning signs. You find elevator banks, signs promising a cafeteria. Left, right, up, or down? You return to the unmanned desk and see the phone is marked "dial 0 for Information." You lift the handset. A voice says, "Yes?" You stammer out who you are, the name of the patient. The voice raps out a floor number, a room number.

"The patient is on the tenth floor. Room 1025," the voice said to me. "Go past the plastic sheeting—all that area's under renovation—and you'll come to the elevators."

Except for that voice, I seemed alone, the only purposeful soul in the hospital. Alone in the echoing entrance, alone in the ample elevator, I exited into the mute, chilled, tenth-floor hallway. Machines hummed. Rubber-soled footsteps whispered. In one of the rooms, a dividing curtain sizzled slowly closed.

In Joyce's darkened room, another patient slept cocooned in tubes and the heavy hiss of oxygen. Joyce lay beyond a curtain. Her vulnerability, over the phone as raw and treatable as an open wound, had disappeared. She had closed up again, the clamshell tight, only a sliver of recognition gleaming past her guard.

Joyce was spread down the bed's shallow angle, a position in which she never slept easily. It throttled and snuffed her breathing. The inadequate cotton gown, a frontal napkin with armholes, exposed more than I had seen even when we were girls. Back then, dressing in our room, we'd without ever discussing it turned our backs, kept our eyes to ourselves. Now, though, it was not only unavoidable but compulsory that I gaze at her body—that after the nakedness and prodding and ridiculously necessary questions she had endured that day, look, as a person who knew her well and loved her, on the body she'd brought with her to this impasse, look at her openly.

She was the same size as the last time I had seen her, but lying down looked larger. I fought down my fright like bile. I forced my eyes not to flicker, not to wince. I forced them to smile despite her untrammeled girth, her helplessness in the cage of flesh. Her belly filled the bed, rested against the side rails. Her short body billowed up from the mattress like a flaming sunrise at a field's horizon.

Three yards' circumference of fat had swallowed her hips. Fat, like a heavy belt of gelatin, mounded and rolled across her. Her bones and organs lay trapped under her belly, the upturned hold of a sunken galleon. Were she to stand, her spine as ever improbably cornstalk-straight, her belly would inflate forward in a creamy landslide, lapping her thighs, a full, fat skirt drooping to within four inches above the knee, like regulation church camp dress. In the hospital bed, Joyce lay encased in the half-dome of herself, a fire in an igloo, the pea in a shell game, a cartoon adventurer buried in an ant hill. Only her grimacing face and head escaped atop the slumping heap.

The swollen trunks of her legs poked randomly from the sheet, her blister-pink calves mottled with beaten-bruise yellow. Her yellow feet were misshapen blobs, wet dough half-risen, wound in fat like yarn balls. Her hands puffed like ski gloves, folded on the crest of flesh just under her breasts. The yellowed arms, dusted with light blonde down, lay thick and quiet. Joyce's thinning brown hair hung unwashed, tangled.

Her face, once a gently rounded square, was now a flat and pudgy wall. The bottom border of the square, the plane of her jaw, had bulged forward like a thunderhead into a massive jowl, pocked with moles and erratically furred with facial hair. This cowl of fat in its buttery skin propped the bones of her skull. Like a whiplash victim, Joyce could not lower her head. To nod, she first tipped her head back, then forward. Her eyes, once the shape and intense texture of Brazil nuts, were now blue, sunken beans mashed between cheek and nose and forehead.

Her eyes, however, no longer looked tortured. In them pooled some small relief, the absence of some edge of pain, some giving up, some giving over to the situation. Around this nugget of peace curdled her annoyance. She acknowledged my entry with a biting flick of her glance and a rigid, impassive pout.

"Hi," I said.

Another flick of the eyes.

I glanced up at the TV bracketed to the ceiling. "What are you watching?"

She shrugged.

"Do you want me to change the channel?"

"No."

I sat in the bedside folding chair. "How are you?"

She shrugged.

"Have they said what's wrong?"

"No."

"Do you need anything?"

She shrugged.

"Do you know when Mama and Daddy are coming back?"

She shrugged. It was the shrug of aggrieved resignation, one shoulder hoisted up, facial muscles leashed and muzzled, hooded eyes steadily focused anywhere but on another human face. The sitcom showered down on us.

"Okay, then," I said. "Right. I'll go check with the nurses. Maybe they can tell me what's going on with you."

She shrugged.

"I'm sorry," said the floor nurse, peering up from behind the monitor at the nurse's station. "There's really nothing we can tell you. You'll need to wait and talk with the doctor in the morning."

"Are you sure? There's nothing you can tell me about her condition?"

"Tests have been ordered," said the nurse. "The doctor can tell you more in the morning."

I traced my steps back down the silent hallway, past the darkened, flickering rooms of patients in the variable grip of prescriptions, pain, and sleep.

"Nope," I said, taking my seat again. "No news until the morning."

"I could have told you that," she said.

"Well, good night, Joyce. Why didn't you?"

She shrugged. "Would it have stopped you from asking?" Relenting, she stretched and wiggled bloated fingers. She squeezed and patted my hand and half-closed her eyes. "I'm just so tired," she said. "I want to sleep."

"Oh, sweetie," I said. The endearment, automatic, unprecedented between us in our adult incarnations, was, I immediately feared, unwelcome. Joyce, in soft, even rhythm, kept patting my hand. "Do you want me to go and let you sleep?"

"No." She brooded. "Well, maybe. But every time I get to sleep, here they come again to take blood. They've been sticking me every ten minutes. Poke, poke. Poke. I sure hope they stop. But they probably won't."

"You know I'm staying in the hospital tonight," I said. She nodded, the briefest lift of her round nosetip. Her hand relaxed. "I'll see you first thing in the morning," I said.

"What time can you come up?"

"As early as they let me. I'll eat breakfast first so I won't have to leave you once I get here." She nodded again. I sheltered her hand between my own, and rubbed it softly.

"You know I love you," I said. She nodded, nearly asleep. "I'll see you in the morning."

She's home from school, trying to loosen the knots that have been in her stomach ever since she saw the girls' clique laughing near her locker. From the closed circle of sweaters and oxford shirts, their whispers and giggles fell like stones on her hunched shoulders. She could feel, as though they were bruises someone were pressing, her straggling hair and high-water, second-hand pants. "Get some real jeans," said one girl, but not to her. "Fat," one said, toward the hallway's high ceiling.

A block of curdled milk weighed down her chest. Her eyes itched. There was nothing she could do, no way to change herself that minute, her hair, her clothes. "Fat, gross," one said, and they all looked at her. She grabbed her books, slammed her locker, then lowered her chin and strode away, pretending she had some errand the other direction. They all knew she had to walk past them to get to class, and behind her they began to laugh.

But it's over now, she tells herself at home. She pours a bowl of corn flakes. Golden, she thinks. Crunchy. The first bite coats her tongue, cold, sweet, breadlike. A rush of relief speeds through her. The tightness in her brain lets go, and worry flees. With each bite, relief blossoms further through her chest. She can breathe again. She eats toward the bottom of the bowl and begins to feel unafraid. The flush of numbness branches, intense, and lasts through her second bowl of cereal. Somewhere in the third bowl, she grows sated, bored. She chases the last flakes with her spoon and drinks the sweet milk.

But she needs the feeling, the banishment of pain and embarrassment. She chases this reprieve with tastes. She lulls her distress into a slumber by waking sensors in her tongue and mouth with fudge-coated snack cakes, fried fruit pies, strawberry jam on bread.

As long as she keeps eating, the feeling of panic won't return. She doesn't yet know she has escaped a bath of panic to be consumed in an ocean of it. She hasn't yet begun to seek panic, addicted to its salve. She only knows she struggled for breath, for anesthesia, and that she ate, and found relief.

A receptionist with a soothing smile and wrought-lace, Kenyan accent took my signature and handed me two keys on a large, rectangular fob. Her directions to the hospital's guest dormitory became a complex tapestry of lefts and rights. My nod of confident navigation degenerated into submissive fatigue.

"Somehow," she said, "I don't believe you are holding all this in mind. Come on. I'll show you the way." She pointed out signposts where I should remember to turn or pass through doorways. Cardiac care. Gastro-enterology. Hospital library. She demonstrated the key-and-buzzer entry system and cautioned me to be quiet as the door closed behind us. "Doctors sleep here," she murmured. We moved past laundry carts heaped with white sheets, toward the creaky elevator. We ascended to the guest floor, a cinder-block and folding-bed bargain of monastical hospitality. The room barely accommodated its bed, a stiff armchair, and two exactly sufficient tables topped with TV and lamp. The bathroom was clean and cold: a shower, a basin with a margin of countertop, a thin, waxy bar of soap, and a steel rack with white towel wafers rolled neatly into its teeth.

I waited in the room until my escort would have returned to her desk, then locked the door behind me and threaded through deserted hallways, down the night-cloaked, glass breezeway to retrieve my baggage and books from the car. I wanted to test my skill and speed in the floor plan, to sleep on knowledge of it. I wanted to be pajama'd, brushed and flossed, stilled and quiet, before I started painstakingly bungling the numbers of the phone card.

She can't forget her fat. She wants to forget that she has a body—to feel a stroll and not her thighs, to feel the dance and not the heave of her breasts, to feel the smile and not the squeezed bladder of throat and chins. Her fat is a nudge at her elbow. Everything she does with her body reminds her of the fat.

It's as if the thing she hates most about herself were shrieked into her ear: You're fat! Shouted at her, every time she urinates or eliminates. Every time she bathes; every time she pulls her underwear up. Every time she orders food. Every time she buckles her seat belt. Every time she bends or stretches. Every time she walks. Every time she makes love. Every time she competes for anything—a job, attention. Every time she poses in a photograph. Every time she does each of these things, a voice bawls out the thing she most hates in herself, the thing she wants most to forget. She feels that everyone in the room must have heard it.

She's fat. They've heard it.

Mama, perplexed at my report, gave a crusty yelp of protest. "Why, we told her we were coming back in the morning," she said. When Mama is tired, extra syllables massage into every word, East Texas drawl unfettered. "The doctors told us wasn't anything we could do while they were running tests. How does she seem?"

"Mad," I said. "Uncomfortable. They're drawing blood."

"Still?"

"Every hour," I said.

"Well, then, maybe if they're running that many tests they'll have something to tell us in the morning. You're staying there tonight?"

"Yeah. They have rooms here in the hospital. You want me to check on a room for you?"

"No, you never know. She might not be there that long." Mama waited for her forming thought the way she'd wait for her eyes to finish sweeping the page of a predictable mystery novel. "I think I'll call LaNita and tell her you're staying there. She was worried. It'll make her feel better. We'll be there in the morning," she said, "probably not as soon as visiting hours but as soon as we can get up there. I sure am glad you came."

Nitin promised to call my boss to relay the uncertain length of my absence. Airy and gentle, he told me what each of the pets was doing—how the dog nudged and begged for attention, how he'd found the cats coiled and sleeping innocently on furniture where they weren't allowed.

"That's all wonderful news," I said. "I love you."

"Hm, hm, hm," he said.

I hung up the phone. I got out my papers. I couldn't do anything with them. I edited another writer's draft, scratched through my corrections and made fresh, equally incomprehensible corrections. I opened a novel, ignored its comforting hedgerows of print. I lay on my stomach, head near the TV, right arm outstretched to turn the channel knob. Like a dog following a fading scent, I circled behind the meaningless color and movement until I knew that if I closed my eyes I'd sleep. I didn't want to turn off the light. I wanted to wake up and have it be morning and me at my sister's side. I wanted what came next. I wanted to get there.

PART TWO: THE ADULT WARD

Joyce, six and a half and stoutly athletic, inhabits a rapidly expanding world. Her world embraces not only perception and desire, but also memory, strategy, intuition, the gummy cement of character and passion. Her world has blossomed past the yellow-curtained bedroom, past our home's floor plan; it has encompassed the honeysuckle-and-cactus-embroidered back yard and the mildly trafficked, treeless block of Seco Boulevard where we live, where our father has planted a willow and an apple tree. Joyce's world has spilled into the streets and intersections of Pleasant Grove and blurs into the towering concrete monoliths of the Dallas metropolitan area. Joyce's world is veined with bright straightaways and 180-degree bends: the noisy, impatient route to Granny's house; the subdued Sunday course toward the Military Parkway Church of Christ; the workaday drives to the grocery store, to last year's kindergarten and this year's grade school, to the Mesquite Public Library. These paths are like charm bracelets, studded with looming landmarks: The Cotton Bowl. Plano's saucer-shaped water tower. The tent-spoke rooftop of Town East Mall, where Joyce is marshalled toward patent shoes, woolen coats.

Joyce's world is large enough now for both Texas Stadium, where the Cowboys play, and Arlington Stadium, home of the Texas Rangers—for a grasp of both the forward pass and a base on balls. Her world is large enough for a field trip expanse of Texas bluebonnets, for the sawfish circling the murky green Fair Park aquarium waters, for the twin faces of Lake Ray Hubbard, with its cool morning fishing docks and its sunburnt picnic tables overrun with yelling children in singlet bathing suits. Her world is large enough for a white-haired Granny and Granddaddy, Mama's parents, in their clapboard urban enclave under the mimosa trees—large enough, too, for a ready recall of all the aunts and uncles, Mama's eight brothers and sisters, of their Texas-bred ruckus and volume, and of an annually multiplying number of cousins playing around the fig bush and swing set in Granny's back yard.

At six, Joyce's world at last includes her own face. She owns a memory of mirrors, a spread fan of family photographs, grids of school pictures. She recognizes herself, the round chin and flirtatious gaze, never at the camera, always at the photographer. Her hair is brown like a pecan shell, thick, straight. Her clover-honey eyebrows are subtle arches of lace over the implacable blue eyes. She smiles in a plump parenthesis of closed lips. In the summer, her broad face tans to the color of pencil shavings, the strong cheekbones darkly shadowed. In winter she pales to soft wheat flour. She knows enough to watch for changes in her body. She sees herself grow, her toes grow past the sandals' edge, her chopped bangs grow long, past her shoulders.

She understands time now. She understands a full five hours, the travel time to Oklahoma, where she visits Grandma Hester and Grandpa Ralph and Great-Grandma Roberts. She understands bundling into the car in the dark and waking with sunrise as Daddy pulls into a truck stop to order plates of pancakes. She understands age and death and birth, the somberness of a great-grandfather's passing and the anxious strangeness of a pregnant mother. She nurtures these sprouts of knowledge in her own world, to which her younger sister's high-chair and car-seat world is a familiar adjunct. She has lived once through my world and understands it ahead of me. She sees that I know little more than a jumble of bright toys, a parade of soft or knobbly laps, a few familiar voices warbling. She grasps significance in the unpleasant surprises before me—injections, spankings, cold bath water—and in the small enticements of our protected child-hood—mud pies, popsicles on their twin wooden blades, blooming redbud trees—and she knows that none of these things are random or new, as they appear to me.

She is lonesome in her world and bored with mine. She begins her campaign. She will teach me her world, make me a citizen.

She starts by telling me where I am. "This is the kitchen. Kitch-en. Mama bought groceries. This is a grocery sack on the floor. If you look inside you can see the groceries. Gro-cer-ies. We're going over to Granny's today. You'll have to put on your shoes. You have two shoes. They go on your feet. These are your feet. My feet are bigger, see?" She is a faucet of commentary. She keeps it up for the next three years, simultaneously culti-vating a family reputation as a willfully silent child, a child capable of sullen refusal, whose speech is infrequent, choice, and forceful. She is stubborn as sugarcane, bearing a reservoir of anger and a violent urge for justice in her hollows.

Mama chases her in a frenzy of immediate punishment. Joyce runs and leaps to the other side of her wooden toybox. She yells at Mama, "I don't have to do what you say! You can't make me!" She plants both hands, leans forward. She eyes her panting mother and whispers, "You can't do anything to me. I'm bigger than you."

Teenaged, still netted in this long bout with our mother, Joyce will tell me, "I don't know why I act the way I do." She'll tell me the story of the chase and the toybox, and will say, "Mama told me once that she and Daddy almost got divorced when they were first married, because he was acting the way I do." She adds, as naturally as an exhalation, "Don't tell Mama you know about that."

But when I am a toddler, she is my private narrator, my vocabulary, a taskmistress yanking me by the hand through a thicket of nouns and verbs. Her patter is as constant as wearing clothes. If I'm with her, she's telling me what I see, what she's doing. It's not that she enjoys talking. She hates waiting for me to catch up.

In the afternoons she arrives home from school and arranges her dolls in a semicircle on the floor around her. She passes out Little Golden books: *Red Riding Hood, Lucky Puppy.* She props the books in the dolls' laps or opens them on the floor. "Now I will teach you to read," she says to them. "You! You!"

She arranges me in the semicircle with the dolls. I sit at the end of the row. I am not the head pupil. Joyce fills a tablet page with overstuffed block lettering, the alphabet and numbers. She flattens a grocery sack in front of me and folds my hand around a Husky pencil. She moves my hand. I copy and trace her letters. I don't have any idea what I'm doing. "Do good and you can sit in the middle with the good children," Joyce tells me.

She can hardly wait. Her world is unfolding, her map is branching outward, a spreading sphere. She doesn't want to go into it alone. I may not have been her choice, but she's been given me. She squares her jaw to the job. She trains me as companion.

I found Joyce in the hospital hallway. She lay flat in her wide, railed bed, a stranded checker piece in the hospital's disinfected 3-D maze. She'd been moved during the night and was moving again. "They say they're putting me in a different bed, too, not just a room. That ought to be fun," she said. "Whoo-ee. Circus."

"Huh," I said, wedging forward to let a nurse steer past with a white-draped cart. "You sound like you're feeling better."

"Not really," she said. "But I got some sleep."

"Have you seen the doctor this morning?" I flipped open my small, fat spiral notebook and uncapped my pen.

"Oh. People were coming and going all night," she said. "I don't know who was who. But nobody told me anything."

The nurses behind the elliptical curve of the station had hands that moved like water currents. They had eyes that, even as they focused like a burning lens on my questions, processed the panorama of action, wasting no glance, recording the full field of vision. A nurse looking up from his or her task, oath-bound, must respond to need, to pain, wherever it sneaks into view. Looking up is no small concession. "There," said Nurse Dorothy, pointing a fingernail the color of a caramel apple, "Ms. Pai, that's your sister's doctor in the hallway. This might be a good time to catch her before she starts on rounds with the others."

Dr. Kamath had stopped beside the moored raft of Joyce's bed. She bent forward. Her shingled, black ponytail curved forward over her slim shoulder. "Joyce, how are you feeling?" she asked, lifting Joyce's wrist, checking each of Joyce's eyes.

"Okay," Joyce said, nearly wiggling with relief at having been asked. She smiled at the doctor, her hesitant, round-eyed smile—her oh-you-flatter-me smile, her did-I-do-good-Teacher smile.

Dr. Kamath was slight and upright, a chandelier pendant in pristine lab coat. Her voice was as light as cumin-seeded cracker bread and as definite as a chain mail slap. She smoldered with questions; they were buried in every statement. When she spoke, her mouth moved in tight, compulsory-figure curves; listening, she gazed as though she were squeezing my face. Her black eyes flickered with subtle impatience. She listened as though she were a Balinese dancer holding a difficult pose. She could hold it forever, but hoped you would not ask her to do so.

"And who is this with you?"

"My sister," Joyce said.

"You are her sister?" asked Dr. Kamath. Her head popped up, and she inspected me sharply. "Your parents are here?"

"They're on their way. They'll be here later this morning. Doctor, if you have a moment—when they arrive, what can I tell them about her condition?"

We both looked down at Joyce, who lay studying her fingernails, glancing up at one or the other of our faces. She listened the way a child listens, drawn by tones and postures, distracted during the most fateful of phrases, not quite aware that she herself is the subject of discussion. Dr. Kamath flashed the curved contraction of a smile and softly pressed Joyce's shoulder. Then she walked me a step away from the bed.

"But where are you going," she asked him, and he looked uncomfortable and said that Jennifer had invited everyone to a pool party, and she said, "I don't have a swimsuit." And he said, "You aren't invited. Jennifer," he continued slowly, "is apprehensive because of your weight."

"Do you mean she thinks I would be uncomfortable?"

"No," he said, "she thinks seeing you in a swimsuit would make everyone else uncomfortable. And," he continued, "I am really angry at you for putting me in the position where I have to face my own apprehensions about your weight, and I am really angry at myself for having them."

"Ah," she said. "Have a good time at the party then. There's nothing I can do about my weight between now and six o'clock tonight and nothing I can do at all about your apprehensions."

But she didn't feel that brave, and she still thinks about it every time she puts on a swimsuit. People can get embarrassed just looking at her.

She's always felt a little sorry for Jennifer, who was so vulnerable to appearances, but not sorry enough to stop wondering whether karma will leave Jennifer's child with a bad burn or an amputated limb so that she will have to teach him over years and years that he is okay no matter how many people avoid him or look at him strangely.

"Her kidneys are failing," said Dr. Kamath. We stared at each other like mirror mimes, she studying my face intently as I did hers. "This is why her skin is jaundiced. We do not know the cause."

"I see," I said. I poised my pen on the open notebook. "What indicators do you watch for kidney function?" I asked.

The doctor's gaze turned to dubious assessment. I stood adamant and prepared, as though listening were my Olympic moment, my dead lift. Dr. Kamath narrowed her eyes; I thought she was preparing a rebuff. Then I realized she was organizing a list.

"There is urine output, of course, which in her case is minimal. Then there is BUN," she said.

I wrote the initials in the notebook. You pronounce each letter separately. B. U. N.

"This measures the amount of urea and nitrogen in her blood. These substances are not being removed by the kidneys. Then there is creatinine, which is a similar test for a different substance. Joyce's levels are BUN at 109 and creatinine at 6.9."

"What are the normal levels?" I drew a table in the notebook, headed it BUN. Creatinine. On the X axis, the date. Dr. Kamath looked on as the ink lines crisscrossed the page.

"BUN is normal at 20 to 25, and creatinine around 0.9." Dr. Kamath tipped her head and paused to make sure I would not look away. I capped my pen. Then she spoke quietly. "Your sister is a very sick woman," she said. "She is gravely ill. You must understand this."

"Yes," I said, locked in her stare.

Dr. Kamath nodded, watched me bite my lip, watched a question form.

"Is there more?" I asked.

"Her white blood cell count is extremely high, and we do not know at this time what has caused this."

"What is her white blood cell count?" I asked.

"Thirty-seven thousand," she said. I uncapped my pen.

"And what is a normal level?"

"Ten thousand," she said. "It was around fifty thousand when she arrived."

"Further," said the doctor, "Joyce has cellulitis, which is a deep skin infection, across her lower abdomen. Have you seen? No? Well, when you do, notice how the skin is inflamed. The elevated white count is possibly due to this cellulitis, but we are not certain of it. She also has a yeast infection which appears to have been untreated for some time. The most important things at the moment, however, are the BUN and creatinine levels and the fact that she is not producing urine."

"What happens now?" I asked.

"We will continue to run tests to see if we can find the cause of the elevated white cell count and to find what is causing her kidney failure. We will begin a course of treatment to attempt to arrest the kidney failure and watch for the kidneys to begin functioning normally."

She was finished. Much longer and the elegant pose would break, for which, I felt, she would not forgive me.

"Thank you, doctor," I said.

"Joyce, are you feeling any pain?" asked Dr. Kamath.

Joyce pondered, squinting into the middle distance. "No," she said. "Just my arms where they drew blood."

Dr. Kamath frowned. "That's good," she said. "If you begin feeling any pain whatsoever, tell a nurse or your sister immediately." She looked up at me, daring me to grab the gauntlet. Joyce ought to be in pain. Like a nerve-damaged patient who can press her hand casually to a scorching iron, Joyce would perhaps not recognize pain until it became agony. My eyes watered. I gritted my teeth and inclined my head. I could spy on her pain. I could call for help. Dr. Kamath's expression relaxed. She adjusted her clipboard in a motion that announced she had been long expected elsewhere. "Okay?" she asked Joyce.

"Okay," said Joyce. She batted her eyes a couple of times. She smiled at Dr. Kamath, her innocent and reassuring smile, her I'm-so-glad-you-came-today-drive-safely-you'll-come-back-soon smile.

She's trying to feel better. She's trying to make the want go away. The food tastes good. It obliterates the want in her mouth like whitewash obliterating filth on a wall. As long as she keeps pouring the pleasure of food into her mouth, she doesn't feel the flaying sensation of want.

But when the food is swallowed, the want returns, howling. She doesn't know why her body feels this way, and she only knows one way to make it stop.

Afterward, she feels sick. Her full stomach, her full intestine feel like fists kneading her body from the inside. She wishes she really were ill, so she could throw up. She's not a purger. Feeling sick is stronger than feeling want. She'd rather feel sick than feel want. But she also feels shame. She feels ugly in her fullness. She knows that what she's done is ugly, that she would turn even her friends away in disgust and pity.

She feels crazy. She knows she's hurting herself. Why can't she stop? Why won't she stop? She's making herself fat. She desperately wants to hide her crazy behavior. But what she wants most to hide, she announces to the world with her own body. Her tears roll down her face, and her hand shakes as she lifts the full spoon to her lips.

Orderlies taxied Joyce into a private room. Comfortably angled upward now, she could see a thin trapezoid of sky framed in the window. I sat in a low-slung armchair and studied her face. A tidy, white mountain, she lay unmoving, her knotted hair trailing in stray whisk-brooms across the pillow. Bags of saline and antibiotic solutions, a bag of blood, dangled from the IV stand. Thin tubes snaked into her bed and along her arm, disappearing below a band of white cotton tape.

Kidney failure. Two raging, known infections. Possibly another even worse, not yet diagnosed. Death split into multiple snarling bodies and circling her like a wolf pack. Where is she in that rich Sahara of a mind? Is she lost, or merely wandering shifting dunes, fear and desire, fever, antibiotic hope? What does she want to say that she cannot? Does she find any power within herself? Does she know a way back?

Ugly impulses fought inside me: vindication at her plight—I'd told her, hadn't I? I'd tried to tell everybody . . . Revulsion at the thought of her pain, despair at the sight of her soft, improbable mass; sickening fear that anticipated consequences were true, that her life was brought to a close; guilt for thinking that only the negative was probable. Who was I anyway, to think she'd die? Would I want the doctors thinking that? Would I actually forgive them if they wrote off the fat woman? Could I forgive myself for that? Didn't I think she was worth saving? Didn't I believe in her strength? Didn't I love her? Vying with this host of perverse voices, my brain kept churning quietly: Learn everything you can. Find out what's happening to her. Search for death's loopholes, the heralds of recovery— be ready to throw your leverage, your intelligence, your dedication, behind her slightest turn toward health. She needs your help. She can cheat death. It's a long road back. Be here to help.

Joyce cleared her throat. She patted the sheet with her hand.

"I'm here," I said. I felt as if I'd slipped in mid-deadlift and dropped the loaded weight bar on my chest.

"I want you to do something for me," she said, rasping, drowsy.

"Anything."

"Would you mind?" Her face bloomed with hope and relief. "Ann, can you go buy some clippers and trim my toenails?"

The dead weight of drama popped like a soap bubble, like a recurring nightmare. "Uh," I said. "Well. Clippers. Sure I can."

She drew and exhaled a moist breath between each sentence. "You'll have to buy the heavy-duty kind. My toenails are real thick. They scratch me and it hurts. I sure would appreciate it. If you want," she said, "you can go now. There's nothing for you to do, is there? I'll try to get some sleep. When Mama gets here I won't be sleeping, that's for sure."

Good God. Where is that dead weight? It's supposed to be across my chest. "You have the nurse's buzzer," I said.

"Yeah."

"Okay. Huh. You want, what, a magazine or something else?"

She shrugged, the tick-tock shrug of lackadaisical patience. "I'm okay," she said. "I guess just the clippers is all."

"I'll be back soon," I said.

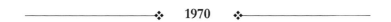

1970

To a three-year-old, the world is mostly floor space. It fans and swells like a pop-up book. One opens its pages, revisits furniture and family, until tables become touchstones; shoes, signals. The upright piano one's sister plays becomes one boundary marker of the predictable world, and the sliding door to the back porch becomes the other. The fireplace, the bath faucets, the garage with its hanging saws and hammers become the somber wonder that people do get older. The kitchen table becomes times, rules. All the objects that the three-year-old has but recently grasped as physics and words must be learned again. They have other meanings, implications. A sugar bowl is a mother's wedding; a typewriter is a father's parents, far away; a Bible is a dress, a drive, the hatch of pew carpet embedded in a sleepy cheek. Only the floor remains itself, the three-year-old's terrain, her private expertise. Only she understands how quick is the span from floor to pantied bottom. Only she bends to feel with her palms the wax ripples on the linoleum, as cool and soft as her grandmother's skin. Only she sprawls in the floor, wallows on the floor, communes from the floor with the undersides of dining tables and the slipstitched hems of dresses hung in closets. But then, her older sister, in a grand concession to further a campaign of knowledge, reaches back into babyhood. She joins the younger sister on the floor. We sit cross-legged in the vast, beige tundra of the living room's textured pile. My left knee wedges snug under her right. Joyce spreads the story of Puss in Boots across our laps. She reads to me, her deft, imperial finger pressed under each word in turn.

Daddy scrolls Santa-print stationery into the gun-gray Smith Corona. "Extending best wishes at this season from all the Vandivers," he types. He recalls himself in third person, as though he were a distant truth. "The father of the family, Norman, is a year older and wiser, we trust," he chronicles, "a little more bald, in the Vandiver tradition, but happy and contented as he nears his middle age.

"The mother, Toppy, in the Smith tradition, has grown a little, and also received a few gray hairs. She goes happily from day to day caring for the family, and tries to keep everything in reasonable perspective."

"Y'all stop fussing and get down for your nap," Mama scowls. "Yes, you, too, Joyce. You big girls aren't too big for a nap."

"Why do we have to sleep with the babies?" Joyce folds her arms.

"Y'all wanted a pallet on the living room floor, and I made you a nice big pallet. It's big enough for all y'all. Now lay down and go to sleep."

The quilt pallet fluffs across the living room floor. Seven cousins point like boxed crayons. We wiggle under the pink cotton sheet. I crawl over my cousin Karen. "Oof," Joyce says. "Watch it."

"Can I sleep next to you?"

"You're here now, I guess." One by one, we calm ourselves. Our cricket legs stop kicking; our spasmodic announcements cease. Joyce whispers into our gathering sleep. "Hey," she whispers. "Hey. You all want to play the tickle game?"

"No," we whisper back.

"It's not a real game," she said. "I tickle Ann's arm, and she tickles Karen's, and Karen tickles Rebecca's, and we go on like that, then we all turn over and tickle the other arm. Like this." She perches her fingernails on the crook of my elbow. Slowly, she draws her fingertips up and down my arm. She touches me so lightly that it feels like air moving on my skin. "Tickle," she says. I reach out to my cousin Karen. I caress her arm the way an escaped pillow feather would blow across it. She hums in pleasure and reaches toward the next cousin.

"Won't this put us to sleep?" asks Rebecca.

"That's how you win," says Joyce. She's right. It's so nice that you don't even feel it when the tickling stops. You don't even fight your own hand falling.

"The next is our only school child, Joyce," Daddy types. "She is the leader of the girls, helping in her own way to raise the younger ones, and doing it very well. Her school work makes us proud of her. She tries hard in all her undertakings, thus maintaining the high standards which have been the Vandiver family tradition, and which both parents recall from their earliest days."

It never occurs to us to sleep separately. In overnight stays at grand-parents' houses, Joyce and I tuck together into a guest room poster bed, or atop quilts layered like flaked pastry on the floor, or into a roll-away cot where like shoes in a box we sleep with our heads at opposite ends and our feet flattened against one another's ribcages. At Great-Grandma Roberts's, we snuggle on either side of our grandmother. "To keep my feet warm," Grandma says, kissing us and rubbing our backs, stroking our hair.

In the years when Joyce is allowed a later bedtime, she'll sit hunched in the kitchen, finishing wide-ruled lines of social studies answers. Waiting, I lie awake in the dark until I can cast the magic spell that wards away the evils of the dark. I lie awake until I can tell her goodnight and hear her say goodnight to me.

In our house on Seco Boulevard, the beds point like disjointed clock hands toward the center of the room. On bright days, the sunlight spills across the toyless floor and turns the wood planks into a plate of honey. On clear nights, stars spark through the window's protective iron curlicues, through the stray tendrils of white honeysuckle.

And on a starless night, in the clenched fist of a midnight thunderstorm, I whimper until Joyce pads down the hall and shakes Daddy awake. "Ann, it's just noise," he says.

"No, it starts fires," I tell him, startled that I know this and he doesn't.

"Where'd you hear that?" he says. In her bed, Joyce pulls the comforter over her ear.

"On the news," I say. The thunder peals again, and near the harbor of my father's lap, I shudder and moan.

"Listen here," Daddy says, patting my hand. "Sit up. Sit up, now, and I'll show you something. The next time you see lightning, start to count. Count until you hear the thunder." We wait with laboratory earnestness. A hot, white hand fills the upper windowpanes. He nods. I count.

"See, that's twelve," he says. "That lightning is twelve miles away. That's a long, long way. That's so far away you can't even imagine it. There's no way it's going to get you from that far away. Now if it storms, that's what you do. There's not anything to worry about." He leaves me with this new toy and its component permission to play past bedtime. I quiver like a plucked rubber band and wait for the lightning's fingers to stretch again. Three. Four. Five. The thunder drums and tumbles, like dreaded canned green beans into a saucepan.

"You can count to yourself. You don't have to do it out loud," Joyce mutters from the tight swaddle of her comforter.

"Is it real?" I ask her.

"What, the counting? Yeah," she says, "I learned about it when I was a little kid. Now for crying out loud go to sleep. No, wait!" she says. "I thought of it. You know what Granddaddy calls thunder? He calls it potato wagons. Like a big wagon of potatoes broke open and all the potatoes rolled down a hill."

Thunder booms; it hammers in my bones. I gasp and can't stop shivering. "Joyce?" I say.

"Mm."

"W . . . watermelon wagons."

"Hee," she says, "bowling ball wagons."

"I'll give y'all some wagons if you don't quiet down and go to sleep." Mama glowers in the doorway, her hair parasoling her ears in black spikes and her hand on a nightgowned hip. "I mean it now." She turns and grumbles away down the dark hall. "And won't be any more watching the news 'til I say so."

Daddy types, "Next is the three-year-old, Ann. She is the apple of her daddy's eye. Opposite Joyce in about everything from eating to talking. She is a real orator, and keeps everyone smiling wherever she goes. Screaming at the doctor one minute, smiling at him the next, and comforting him by saying, 'That wasn't so bad, was it?'"

My parents' bedroom faces the street, so the curtains are closed unless Mama sits sewing. The round, beveled edges of wooden flaps lift apart from the center of the sewing machine's cabinet. Mama's hands dance like a switchboard operator's. She steers the fabric, teases the tension dial, trips the presser foot lever. The sewing machine whines its laborer's aria. The needle and faceplate shine like dentist's hooks under the tiny, blistering light bulb in its recessed cove.

"Get out from under there," Mama says, and kicks lightly to dislodge me from my sneaked post near her feet. I look up at her resolute, slanted black eyes. She has her mother's Irish paleness, her German father's high cheekbones. She and her eight brothers and sisters are taken sometimes for Cherokee, sometimes for Chinese. "Not everybody who ran all over Germany had fair hair and blue eyes," she says. She and her siblings are Texan, fiercely; all carry like sack lunches their memories of rural work and want; all still answer to nicknames given them as children by their father.

"You know Mother says I need to let you sit and watch me sew. That's the way little girls learn, she says. But I tell you what, I can't hardly stand it. I can't watch what I'm doing when somebody's watching me." As if to prove her point, the needle stammers through her finger. Red cotton thread trails from its javelin, through her hand. She cries out, grabs her fingers, looks at me and presses her lips together, and runs into her adjoining bathroom. Later that afternoon, I crawl down the hall to eavesdrop on the machine's brawling song.

Mama feeds the sewing machine broadcloth, calico, polyester, flour sack cotton; from the machine pulls rompers, pantsuits, princess dresses, yoked and gigantically collared shirts. Joyce, in the A-lines Mama favors, looks set to run, ready to jump. Her clothes fit her like the petals of a flower on their stem.

When we dress for church, I need help but Joyce doesn't. She gathers a white knee sock and hikes it over her heel in one round sweep. I struggle with my anklets, their toe caps twisting. Joyce never puts anything on backwards. She can reach the hangers in the closet. Her clothes are smooth and trim. Mine rumple; Mama sighs. When Joyce disrobes, she folds her dress before she drops it in the hamper. I can usually find a loose, dusty sock under the bed. Usually, I put it on my foot.

Daddy types, "Last, but certainly not the least now nor tomorrow at the rate he grows is the young man of the family, Andrew Hunter, age 20 months. He has reached the period in his life where he thinks he is the ruler of the roost. Unlike the girls, he was about the meanest, loudest, demandingest, most tearing up kid we had ever seen. About three months ago a sudden change came over him. People say they never saw a child change so fast. However it is still not beneath his dignity to jump on the girls' backs, or to hit them with a book."

The orange sofa is a barge, and we are its cargo. On it, we sail into Saturday cartoons. Any child freshly losing a tooth is deposited, with a damp washcloth and an admonition not to cry, onto the slick, boxy cushion. The orange sofa is home free in rainy-day games of tag. It is the neutral ground at the faraway ends of which two squabbling children are posted to think about what they've done. Someday, the known world's pop-up book will close on the sofa. It will be sold before a move; it will become not an orange sofa but a forgotten volume, belonging to the days when a Dixie cup telephone string seems, to the children hunkered on the floor behind either arm, to arc on the planet's curve.

It will belong to a long-ago, photographed day. Parked on the behemoth orange sofa, Joyce and I wait for the flash cube to pop and swivel. Joyce struggles to hold a hefty, diapered Hunter on her lap. Hunter is as big as me, more than half as big as Joyce, his seven-year-old sister. I suck my fingers and watch him squirm while I slyly remove my right shoe, a patent baby doll. Hunter protests and starts to cry. Joyce props his legs stiffly in place. "Hold still," she murmurs in his ear. "Let Daddy take the picture, then you can jump on me and Ann. I'll let you."

The light dimmed from the hallway. A stethoscoped resident filled the doorway and strode into the room. He had wheat-husk skin and cavern-water eyes, the lean height and white teeth of fortunate birth and secure nutrition, the carriage of a man who makes decisions without wasteful tension and works long hours without drooping. In his baritone hung consonants like softened sheets, implying a stockpile of laryngeal sounds lying unspent in English. "Good morning, Joyce," he said. He breezed around the bed and sat on the windowsill, long legs stretched and crossed at the ankle. He folded a clipboard in his arms, against his chest. I pulled my notebook out and bent the cover around the spiral. "How are you feeling?"

"Okay," Joyce said. Rare confusion hurtled across her face, then dissolved into exhaustion. She wants to tell him something more, I thought, and she can't. She can't think of the words.

"Yes?" he said. "Just okay?"

Another brief attack at sentence structure flashed, and she sighed. "Just okay," she said, and shrugged one shoulder.

"I see," he said, then tilted his chin toward me. "I'm Dr. Abu." He launched lightly from the windowsill and extended a long arm. He shook my hand, pressure in the palm, heel, and thumb, fingers curled lightly. A surgeon's grip. His smile was a slow-burning candle, a thaw. It promised an expertly sharpened but sleeping defense. "This is me," he said, showing off the Persian name embroidered on the lab coat, a K and H trailed by an unfamiliar combination of letters. "It's a little difficult for most people, so everybody calls me Dr. Abu."

My smile was a butterfly hunt—no blinking, ready to pounce, prepared to wait. "I'm Joyce's sister."

Dr. Abu flopped back the sheet from Joyce's toes. "What's your name, Joyce's sister?" He gently turned her feet, touched each of her beery yellow legs. "You'll have some more tests later today," he told her. "There's more blood work. And we'll do an ultrasound on your legs and stomach."

He sat back on the windowsill, cocked his head like a painter in front of a mural canvas, puzzling out the next brushstrokes. "Questions for me?" he asked Joyce.

Joyce cast her gaze to one side, forced a rapid audit of the mental surface. Questions waiting there? "No," she said.

"No questions, fine," said Dr. Abu, nodding his leave and walking across the room. "I'll be seeing you in a while, all right? When we're here on rounds."

"He's nice," I said to Joyce, writing in my notebook: Abu. Ultrasound. "Did you see him last night?"

She shook her head, tapered her eyes, a snub of irritation. "Don't ask me that," she said. "I don't remember."

She had a professor in college who described overweight women by saying they obviously loved to eat. Women who obviously loved to eat figured into so many of his stories that it was clear he thought of women as two types: those who obviously loved to eat, and those who were normal and warranted no physical description whatsoever.

I obviously don't love to eat, she thinks. She hates to eat. Her body chains her to food, to eating, but she doesn't know when or how to stop. She's zombie-like, obedient to her desire for second helpings of lasagna, second saucers of cheesecake, free once her ticket is punched in the cafeteria. What she would do for vending machine pop tarts! She changes her pennies for nickels and dimes at the bookstore; she steals loose change. She begs from friends. She eats the food in their dorm rooms when they've gone to take a shower. She asks others at the table if they want their unfinished portions. He thinks she loves that?

He thinks she loves the humiliation, the debasement of taking a third scoop of cobbler while the rest of the family takes one? He thinks she loves masking her panic and her self-loathing with inane chatter? Don't know when I'll have another chance to have a slice of this. I've been so good on my diet lately, this is a real treat. It's only once in a while I eat sweets.

He thinks she loves that she can eat an entire box of cookies and then greedily lick her fingers to gum up the crumbs? He thinks she loves that she can finish the whole two-for-one burger deal with double fries, feel queasy from the grease, and still want to eat? Still eat a full meal, in fact, only thirty minutes later to cover up the fact she ate two hamburgers and two fries by herself, in her car? Doesn't he think she knows that only an insane person would keep eating?

There was a girl, and, well, let's just say she obviously loved to eat. She wonders whether it affects her grade that looking out on his classroom he sees her and thinks, yes, you obviously love to eat.

She hates it. She thinks: You simpleton.

Mama and Daddy had set up residence in the room's armchairs. Mama fussed in the contents of her purse, clutching it against the tidy duffel of her rotund torso. Daddy sat with his fingers interlaced across his plain, square belt buckle, ball cap pulled low on his forehead, the *Dallas Morning News* folded on his lap. He wore his newest, darkest jeans and a long-sleeved flannel plaid shirt. Mama and Daddy both looked pressed, rested. Mama smelled like fabric softener. Daddy was cleanly shaved.

Joyce rolled her eyes at me. I grinned and gave her a thumbs-up. She drummed her fingers on the bed. I wasn't to mention any toenail clipping until we were sure it wouldn't excite the dust devils of maternal comment.

Mama's voice was calm as banana pudding. "Well, where've you been?" she said.

"Just out for a walk. There's a drugstore over in the shopping center. Looked like some places to eat, too. Have you seen the doctors?"

"No, not a one. There was a nurse in to take her breakfast things away but that was all."

Mama's incidental baggage—her sweater, her novel, the empty plastic sacks in which she'd carried Joyce's clothes—marched across the padded bench below the window. I began to stack the items, clear a place to sit. Mama took the things from my hands and restacked them. "I put Joyce's nightgowns over here in the dresser," she said. "Joyce, I brought you two nightgowns and couldn't find the third one. Oh, and I brought back your clothes and your shoes from yesterday. Everything's over here in the drawer."

Joyce nodded numbly. I perched on the edge of the padded bench. The four of us sat calibrating our eye contact, measuring how long a silent glance lasted before it became a stare, locating fixtures in the room at which the glance could be casually shifted without appearing foolish, obvious. Joyce scowled, irritated at her unremarked centrality.

"Well, what'd you find at the drugstore?" Mama said.

I passed a permission-slip glance to Joyce. The ball of her chin depressed the pillow of her neck.

"Toenail clippers," I said.

"Toenail clippers!" Mama said.

"Yeah. Toenail clippers." I handed them over. Mama held them at plump forearm's length. She looked down her nose and shifted her scrutiny between the upper and lower lenses of her bifocals, first at the clippers, then at her daughter's exposed feet.

"Now, that's a real nice thing. I wouldn't have even thought of it. And yes, her nails sure need some clipping." She handed them back. "We were planning on that last week, weren't we, Joyce, and we didn't get around to it what with working the air show and all. That's good, y'all thought of it."

"Well, Joyce thought of it, not me," I said. "I'm just the errand girl."

"Joyce, do you want me to clip your toenails?" she asked.

"No," said Joyce.

"Are you comfortable there? Here, let's move the tray closer where you can reach your juice glass." Joyce submitted with a grimace, but her face smoothed as she watched Mama fuss around the tray table, retrieve the nurse buzzer from the furrowed sheet, and study the bed's incomprehensible lifting mechanism.

Daddy shifted in the armchair, chin in hand. He scanned the hallway, patiently as if in the beaten wingback chair at home, where he by habit would sit motionless at the end of a day's work, watching songbirds feed in the yard. He twisted a look upward at the television. I caught his eye, and from under his cap brim he gave me the wide-eyed, quick shake of the head that signalled troubled thoughts outstripping his previous experience. I walked over and gave him a light punch on the arm. He'd have answered equanimably, as always, if I called him pal, or you there, or by his first name. So I called him sir. It amused us both, for only a fool confuses title with respect. "How you doing, sir?" I asked him.

"You tell me," he said, drawing the words slowly like raked grass.

"We've seen two of the doctors. You want to hear what they said?"

"I suppose I do," Daddy said.

"What a good idea," Mama said, "to carry a notebook. How did you think of doing that?"

"Just what I do," I said. I told them about the infections and that the doctors were still trying to find the cause of her high white count. "And you know about the kidneys," I said.

"No," Mama said. "No. What about them?"

Christ help me. The startle and disorganization, did they see it? Mama has stopped rustling in her bag and Daddy has tilted his good ear at me. They're waiting, and I don't know how to compose a voice on words both easy and unsparing. What did Dr. Kamath look like? Use her tone. Do not look like you want to run away.

"Joyce's kidneys are failing," I said. The distortion of expression was immediate and fierce. Mama's black eyes grew blacker, angry, reflecting white pinpoints of light, and then they moistened with worry. She pulled both lips into a bite as though to keep from crying out. Daddy stared at Joyce lying in the bed. Joyce's face didn't change. She fostered a steady pout, an I've-heard-this-already weariness. I kept my eyes on Mama. Daddy would watch and listen, his reactions deep as ocean trenches. But if Mama's imagination and emotions careened too fast, she wouldn't be able to steer through the facts, would overcorrect with platitudes, guesses, falsehoods to calm herself. I'd need to watch the track ahead, pad the safety rails. "Now, the way the doctor talked," I said, "it's serious but it's not irreversible. Isn't that what you gathered, Joyce?"

"That's right," said Mama. "If it was worse she'd be up in ICU, wouldn't she?"

"Wait, now," I said, swung in the centripetal pull of her lurch toward a sunny denial. "They said it was bad. Really bad. But they've started her on a course of treatment and they're watching to see if she responds. They're supposed to come in on rounds. I'm sure they'll tell us more."

Mama and Daddy gazed at Joyce as though she were a nature show, in which the young of some species already facing extinction ventures out alone, innocent prey of the growling hyena. Without looking up at them, Joyce fattened her pout.

I sighed. By family etiquette, as I had forced us into a barrage of unpleasant thoughts, deflection was my obligation also.

"So, is Hunter coming up to visit?" I asked.

"Oh, I don't think today," Mama said. "They just got in from that long drive and they need to rest and get settled in."

"Where are they staying?"

"With us," said Mama, "I suppose. Until Hunter finds a job and they find a place. That boy of his sure has grown."

"He looks just like Hunter," Daddy said.

"Oh, he sure does," Mama said. "Oh—LaNita called and said they'd be up for a visit later today or tomorrow. Lanette's coming with her."

Good. Lanette, my cousin—skydiver, aggressive listener, two-fisted curator of experience—had studied medicine and was now a social work case manager. Tall, blonde as sweet corn, with a voice like rum and coke, Lanette was fearless and poised to help those near her. She knew how to read lab results and how to make my father laugh. She also knew what it was to love the dying. An ally was coming, a second opinion.

"Reminds me. I've got something here," Daddy said. He pulled his glasses from his shirt pocket, slowly unfolded them, and settled them in place. He reached into the pocket again, sticking his tongue out in concentration, fishing for a small piece of folded paper. He unfolded the paper, read its contents, and handed it over. "I need that back," he said. "It's Lanette's cell phone number." I leafed to a new page in the notebook, wrote, Important Numbers. Below Lanette's name, I wrote, Harry. St. John. Home. Parents. Fill it in, I thought, something to do later. God knows, the hours are going to stretch.

She lives one life in secret, in the body that hides and eats food privately, gorges and binges. In secret, she creates her other body, her public body, a body that behaves itself and never betrays her eating seizures. Near co-workers and friends, her public body keeps the social faith of good mood, prompt arrival, attentive listening. It pointedly ignores snacks, buffets, boxes of doughnuts contributed to office camaraderie. But the public body exhausts itself containing the secret body, the one out of control, the furious one. The only way to keep that body and its rampages secret is to let it rage in private. So, when she's alone, her public body disappears along with its good mood and pleasant smile, and she lives inside her secret, with its violence.

Between ten and eleven, as they would every morning afterward, doctors descended on the room like cicadas on the summer quiet. They assembled around Joyce's bed, the attending physician on one side as if at a lectern, and the interns and medical students opposite in a tight choral-ensemble knot, pens poised over their clipboards, expressions disinfected of surprise, puzzlement, dismay.

Dr. Abu detached himself from the reef of students to circle the bed and stand by Dr. Patrick. Dr. Kamath remained in the pack, exchanging quiet comments with the young nephrologist, Dr. Bemeka. The two of them and Dr. Abu ignored the students, passed wordless instructions and questions across the room to one another.

Dr. Patrick, toothy and sun-weathered in his late forties, looked, like all the full medical staff, somehow coiled, as though he were a fencer with the button off the foil, repressing his quick, irreversible reach. "I'm your attending physician," he said to Joyce. "The other doctors on the team may rotate on and off. Now, what have you been told this morning?"

"It's my kidneys," Joyce said. She folded her hands on the crest of her high stomach like a child preparing to lay its head on its desk.

"That's right," Dr. Patrick said. "And there are some other things we're concerned about." He repeated the earlier lists of ailments, reiterated planned tests. The student physicians inspected Joyce's skin, noted conditions, scribbling on their clipboards. I jotted words, an index germinating in the notebook. Edema. Jaundice, degree of. Abdomen, relative hardness in. Blood loss, unexplained.

Dr. Patrick watched me while he talked. I'm like a front-row student masking sleeping classmates, I thought. I pulled my stare from him and looked instead at Mama and Daddy and felt a funhouse dizziness. The three of us seemed suddenly small and distracting on the margin of the standing throng of doctors, in the dim edge of Joyce's spotlight.

"Because of your size," Dr. Patrick said to Joyce, "some tests we would like to do aren't possible. So we're still working out the best course of tests and treatment."

"Well. Don't stop trying," Joyce said, an onlooker's cheery proposal.

He choked on a laugh. "Okay," he said. "We won't." He nodded to the phalanx of students and doctors. They began tidying their phrases and capping their pens.

"Do you have any questions, Joyce?" Dr. Patrick asked.

She shook her head, her eyes large with first-impression willingness. "You explained everything I would ask," she said.

"Do any of you have questions?" Dr. Patrick asked. Daddy, face empty, shook his head like a pupil mistakenly placed in the advanced class who suspects with disappointment and relief that the teacher will simply move on to the next name in the roll book. My mother cleared her throat. "No," she said.

I narrowed my eyes at Dr. Patrick and opened my mouth. He raised an eyebrow at me. I glanced at my parents, blinked, shook my head, smiled. He smiled back. The clutch of studious attendants decamped toward the door.

"Well, now, Joyce," Mama said, "I didn't expect . . . there sure were a lot of them. Were there that many around all last night too?"

Joyce curdled her face in annoyance, loosed a soft, disdainful grunt. I stretched and said, "I'll be back in a little bit." I strolled out the door, then hurried behind the fleet of lab coats. I tapped Dr. Abu on his elbow. He turned, paused, checked the progress of the team leaving him behind, and inclined his head. "Yes," he said.

"Excuse me," I said. "I'm sorry. I have some questions."

"Yes," he said, gently as rain in sleep, gently as though he'd expected it. He watched his colleagues funnel into the next room, and he worked not to fidget.

"When can I talk with you?"

"I'll come back after rounds," he said. "About eleven. I'll find you here—but if you like, look for me by the nurses' station."

 **1971**

Joyce lays the violin gently in its case, fitting its belly and then its neck into the velvet envelope. The violin shines like bath water. No fingerprints, no smudges mar the syrupy curves.

"Why can't she play anymore?"

When Joyce draws the bow on the strings, the crystalline notes bump one after another like ticketholders at a turnstile. She retracts her short, stiff fingers, welted with deep marks. She grits her teeth, presses her round chin into the black pelvic curve of the chin rest. She twists her fingers, a forced march, down on the slicing strings. She kisses the bow to one taut line. A pure, defiant tone detaches itself and floats, a golden bubble.

"Why? Why can't she play?"

"Shh," Mama tells me. "Joyce needs to concentrate on what she's best at."

Joyce sits on Mama and Daddy's bed, one tan leg crooked, the other dangling off the mattress edge. The fingertips of her left hand rest on the lip of the open violin case. Her hand droops, her eyes fill with captive tears, and her lower lip works once, like a sparrow fluffing its wings. She won't look up at Mama and Daddy, at me. She looks at the violin, at the creamy puddle of its maple grain.

Compared to the sleek violin, the upright piano is cartonlike, dull, prone to gather dust. But at the piano, Joyce's hands never hesitate. Her fingers dip, lift, caress the keys, and music pours across the floor, a rising floodwater.

She practices every afternoon. Sunlight filters through white sheers onto buff folios, onto a carnival of black dots and lines. The metronome clucks softly, waves its silver hand. I settle into the crawl space between the piano and the corner of the room. I hug myself into a ball and lay my ear against the wooden piano case and close my eyes. I hear the hammers hit the wires, the muffled thump and buffeting vibration. The music travels from Joyce's fingers onto my eardrum and down my spine. The notes spread like tree roots into my ribs.

Her understated touch domesticates wild music. Passages that other students frill with romantic pauses and crescendos, Joyce paints as private and complicated discussion. She strikes at fortissimos phrases, frees the chords, decorates them with their own resounding echoes. Her hands greet the melodic line, then curtsy and recede in decorous meter. Her arms float like a ballerina's. She uncurls a comma of a smile toward the sheet music. Her blue eyes flash, dark as hydrangea petals. The music pours through her as through a terraced fountain; through me, as through a fish.

But now, she rests her limp stare like an offering on the violin. Her eyes grow gray, like rainwater puddling on a window frame.

"You can't do everything you want, always," Daddy says to her. I look up in surprise. Daddy looks the same—his lanky pitcher's-mound posture, the thinning crest of blond hair, the narrow chin pointing away from the pale blue eyes—but his voice carries a new, arresting tone. Normally, Daddy's soft bass-baritone is warmly creased like a walnut shell, a teasing laugh buried in it like a pitchfork in garden clay. But now, he holds each word in his mouth, almost singing, with a slight rise, a long fall, like a creek descending over rocks at night. In the dark of this voice spread searchlights: experience, adjudication, decree. It is the voice of probable fate. In this tone, Daddy explains the way things are and are to be. It is not the voice of reason, but of conclusion. It is the voice that Settles Things. Daddy watches Joyce with patient commiseration. "Sometimes you have to pick one or the other," he says to Joyce.

When you have to pick, money is always mixed into the smell. Joyce wrestles the humiliation of having forced our parents' hands. If she were better at the violin, she could keep doing both. But it's not so, and the choice is hers. She can stop piano lessons and devote herself to the violin, or she can relinquish its delicious torture and train entirely on the cool black and white keys. She knows which choice Daddy thinks is wisest. She knows it mustn't influence her choice. She picks.

"I love to play the violin," she tells me in our room.

"I like to hear you play the piano," I say. "You play good."
She never talks about the violin again.

Dr. Abu stood at the nurses' station, head bowed over his clip-board, hand and pen waltzing over a page. His trim beard pointed down his beige shirt's button placket. His white coat buckled around the back of one knee. I stopped at his side, waiting. He looked down, surprise fading quickly, a smile melting upward under his sleek black mustache.

"Yes," he said. "So. You have questions."

"Right," I said. "I sure do appreciate your time. If you have time."

He clipped his pen and steered me with a quick tip of the head to the far end of the nurses' station. "Certainly. That's not a problem."

"Great. Okay," I started. I laid my square notebook on the counter-top, left it closed. Dr. Abu's eyes focused on my face as though he were reading ancient lyrics from a scroll. I looked into his eyes, unrolled my intent, trusted his literacy, his savor of silent language. "I understand the kidneys—the cellulitis—the elevated white count. First—does the medical team believe yet that you know the extent of Joyce's illness?"

"No," he said. He shook his head, leaned against the countertop. He granted us a slender hesitation. It would not be safe to continue if my gaze wavered, if my attention capsized into my own feelings. I'm steady, I tried to tell him with my eyes. Steady as a coroner. Go on. "We strongly suspect another infection. However, Joyce isn't exhibiting the signs that would be consistent with such an infection."

"Signs?"

"A high fever, intense abdominal pain," he said. "These would be consistent with the types of infections we would naturally attempt to diag-nose."

"What types of infections do you mean?"

"Infections in her internal organs," he said. Next question.

"Dr. Kamath explained to me the tests for kidney function," I said. "What other indicators are you watching most closely to diagnose additional conditions?"

"Her white cell count," he said. "We'd like to see it come down as she begins to respond to the treatment for the cellulitis. For the kidneys, of course, we watch urine output, BUN, creatinine, her altered mental state. The unfortunate thing," he began, and rubbed his beard. "The unfortunate thing at the moment is the difficulty both of diagnosis and treatment. You see, the antibiotics that can treat the infection can worsen the kidney. While we wait and treat the kidneys, which at the moment is the most important treatment, an untreated infection may become extremely dangerous."

"I see. You mentioned—that is, you mentioned an altered mental state?"

"Yes, of course. She doesn't respond to communication; this is what we've noticed most."

"Oh," I said. "Um. I'm not sure what you've seen. I'd say she seems sluggish. But otherwise, her mental state—her attitude—is scarcely altered."

"You're joking," he said. "No, I see you aren't."

"Yes," I told him. "What you see is—well, it's Joyce. It's worse when she's in physical discomfort, or in a bad mood. You won't get a response, no matter how badly you need an answer, if she doesn't feel like talking. Also, she thinks other people can read her thoughts. She becomes in fact irritable when others don't respond appropriately to what she hasn't said. That's not an aberration."

"Ah."

"That's her."

"Ah."

"On the other hand, she seems to want to comply and help; she seems in good spirits. Actually, this is as open to conversation as I've seen her in a long while. A couple of years maybe."

"Really," he said.

"The other thing you ought to know. Our family—my father's family—has an unusual tolerance for pain. My grandmother, for instance, fell and badly sprained her hip and ankle. She said it tingled a bit. Joyce—well, she'll go to great lengths not to complain. If she can imagine it worse, she won't call it pain."

"Go on," said Dr. Abu. "Whatever you can tell us helps."

I nodded. "Another question. About the indicators. What are the levels of BUN and creatinine you'll need to see, and for what period of time, to know her kidneys are improving?"

"May I ask," he said, "how you come to be so interested in this information?"

"Well, like I said, Dr. Kamath explained these tests." My turn to hesitate. The path led off a traitor's plank into icy, choking waters. A spark of anger fizzled in my chest at my parents for making me admit these things. "Doctor, I find myself in—well, what I think is a situation. We're not talking about a short hospital stay, no matter what, are we?"

"No. Because of her physical condition, Joyce's recovery is likely to be several weeks, even in the best case, that the kidneys improve and the other problems come to nothing. And we don't believe that is the case we're in. We believe her life is in danger."

"I thought so," I said. "And so here's a problem. I live in Kansas. A little over five hours away. Sooner or later, I'll need to go back home. Now, my parents will be here . . ." The spark, the raw edge of the plank, the churning ice below. "But they don't appear to grasp the situation. They're not—they're not trying to find out, to deal with the particulars. It's hard to tell how much they understand of what you're saying."

"We've noticed," he said. "Ann, is your father all right? We've been worried about him. Sometimes he seems to have removed himself entirely, not to hear anything at all."

"He's worried," I said. "He's all right. He's listening. But he won't ask questions. He might not even talk. Neither he nor my mother will ask questions. They'll hear what you're saying, but whether they understand its consequences . . . I don't know that they're going to be able to answer questions you have about her. I don't think she is, either."

He nodded. "That's what we've seen," he said.

"You know, she's lived with them this past year. They've not been able to confront her, confront the seriousness of her weight. I suspect they're fully occupied, coping with Joyce's hospitalization. I don't know whether they can yet try to cope with her illness."

He nodded. "It's consistent with what we doctors have said, ourselves. Does it help you to know that?"

"Yeah," I told him. "It's not—nice. They're hard things to say. But someone in the family needs to understand what's happening. If for no other reason, to help my parents. It's true what I think, isn't it? That they might need, at short notice, to make important decisions about her care?"

"Yes," he said. "That's distinctly possible."

"Does it help Joyce? That I keep track of her condition?"

"It helps Joyce. It may help us. It will without a doubt help your family."

"Then I'd like to be able to get the status of those indicators on a daily basis. I'd like to know what I should be asking about. I want to know new developments, anything you find. And I need to be able to call from home. I know I can't talk to you. I know what you're doing right now, standing here with me, is an enormous amount of your time. And I know the nurses can't give me chart information without your OK."

Dr. Abu nodded. "I can add it to her chart," he said, "that you're to be told her status. You can call and ask for information from her chart. I'll sign for that."

I break the surface, bucketing a watery breath into ice-crazed lungs. "Thank you."

"But I have questions, too," he said. "Anything more you can tell us about her history and her condition will be helpful. How did she come to be so overweight?"

"She wasn't overweight as a child," I told him. I paused, thinking back. "She was slightly overweight in high school, gained weight in college.

After college, she began to gain weight rapidly. She tried diets, but didn't adhere to them very well. In the first five years after college, she became obese. I don't know how much she weighed. She looked maybe seventy-five percent of her current size, maybe a little more. Then—it was like her body stopped. It just stopped helping her. It was like her body said, fine, if you're going to gain weight, let's gain weight. No matter what she did, she gained and gained. It didn't stop."

"But what is the cause of her overweight? Has it never been diagnosed?"

"The last time she went to a doctor was a year and a half ago. I only know her report of what he said: that she needed to lose weight, that she was on the borderline for many conditions, none of which she specifically would name. She reported that the doctor told her she was healthy, except for her weight. I didn't believe her. She wouldn't say any more about it." Next question.

"What can you tell me about your family medical history? Is anyone else in the family overweight to a similar extent?"

"Maternal grandmother, heart disease. Paternal grandfather, Parkinson's and diabetes—she mightn't have diabetes?" He shook his head no. Tested. Negative. "Brother, cancer of the sinus, operable, now in remission. Also kidney failure once, due to heat stroke during basic training. Overweight in our family—to this extent, no. On my mother's side we have overweight and obesity in both children and adults, with the chronic conditions you'd expect—diabetes, high blood pressure, impaired range of movement—but no history, that I know, of acute illness like Joyce's as a result of overweight."

"That's more complete than what's been told us," he said. "Thank you."

We studied one another briefly, glanced down at our respective pens and papers, shifted to starting-gate posture. "Any more questions for me today?" Dr. Abu said, acknowledging the spray of signals.

"Oh. One more. Is there anything we haven't discussed that Joyce has been diagnosed with?"

"Let's see," murmured Dr. Abu. "She's anemic."

"Thank you," I said, hoping something in my eyes indebted myself to him, separated this thanks from the daily tank of shallow, parting thanks.

"Any time you have questions, or want to talk about Joyce's condition, you can leave word with the nurses that you need to speak with me."

"Doctor. Thank you."

"Make sure the nurses have your phone numbers on her chart. Oh, and Ann—"

"Mm."

"In the next few days, be careful what you tell your parents about her condition. The best thing all of you can do for Joyce is to keep your own spirits and hopes up, and to stay positive with her."

❖ 1972 ❖

Adults don't believe the world is big, but that we are small. Learning this is like a trick of vision, like seeing a disguised door creak open to reveal an ancient, fully furnished wing—the adult ward, which becomes visible when you see yourself as they see you, a small creature within it. I wander through its rooms, touching and identifying adult things, dividing them from my own.

Sermons belong to adults; Bible stories, with their loaves and fishes and lions and jasper gates, belong to me. Transit, the stench of gasoline and thrum of engines, belongs to them; the vined and forested back yards to which I am remanded with playmates, to me. Blackboards belong to them; the Big Chief tablet, to me. Late evening card games, with perfumed friends laughing around the folding table, belong to them; the evening star and the constant forgetting that its wish isn't supposed to be called a prayer, to me. Work—the invisible buildings that make people tired of being themselves—belongs to them; their laps belong to me.

Joyce, with almost a decade piled into her body, belongs to both worlds now. She sleeps over at friends' houses; helps our neighbor roll newspapers for his route. She can see over the sink. She washes dishes and doesn't break them. She can whistle, swim, write paragraphs in cursive. Her books aren't made out of laminated cardboard. She sits in the Falcon's front seat; she helps pick out groceries. Yet Joyce still sees imaginary animals, names them all Herman; she grabs my hands and swings me in circles; she soaps my back in the tub and draws letters and cartoon faces in the soap. I want her to belong to me.

"How much older are you than me?"

"Four and a half years," she says.

"What's a half?"

"Your birthday's May. Mine's December. You're five. I'm nine. That's four years older, right?"

"Yeah."

"Well, on my birthday I'll be ten. But that's not five years older because it's not a whole year since your birthday. It's only a half year. I was four and a half when you were born."

"Oh."

"Oh, what."

"How do I catch up?"

"You big dummy, you don't catch up."

"I want to."

"Well, too bad. I'm four and a half years older for good. There's no such thing as catching up."

Daddy ratchets the typewriter platen. Holly-bordered stationery pops up behind the metal clips. Daddy strikes the round keys with his index fingers, and the Christmas letter strays slowly down row after row, like a tourist in a rose garden.

"As the year 1972 has drawn to a close I sit down to think back over this period," he types. "For the most part it has been a very good year for the family. We enjoyed good health, had no broken bones, and few illnesses.

"Ann got two teeth filled this year. She said she was an average child as the average number of teeth filled by teenage is 11. She watches commercials. Joyce was notified that she wasn't average as she has no cavities.

"I am trying to uphold the Vandiver tradition that the older you get the less hair you keep, and what we are left with is gray. Over the past year I have lost a little more and the gray is trying to creep in. Peavey Company is still my employer and we keep putting out that good American Beauty Flour.

"The mother in the house, Toppy, has to cope with bigger and louder children as the years pass. When all three kids are in the TV room the volume is turned up about two notches. She still has the same problem with her eating. The Smiths really do like to eat a lot and hope to look like Debbie Reynolds rather than Kate Smith."

Joyce and I sit at the kitchen table. Mama and Daddy have carried Hunter to their bedroom to watch TV; all the melamine plates are cleared away but Joyce's. Her plate sits centered on a green placemat that's embroidered in pink with her name. Joyce's long, brown pigtails fall forward over her shoulders, the pink orbs on her hair elastics perched atop each ear. Lost in her pout of sullen frustration, Joyce stares at the remnants of her dinner. Her eyes narrow, her eyebrows flatten into oppressed lines, and her cheeks flush. She wants more than anything to cry, but grits her teeth and refuses. She fixes her gaze on the plate, on its last smear of potato and gravy, on the three radishes, their peppery red skins and flat white lids.

"I'm not going to wait all night here for you," Mama's said. "But you're not moving from that table 'til you eat them radishes. Ann, you get down and go play."

"Okay," I say, but I don't move.

"Eat one of them," Daddy tells Joyce, and follows Mama down the hall.

Joyce glares at the radishes. She shifts her gaze from plate to my eyes and back to plate again. "I'll be sick if I eat them," she whispers to me, miserable, enmeshed in the injustice of obedience. "I'll throw up. Ann, I can't do it."

Decision churns inside me like a paper scrap in a table fan. I know that spankings are terrible with mortification, combining pain with public embarrassment, much like when you realize that if you stand up you won't make it to the bathroom in time. You can't do anything to make a spanking stop. But Joyce's face crumples with grudge and revulsion. "Listen," I whisper.

"What," she bats back, as though I want to distract and cheer her.

"No," I say. I motion with a glance toward the hallway. "Listen for them." I reach across the table. I scrape my front teeth down the hot curve of a radish, peeling a chunk of its skin and flesh. I drop the gouged globe on her plate and apprehend the loose bite between my molars. Daddy appears around the door frame.

"Toppy, she managed a bite," he calls.

"May I have another glass of water," Joyce says. A tear of relief jostles out of her left eye.

"You can be excused now," Daddy says to Joyce. I bear the radish fragment between my teeth until we reach our room, then chew it happily.

"You know I can't eat your beans for you next time," Joyce says.

"Ewwee," I say. "I wouldn't ask a dog to eat beans for me. I like radishes."

"You're nuts," she says, and jumps on top of me on the bed and hugs me, and musses my hair with both hands.

"Joyce turned 10 in 1972," Daddy types. "She is now in the fourth grade. Her homework and piano take up a good deal of her spare time. Ann has reached the age of five and attends kindergarten where she and the teacher try to keep the class straight. Ann reads and understands very well, which keeps her teacher on the defensive."

A year ago, the nouns above Joyce's pointed finger condensed into dewy pictures, the verbs into sympathetic twitches in my arms and legs. Under Joyce's tutelage, I study the vast wall of the Saturday's paper front page. I stare at black blocks of text until words leap from the columns. On Saturdays, Joyce and I sit flanked by stacks of library volumes—*Thumbelina, The Great Brain, How Fish Swim.* Joyce reaches across the tower of books and pulls my hand out of my mouth. "Only babies suck their thumbs," she mumbles without looking up from her book.

"Thanks," I mumble back. I keep forgetting. My salty thumb returns, a homing dove to its roost behind my front teeth. Joyce has promised to help me. Mama and Daddy wince and grumble and yell when they catch me. Joyce, grasping the reason and the rule and the punishment and the inebriating desire that drives digit toward lips, has made a deal: she won't tell Mama and Daddy when she catches me. But I have to let her help me stop. She'll figure it out. She reaches over again, absently, grasps my fist and forces it to my lap.

"Only babies suck their thumbs," she says.

"The year ended with the family spending the Christmas season with my parents in Ponca City," Daddy types. He pauses to think of the list of Christmas visitors, his aunts and uncles, his mother's friends and cousins. "Had we been a few hours earlier we could have seen Herbert and Marie Scriven, Doris and Harve Mayhew, and Walter and Norma Vandiver, but nosy old me spent about an hour going through Pawnee Bill's home and area in Pawnee."

The gifts are opened. Creased paper and dissolute strands of curling ribbon waft in dunes across the floor. Great-Grandma Roberts has cradled each of the small children in turn in her lap, kissed us with her gardenia-

petal lips, and fussed over our smartness, our handsomeness, our goodness. We wriggle out of her lap and return to our tea sets and fire engines.

Great-Grandma Roberts's daughter, our Grandma Hester, clinks
dish lids and sinks spoons into cranberries, baked apples, sweet potatoes.
Mama and Aunt LaNita hustle plates and cut-glass water tumblers into
their billets around the long table. "Y'all, dinner'll be ready in a minute.
You kids get washed up."

"We need to get the rolls on yet, Toppy." Grandma Hester chides
Mama and pokes spoons into jam pots. "And the gravy's not done."

"Go on, get washed up," Mama tells us again.

Daddy, Grandma Hester's son, sits with his father and my uncles
and the oldest cousin, Jim. The men will drift back to the corner after the
meal, to quietly tell of houses and yards and cars and jobs and to share
hometown news of school friends and faraway relatives whose names oxi-
dize into family mythology. After the meal, the children, our mouths still
tingling with turkey juices and Great-Grandma Roberts's sugar-latticed
cherry pie, disperse to the adjoining rooms to play.

My older cousins unfold a board game. Joyce sits cross-legged at the
board's margin and sorts the plastic pegs and cards. I fear my cousins. I
hunch mousy and bucktoothed next to their long limbs and smooth pre-
teen flips and ponytails. They're tall; they walk quickly and swing their arms
boldly; they find our Texas accents unspeakably ridiculous.

"What color can I be?" I ask.

"What color kin I be?" my cousin Lanette mimics. The girls giggle.

"Go play with the little kids," Brenda says.

"This game's too old for you," Paula offers. "Didn't you get a tea
set? Jana will play tea with you."

"Jana's too little. She runs away with the cups."

"Well, you can't play here," Lanette says.

I tap Joyce on the shoulder. She's still sorting cards. "Joyce," I nudge
her. "I'm not too little. Say so."

Joyce shrugs one shoulder and grimaces around the board in an
appeal for sympathy. She stands and brushes her plaid skirt down with

both hands. "Come on," she says. She puts her arm around my shoulders and walks toward the door.

"I can play."

"I know you can," she says, "but not right now. Don't bother us."

I stand outside the door; she stands inside the threshold. Lumps of confusion whirl in my throat like cotton candy on a stick. "Grandpa will read you a story if you ask him," Joyce says. "Hey, don't start without me," she calls. She shuts the door. She lets go of the knob; it pops back around to rest, the latch snug in the recess. I rest my forehead on the door's thick paint.

"While in Ponca we gave Grandma Florence Roberts a premature birthday cake," Daddy types. "She will be eighty years of age in January of this year. Typical of all women (windy), she blew out all of her candles.

"Hope this letter finds your family in good health and no one forgot to eat his New Years Day peas if you believe in that sort of thing."

Mama and Daddy drove the dusky hour through the Oklahoma countryside from the hospital to their home before night fell. We reconvened the next morning in Joyce's room. I was knotted with the lumpiness of the dormitory mattress, the lumpiness of the hospital cafeteria powdered egg breakfast. Dr. Patrick and the shadowy pack of doctors had come and gone, had said there was no improvement, had drilled me with the numbers of BUN, creatinine, arterial blood gases, and white cells, and had said they were discussing options now if her kidneys didn't respond to the medicines.

"What did the doctors say this morning?"

"There's not much change. They don't think the medicine for her kidneys is working."

"How do you feel?" Daddy asked Joyce.

She shrugged. "Can they come take this food away? This toast and eggs is sitting here for hours. I'm disgusted looking at it."

"Well, I don't think you need to worry so much, Ann. When we talked to the doctors yesterday, that nice one, what's his name, Abu, he said they were just waiting to see that the medicine started working and that it might take a few days."

"Ah," I said.

"You know Lanette came and brought her mama last night."

"No," I said. "Did you talk to them?"

"A little while," Mama said. "They didn't stay all too long. LaNita didn't want to be away from Troy. It sounds like he's not doing well at all. LaNita's just not able to face it," she said. "She needs to let him go and she's in denial. She says he's getting better."

"It's just sad to hear," Daddy murmured, standing at the window, looking over the angular quilt of hospital rooftops.

I dialed Lanette's number that evening after Mama and Daddy had gone home again. "Hey," she said.

"I hear I missed seeing you."

"Ann. Joyce isn't looking good. You know this doesn't look good."

"Yeah. I know. Did Mama and Daddy tell you what the doctors said?"

"Your mom said there was some kind of infection, but she couldn't remember for sure what it was. And she said Joyce's kidneys are improved."

"Well," I said, "No. That's not right."

"Yeah," Lanette said. "I know. I could see it from her chart."

"Mama and Daddy don't seem to be getting the information," I said. "Even when it's told directly to them."

"I'd say you're right," Lanette said. "Your mom seemed to be taking it kind of lightly, and your dad didn't say anything about Joyce at all."

I sighed.

"You're going to have to follow up on absolutely everything," Lanette said. "You're going to have to talk to the doctors and nurses at least every day, maybe twice a day."

"I figured."

"Make them tell you her lab results. Make them tell you what they're thinking. Ann," she said, with a moment's pause. "I hate to ask this. I'm sorry. I feel bad about it, but I couldn't stay in the room with her. Were they able to do anything about the odor?"

The women in her Bible study group all wanted to lose weight. They put a dollar in a pot each week, wrote their goals on a chart, and recorded their losses each week. At the end of two months, the woman who had come closest to her goal would get the money. So every week she stepped on the scale. At first, she lost a pound. Then she didn't lose anything for two weeks, and then she gained a half pound, and then she gained a pound every week or two, feeling buffoonish as the rising numbers went on the chart with everyone else's falling weights. No one mentioned it. Frightened by her inability to turn away from food, she wanted to talk to the women, ask for help. But she felt like an imbecile, deficient amidst their success. It'll be over soon, she thought, and at least I won't have to face the weekly reminder that other people can control their eating and I don't know how. The two months ended, and the woman who had come closest to her goal brought a big salad to share, and the group had a party. She felt happy that the publicity of her failure was over, and happy to be in this group of women feeling good about themselves. But wait, said the woman who had won the prize—we have something for you, too. Close your eyes. She closed her eyes. She felt a loop of string slip over her head. A heavy posterboard sign hung from her neck. The women began to laugh and applaud as she opened her eyes. They'd labeled her: Don't Feed The Animals. Her ugliest, secret truth swung like a leper's bell. Heads turned around the room. The laughter spread.

The nurse scowled at Joyce's bed, testing its controls. "I don't know why you're in this bed," she said. "It's so old I don't even know how to work it. There's a way to do it by hand, but I'll need to go get Dorothy. I think she's the only one who knows how to work this kind. Hang on and we'll get you raised up where you're more comfortable." I suspected the new bed had less to do with Joyce's size than Joyce's lack of insurance.

"Is this bed uncomfortable?" I asked, after the nurse had gone to fetch the proficient Dorothy.

"No," she said, "it's about the same, only more inconvenient. It takes them forever to come anyway when I buzz and then nobody knows how to raise it up."

The changed bed may have been a fiscal practicality. The change in rooms had been a prescription. They'd moved her for the shower stall, a small room itself, four feet by six feet. The shower's yellow tile beveled cleanly against the linoleum bathroom floor, no ridged lip separating the surfaces. A heavy-gauge plastic curtain hung on steel shower rings, and a steel-framed chair, like lawn furniture no one has carried indoors before a storm, sat near the drain. The shower nozzle bloomed from a snaking, stainless steel tube. Entering the room, a visitor saw the shower first. Joyce's bed lay beyond. I could see her feet from the doorway, but had to pass the shower corner to see her face. The nurses were at her bedside now, cranking the upper half of Joyce's bed into a more vertical line.

"She'll have a shower today," the nurse said. "In a few minutes, actually. You might want to go out for a while. Or Joyce, do you want your sister to stay?"

Joyce shook her head no. No watching as she is levered out of bed, stripped of gown, maneuvered wobbling in her hula skirt of naked flesh. "Tell Mama and Daddy to stay out, too," she said.

I came back too early. Checking, I peeked around the doorway's blue swag and saw her slumped and quiet in the shower chair, her back to the door. Water cascaded over her naked shoulders, over the cords of her hair, over the chair. My chest tightened as though cold air were being pumped into it. I couldn't speak. I couldn't recognize her body as a body. Her back and shoulders looked hunched under an heavy, silken pack of white pelts. Her immense buttocks collided, flattened pale planets, biologically incomprehensible. The fat, wet sandbag of her naked left thigh squashed against the shower chair. I backed out, sobered and awed.

When I returned, Joyce lay with her arms at her sides, the saline line looping away to the IV cart. A college basketball game blurred across the TV. Her daybreak-blue eyes darted back and forth, calm and concentrating. And her smell was gone. Her smell, the rotten soil perfume that turned strangers' heads away involuntarily, shut down their faces, was no more. It was as though a suffocating pillow had been lifted off her face and placed on mine. I had wanted to believe her smell sprang from internal causes. If internal, then I wouldn't need to tell her she smelled bad; there'd be nothing she could do about it. I didn't want it festering anywhere near me, the common prejudice that fat people smell bad. I had refused to think that she smelled bad because she didn't clean her challenging body properly. But now she had been expertly cleaned, and the odor was gone.

The odor had begun to cling to her four years ago. The smell was at first a faint tang, but as the stew of months simmered, the smell encapsulated her the way a blister encloses a splintered wound. Her body smelled sweet and rancid, like old vegetables in sour oil. It was an odor that arrowed to the back of the throat and clotted there, the odor of dead mice, the odor of deep, clammy folds, of sweat and urine trapped in dark, soft hillocks of flesh that were impossible for her to reach. Her vast body required a daily groundskeeping vigilance beyond the slender hygiene of another woman's ten-minute shower. The odor of putrefaction compiled on her like exhaust grease on city brick.

Her car was soaked in the smell, as though a liquefying corpse had been sewn up inside the seats. Her clothes and her bedroom carpet held the odor like juice in the pores of a sponge. The smell remained to her a faint tang, didn't foul her own nose. But she knew. She tried to mask it with perfumes, lotions. She bought and tried new body sprays, discarded the old, ineffective cans.

The odor was one of the reasons she had been dismissed from teaching. Had there been complaints from parents? From staff? "It's not just my weight and health," she'd told me, when she called to say she and the Dallas Independent School District had agreed on mutual leave. "There's another—there are other problems. One. But it's too embarrassing. I don't want to tell you."

"But I know what you're talking about," I'd said. I'd gulped. I'd felt the old shame wash back up my gullet, make me want to ball up like a pill bug and roll away.

"How could you?"

I'd transformed my voice into a steel plate so it would not become a reservoir instead. "Because I had the same problem, and people had to tell me about it, and I felt so terrible I wanted to die. I felt dirty and ashamed and mad, and didn't know what to do about it."

"Well," she'd said, cutting me off. "I'm working on it. I'm taking steps." But the odor remained and saturated every fabric surface where she sat or slept or in which she swaddled herself.

The nurses bathed her, every puff and fold, delivered her skin of its wastes as a cow of a breach calf. The first time in Joyce's adult life in which another human touched every inch of her bare skin, she was touched with care, with compassion, to be cleaned, to clean where she could not, how she had not. Bathed, she smelled as she had when we were young, like soap on a clean washcloth, like wilted white honeysuckle, faint and faded in a water glass. The nurses cut her hair's long mouse nest. It lay now, thin, but combed and shining, on the pillow, its fresh ends wafting just above her shoulders.

"Sure felt good to be up out of this bed a while," Joyce said.

She must be lazy. How else could she stay fat? She must be stupid. How else could she ignore the simple equation: fewer calories, more exercise? She must be dirty, unhygienic. If she's sloppy about her weight, her habits can't be clean. She must be boring. How could she be doing anything interesting, active, and get so fat? She can't be trusted with challenging assignments. She obviously hasn't the commitment, the follow-through. She must be poor, or bad at handling money. Otherwise, she'd put some resources toward weight loss treatment. She must have social problems. If she treats herself badly, how could she be a friend to others? She must not be trustworthy. If she lies to herself about her weight, won't she lie about other things? She must have poor taste. The clothes she wears are cheap, unflattering, and pinch and bind. She must not care about her appearance. She's fat.

She must not care.

"The odor's gone. They showered her today."

"I feel bad having to say anything about it."

"I know," I said.

"I'll give you some advice," Lanette said.

"Please," I said.

"Will she talk to a counselor?"

"Maybe," I said.

"I told Joyce this already, so maybe she followed up. If she'll talk to a counselor, there are psychologists and case workers on the hospital staff. She can request a visit from a counselor."

It made sense. There'd be a long road back to health for Joyce, and she'd never reach physical health without addressing mental challenges, surely packed in her like a lifetime of old photographs in a box. "It's good advice," I said.

"And if she won't ask for the counselor," said Lanette, "you need to do it for her. She needs to talk to somebody." When I didn't answer, Lanette said, "I'm serious. If she doesn't do it, and you don't do it, I'll come back down there myself to get her some counseling."

Lanette had seen it, then. Joyce would have, to Lanette as to the doctors, smiled and answered like a Southern lady entertaining company, like our Grandma Hester in the manic phases of dementia, when she was polite and girlish, flirtatious and simple. The need to escape the horror of her body might smother the need to ask for help.

"You're the best," I said. "I'll talk to her tonight."

"Be sure you do," Lanette said. "She needs you."

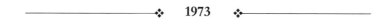

❖ 1973 ❖

By Thanksgiving, with its construction-paper turkeys and coloring-book cornucopias, I am a veteran of first grade. The sticks and bulbs of pencilled letters march in step across the coarse-pulp paper with its dotted-line rule. A red-haired boy who pretends he is Prince Valiant chases me on the playground, and I in turn chase a fifth-grade boy, Alex of the fox-slim face, who sits next to Joyce in her class.

Joyce is a veteran of everything. She knows two Bible verses from every book of the Bible. She writes to a Rhodesian pen pal named Debbie. At ten years old, her assertive finger work and Swiss-watch rhythm caress a Bach sonata and earn a superior rating in the city-wide piano auditions. State representatives and Dallas county commissioners clip the newspaper article and mail the copies to Mama and Daddy with congratulations. The aunts and uncles purchase and deliver extras. Joyce's faintly amused, square-jawed face peers out from dozens of newsprint strips. Joyce pastes one in her own scrapbook. Mama sends copies to the grandmas in Oklahoma and sighs. Joyce has asked Mama not to come to any recitals. When Mama's in the audience, Joyce's stomach hurts from nervousness and she can hardly walk to the stage. Mama stays home, while Daddy takes me to a back row of the auditorium. I can't see the platform, and by the time Joyce plays, I've fallen asleep, my blond bob tangling on Daddy's pant leg.

Our passions have begun to secrete, like the soft folds of exoskeletons, from our daydreams. Our inclinations become visible to our parents and ourselves. We know ourselves not only as ourselves, but as others know us, by our reputations and obsessions. Joyce walks ahead of me in this house of mirrors. With relief, I recognize her, regardless of her multiple, shifting, public definitions. I know her not as others do, by her passions solidifying, but by the stubborn, fluid form beneath, her willful and alert joy, her disdain for liars and the jaded.

Joyce's passion is collection. She accumulates Dick Tracy comic strips, stacking them in a lunchbox she has decoupaged with collected stamps. She saves her allowance and buys books. Joyce's bookshelf, a cotillion of trim paperbacks, tantalizes her younger siblings. Hunter, rowdy, his impulses explosive, is not allowed to touch the books. I'm allowed to hold the ones she gives me. "You're ready for chapter books," she says one day. "You shouldn't be reading little kiddie books anymore."

"How long does it take to read a chapter book?" I ask. Chapters are a craved mystery, like recipe ingredients, like the Holy Trinity, complete in themselves, yet when combined inseparable from the whole.

"Let's find out," she says. She dethrones *Viking Adventure* by Clyde Robert Bulla from its slot on the shelf. "Come on." She posts me on the living room carpet. "Now read the book. Don't move until you finish. I'll time you."

"What if—"

"Oh, good grief. If you have to go, yell at me and I'll stop the time until you get back."

I can barely finish all the pages. I skip the words I don't understand; Joyce won't tell them to me. We repeat the exercise every day until I can read the whole book in thirty minutes. Every day, Joyce quizzes me. "What put an end to Olaf's fighting days?" A wound. "How did Sigurd prove he was old enough to voyage to Wineland?" He lifted the test-stone. "What did Sigurd say when Rolf did not believe in Wineland?" I know what I have seen, and no one can take it from me.

In the pencil illustrations, the young Sigurd climbs a rope hand over hand in his lessons as a young Viking warrior. Even on the day I pass the test, I stop to look at this picture and imagine the rope end dancing between my feet.

"You can speed read now," Joyce says, "and I'm going to be a great teacher."

My own exoskeleton is a pudding of desires to organize, to direct. I invent clubs, of which Joyce and Hunter and I are sole charter members, through which, I dream, we will change our lives, create great things, harness and leverage our will. None of the clubs lasts more than one meeting. But for an afternoon, all pride and anticipated residence in the future balance on the plan to accomplish. I worry that I haven't hidden my pushiness well enough, and that being older Joyce may be offended by relegation to second in command. "It's okay for you?" I ask her. "Not being the president?"

She stiffens her face, her eyes blank but shifted away, a look I don't yet recognize as stifled laughter. "You really think you have to be president of everything, don't you."

I gum at the question, search my conscience. "Well . . . yeah. But I don't know how to do anything else."

"I don't care. I'd rather be the secretary," she says, her assertion like a chalkboard pointer tapped loudly against the correct response. "Everybody likes the secretary."

Joyce schemes when she needs to. Unlike my grandiose machinery of plans, her schemes are methodical and unannounced. "Please, please take the wheels off. Just for a little while," she says to Daddy.

"Now, Joyce. You know Ann can't ride that bike without the training wheels. She's too little. Y'all both need to take a turn."

"But she's not riding now. Please, just for a while," she says. Daddy sighs and puts down his book. She finds me stripping paper peels off crayons. "Put that stuff away," she says. "Come on."

"Why?"

"Shh. Don't let Daddy hear you. Just come on."

The purple bicycle tilts against its kickstand in the driveway. Faded pink vinyl streamers dangle from white handle grips. A mod splatter of pink and purple daisies patterns the vinyl banana seat. Joyce wheels the bike to the starting line, the sidewalk's concrete seam. "Get on," she says.

"No." My pulse swells like a jumbo marble in my throat. "Please don't make me. I'll fall off."

"You're big enough," she says. "I know you can do it. I watch you ride all the time. Look, I'll hold on to the sissy bar, and we'll go slow, like this."

"You'll hold on?"

"I'll hold on."

"You won't let go?"

"Oh, good gravy, Ann. I won't let go." And in one of the great, honorable lies of childhood, as beautiful a lie as the rainbow's pot of gold, she becomes the person who lets me go. The bike stops wobbling; I pedal faster; she can't be running so fast—she bounces and leaps on the sidewalk behind me, springing from her sneaker toes, her arms pinwheeling. "You're doing it! You're doing it!" She runs to me, claps her hands. I improve my shaky equilibrium with every pedal press. I waver back down the sidewalk toward our house. Joyce skips and bounds beside me on the neighbor's lawn.

"Now you have to show Daddy so he'll believe it," she says.

"He didn't know?"

"Why do you think I made you be quiet? Silly. You could have fallen over and busted your head open."

"Oh."

"I'm a good teacher. You didn't bust your head. No more training wheels, no more training wheels," she sings. And with the chapter books and the bicycle, her campaign is complete. I can read anything, ride anywhere. She has cracked her world open for me. I can plunge my hands in it now without her help. It's more than she intended.

Mama and Daddy had gone home for the day. I tried to clip the yellow plates of Joyce's toenails. Her foot mashed gently in my hand. The crooked cakes of keratin jutted from the nail beds, like tiles inexpertly set in excess mortar. The industrial-strength clipper dented but could not slice the thick, yellow textile. Its surgical curve bit into her toenail like a box knife into PVC.

"How long has it been since you did this?" I asked.

"I don't know," she said. "Long enough, evidently."

"Well. I'm not having much luck, I'll tell you that." The steel edge slipped, and I jabbed her big toe with the sharp blade. A crescent of viscous cranberry bubbled up and slithered toward the sheet.

"Ow," she said. "No, don't stop. Keep trying. Whatever you can do is better than how they are now."

I gave up sculpting a cherry-cordial shape and instead mitered the sharp corners, chipping away the flint arrowheads that rubbed the adjacent toes. "Okay," I said. "There."

"Thank ye," she said. She bore old-style, East Texanisms in her speech the way a country woman wears an apron. Figures of speech are not merely decorative but also worker's wear. They are not worn like fashions, to foster an identity, but with respect for the kitchen's tasks. East Texas expression shielded Joyce from the splatters of lax and crude popular speech; she was not less than her society by rejecting its slang, but more, by choosing words it never used, old-fashioned, countrified, alien.

Her genteel thank ye invited me to stay. A thanks, deliberate as a whittled stick, was a poked bestowal of merit, a suspension of Joyce's shrugs. For Joyce shrugged, looking directly at her opponent, to mean, Continue. She shrugged, looking away, to mean, You're going to do what you want anyway. She shrugged, wincing, to mean, I don't care and I'd rather you went away. If you went away when she wanted to keep shrugging at you, you gave cause for grievance. If you stayed when she wanted you to go, it proved her right: You're going to do what you want anyway. But when she bow-tied the apron strings of courtesy around her conversation, she meant to discuss, to wonder aloud, to have company.

"I'm so sorry you're in here," I said.

"I know," she said.

"I'm glad you went to the doctor. I know that must have been very hard for you."

"It was," she said. "I didn't want to tell anybody something was wrong. I could feel it. It hurt. I couldn't eat."

"I know how hard it was for you to ask for help," I said. "I want you to know. I think you were incredibly brave to do it."

"Thank you," she said. She looked at me as if appraising a used car. Could it be true? Did I understand how hard it was? Her eyes softened, dilated to blue clouds around black seeds. I folded the softness inside me, her welcome of my nearness.

"How long did you wait? When did you know something was wrong?"

"A few days before. They were off busy in town with their air show," she said, scrubbing at the faint residue of an accusation to reveal a more generous understanding. "You know how they volunteer to work at the air show every year. They were going to be all finished with it late on Saturday. So I told them on Friday that after they were done with the air show, I had to talk with them about something. I told them I'd tell them on Sunday."

"Weren't they curious? Didn't they ask?"

"Oh, you know how we all are," she said. "They weren't going to go poking around in it. I didn't want to spoil their plans and all for Saturday. I shouldn't have waited. I know, I shouldn't have."

She held her chin up like a bride's bouquet. She cast a soap opera star's half-lidded gaze of tragic revelation toward the empty air above the bed. I thought she was ready to make a joke. A laugh had already begun to cyclone high in my belly when she spoke, caressing the words like heirloom pearls. "I guess I had to reach rock bottom," she said. "I guess I had to reach rock bottom before I would ask for help."

She eats prodigiously, a whole box of corn flakes at a sitting, a full Chinese dinner ordered, then a whole frozen pizza. She doesn't feel, while eating, the grotesqueness of this marathon. Later, she's horrified. How could she do this to herself?

She admits it: eating feels good. When she eats, the only reason to stop is if something interrupts her. The stomach rarely complains, the intestines don't groan. She might get bored of eating, but it never stops feeling good.

To stop eating when it still feels good, her mind must be stronger than her desire to eat. Like a car crash survivor waving at headlights on a dark road, she throws thoughts into the traffic of her appetite. When she eats, she thinks, I am harming myself. When she refrains from eating, she thinks, I am being good to myself. But harming herself feels good, and being good to herself has so far been fleeting, unproven. She values the pleasure of food more than she values positive thoughts about herself. The pleasure is reliable, but she's not used to pride or compliments. She doesn't trust them, the way she doesn't trust the mirror. What she sees may not be real. Her positive thoughts about herself might be merely more of her own flimsy lies.

Some clarity, some happiness in Joyce's voice, prickled up my spine and through the fine hairs on the back of my neck: she was proud. She was waiting to be admired in her extreme struggle. She had actually recognized that she was in trouble, yet had waited to hit rock bottom. She could say she'd survived it. You fool, I wanted to scream. You don't see it even now, do you? Where you are, where you've gone with your body?

"Joyce," I said, dismay and anger in my voice like the low, ambient heat of a forgotten stove. She drew back her head in rebuff, expecting wheedling, nagging. She hadn't thought I'd be crying. "Don't you know what happened to you? Don't you realize that if you hadn't gone to the doctor, in another day Mama and Daddy might have come home to find you dead on the floor? There's nothing noble about it. You almost died."

She didn't answer. She relaxed, exhaustion fading into the depths of her face. Her face was calm and conquered, the smooth face that lulled worries when she held a sleeping nephew or caressed a household pet, gently, to give pleasure. Don't cry, her face said to me. "Don't you know you almost died?" I said.

"Yes," she said.

"Do you know how happy I am you didn't?"

"Yes," she said.

"Do you know what a big fight is in front of you?"

She nodded, the tears now prodding her eyelashes.

"Promise me," I said, "please. Please promise me, you're going to do everything you can to get well. You're going to have to fight. Promise me you're not going to give up."

"I promise," she said.

"Promise me you'll ask for everything you need," I said. "Promise me you won't try to do this alone."

"I promise," she said. "Ann, I just want to get well. I'm ready to get well."

"You'll keep fighting?"

She nodded. "Yeah," she said.

"That's it, then," I said. The marbled slur of television noise tendered itself into our consciousness, and we held our notice toward it like outstretched hands. Joyce waited until the commercial break to speak.

"Did you hear if the counselor was going to come see me tomorrow?"

A warm spur kicked through me. She'd just asked for help. I couldn't remember another time. You're doing it, I cheered through my eyes, through my quarter smile. You're doing it. "I can ask Dr. Kamath about it, or I'll ask the nurses," I said. "In the morning I'll make sure someone's coming to talk to you."

"Good," she said.

"I love you," I said, soberly, as though I had never said it before.

"I love you," she said, fondly, as though she said it to me every day.

Our tattling has at last become credible: the hired babysitter spends her days on the phone or napping in the sun, and Joyce alone supervises us in the shadow of the babysitter's peevish, bossy neglect. The babysitter goes. Joyce, eleven, is in charge. We dare not disobey her. A babysitter might grouse, cajole, and holler, but Joyce will pinch and bruise us. She can sit on a sibling, hold the wrists by one hand, and with the other hand mercilessly tickle. She need not resort to these restraints. Her face has assumed its adolescence—the flashing eyes, the stern jaw, the shoulders and neck stout as an eagle's breast and wing. She can with a steely look silence us, send us running. She can with the jump rope of her smile make my lungs stretch with laughter, make me forget any place not near her.

In the afternoons, she and I elbow one another at the kitchen's double sink, our faces warm, ambushed by sunshine from the windows overlooking our back yard. Joyce swishes soap around a plate and hands it to me. I rinse it under an icicle of tap water. We gossip; we reveal which island castaway we love best and will marry. I love Gilligan. Joyce loves the Professor. We feel a little sorry for the unloved Skipper, but not sorry enough to be in love with him.

In August I start second grade and after five weeks am skipped to third. Daddy explains the opportunity. "It's your choice," he says. "A lot of people really want you to do this. But if you don't want to, you don't have to." Habit turns my head; I look for Joyce. She's been sent out of the room. She doesn't get a say. I nod at Daddy. Second grade's boredom sits alarming and sad in my stomach; I have felt like a stranger, quickly finished with my work while those around me are gripped and busy with challenge. Third grade can be no worse, and tantalizes, unknown, with the lure of an unreadable name on a spinning globe.

"Don't get to thinking you're something special," Joyce tells me. "You're not somebody different just because this happened." For a time, while the aunts and uncles and Granny and Granddaddy fuss and preen over my education, Joyce and I fade into one another's backgrounds, float away as if in separate lifeboats. We discover how to survive competition, how to recede from a sister until she is no more than texture. We discover that when we do rush toward each other again, we guard our sisterhood with an avid conspiracy—our games and conversation are sanctuary, hide-out, homeland, more idyllic and secret as our adventures diverge.

I don't know Joyce's friends. I don't know the secrets she shares with them. I don't know the songs she sings in Campfire Girl meetings, the homework she unwrinkles to show Mama and Daddy. She seems far away. I don't know how to tell her that third grade is worse than second. I don't know how to stop children from calling me names and jeering at my sacked sandwiches next to their school lunch trays. I don't tell Joyce that a girl named Vanessa has promised to be my friend as long as I keep it a secret. Not even Joyce knows that some mornings I hit myself in the stomach in order to convincingly fake illness, to not face recess.

My playmates, daughters of Mama's church friends, don't know me from school. Ashlie and Paige and I raise noise, track dirt, and scatter toys, and we are sent behind the closed pocket door of Paige's family room or to her back yard for leapfrog and house and jacks.

Mama retrieves me from play late in the afternoon. She's working now as an accounts receivables clerk. She's itched to return to work. But now, in the middle of her day, with sniping office workers and the Dallas freeway blender blades behind her, with cooking and cleaning and folding and bathing yet ahead of her, she's weary and griping. "Get your feet in the car," she says. "Would you—look at where your jacket is. It's going—there, it's caught in the door. That's a big grease stain now. You know how hard that is to clean?"

A scant crease in her day-worn cake makeup catches my eye, pulls me in like a bear hug. I'm pummelled by sympathy; I stagger under unexpected love. Her children wreck her. We're loud, we fight and quarrel, and we don't do what she says. We wear her out. We complain about bedtime, and we complain about food we don't like, and we complain when we have to quit playing. She doesn't want to be tired and frustrated. She doesn't want to gripe and be unhappy. We don't make it easy. What a relief there aren't more of us.

I suit up my voice, button into what I believe is womanly camaraderie. I anticipate her gratitude and a blossoming confidence: one of her children understands her.

"Can't you stop wiggling around," she says. "I mean it! Ann!" She turns the ignition.

"I bet you were glad when Robert died," I say.

Mama wheels in the driver's seat. Her breath seems vacuumed from her, leaving her frozen. She raises her hand from the wheel. Her shocked face is squeezed like a slice of bread. "Don't you ever say that!" she screams at me. Her eyes are black and bright with pain and revulsion. "Don't you ever say that to me again! You hear me!"

I am afraid to speak but more afraid not to answer. "Yes, ma'am," I say.

She slams herself back against the car seat and grips the wheel. She grits her teeth and shifts into gear and doesn't talk to me the rest of the way home. I sit still and concentrate on being small and think on my mistake—putting on airs, trying to be a grownup with my mother, not keeping my place. What I've said hangs between us like a target, hangs in our hands like knives.

"I messed up," I whisper to Joyce in the black fog of bedtime.

"It's not the first time and it won't be the last," she whispers back. "So go to sleep."

In the third morning of her stay, waiting for the doctors, Joyce was pensive and jumpy, like a child hiding a gift behind her back. Dr. Patrick checked her chart, asked how she felt.

"I remembered something," Joyce told him. "I think I remembered what might be making my stomach hurt."

Dr. Patrick tensed around the fixed pivot of his smile. His little finger twitched; the fine muscles near his eyes tightened. The urge to act seemed to vibrate from his body, around the anchor of his cool, cavernous voice. "You have some abdominal pain?" Dr. Patrick asked.

"Yes."

"More than before?"

"About the same."

"I see. What do you think might be causing this?"

Joyce's eyes were round and guileless. She scooped out the prepared words like aspirin from a hard-to-open bottle. "I might have hurt myself," she said. "A few weeks ago I needed to go and I stopped myself. I held it in. Maybe I pulled something."

Dr. Patrick frowned, a quick stitch on either side of the smile. "You pulled something? What do you think you pulled, Joyce?"

"I don't know, it just hurt and I thought maybe I pulled something," she said.

"I don't understand," he said gently. "What happened?"

"I held it too long," she said.

Dr. Patrick puzzled a moment longer, reading Joyce's expectant face. Sad decision flickered behind his rimless eyeglasses. Altered mental state, I thought, and watched him let the discussion fly free, no written note to cage it.

"She held in a bowel movement," I explained to him later. "She's afraid she hurt herself doing it." Nurses and visitors milled past us in the hallway. He widened his stance, folded his arms.

"I see," he said. He noted the information and set it aside as one might a spotless fork from the tray of unpolished silver.

"Have you a moment, Doctor?" I asked.

"You'd like to discuss your sister's condition?"

"If you can."

"I'll tell you what we know so far," he said.

No one needs to make her understand that she's fat. She never forgets it. That's why she pretends, in public, that her fat isn't true. It's not polite to admit it controls her, not smart to admit it controls her. She pretends it's not an overwhelming and obvious part of her life.

The weight is no secret. She can't hide her fat; everyone can see it. But no one can see her terrified obsession, or how ashamed she is that she's done this to herself. No one can see she feels like a sick beast, with thoughts of food never out of her mind. No one sees how asinine she feels, publicly picking over the minutiae of calories or sugar and fat grams before privately shoving a barrage of food against her teeth. There are people who have always known food as food and exercise as pleasure. She can never expose to them how she feels about herself. How could they hear it without feeling they're watching a freak show?

"It's such a simple equation," one friend said. "Eat less, exercise more."

But from the inside it's not simple at all. She doesn't remember what it's like not to be obese. She doesn't know how to eat less, since she doesn't comprehend or remember the amount she eats. She doesn't grasp how to exercise more, since she doesn't recognize when she hasn't exercised enough. She doesn't know how to fit herself into the simple equation—but she believes in it, and thus believes herself a failure. No one needs to make me understand I'm a failure, she thinks. She never forgets it.

Daddy chewed on the tip end of one eyeglass earpiece and perused the cafeteria menu board. He and Mama and I shuffled, like dazed cattle down a chute, through the hot food, salad, and drink lines. Mama, neat and sturdy in blue crepe pants and loose-yoked, flowered overshirt, perambulated the long formica-plated dining tables, hefting her tray breast-high. At the table, Daddy folded his glasses, dropped them in the plaid woolen shirt pocket. He stabbed three green beans in slow succession. With his glint of his glasses removed, his eyes were the color of the faded jeans he wore when working in the garden. His shoulders stooped slightly. "Did they tell you she tried to walk?" he said. He rode his voice uneasily, like a boy balancing a seesaw against a slightly smaller child.

"What?" I said. "No. When?"

"Last night. She tried to get out of bed and walk."

"What happened?"

"She got about two steps and fell down," Daddy said.

"With all the tubes and everything?"

"Uh-huh."

"Oh. Oh, what a mess. She didn't say anything about that. What was she thinking?"

(The doctor said, "You'd like to discuss your sister's condition? I'll tell you what we know so far.")

Mama spoke through a bite of hamburger. She warmed to conversation through declarations, like a car coasting downhill before its engine sputters into full ignition. While we spoke, Daddy receded from our noise and ate slowly, silently as though he were alone, his chin dipped and his eyes raised toward the overhead TV monitor. There, firefighters struggled over concrete mountains, and commentary flowed around the rubble like oil around locked gears.

"Well, now, it gets tiresome just staying in that hospital bed, and I suppose she wanted to show she could do it. She's real weak, you know, from just laying there, though."

"That and a few other things."

"Well, mostly from laying there. You can't just lay in a hospital bed and not expect to be a little weak, and what with all that's wrong with her."

("We'd like to do a sleep apnea study. We're concerned about her difficulty breathing. You know she's using a CPAP oxygen mask, several times a day as needed. Her oxygen levels are low. She may in time need a larger ventilator.")

"Did Norman tell you we called the DHS office. They're going to send us out the forms for Joyce to sign. If she can get on the state rolls then the woman there said her medical should be covered. She'll have to get a doctor to say she's medically disabled and couldn't have worked the way she is. Do you think one of the doctors here could probably do that? Or will we have to hunt down whoever her doctor was in Texas?"

("Dialysis could be a next option, yes, in a typical patient who did not respond to the medication for the kidneys. However, Joyce's size and general physical condition present serious difficulties. We don't believe we will move in that direction.")

"You know, Norman, I've been thinking. LaNita has that hospital bed in her garage they're not using anymore for Troy. When Joyce goes home we should see if we can't get it while she's not able to get around."

("We've tried. We can do neither an MRI or a CT scan to find out what might be causing her infection. We don't have a machine here large enough for her to fit in. There is no question of moving her to the closest facility that does.")

"Is Hunter coming up?"

"Oh, Ann, I don't think so. He's having all kind of problems with his car, and he's not wanting to be driving it all over the countryside."

("The chest X-rays are also problematic. A large amount of tissue overlies her chest, and this causes a haze on the X-ray. We aren't able to read the X-rays as well as we need to.")

"I tell you one thing. When we get home she's going to have to eat right and exercise. There's no putting it off anymore. Won't be any more excuses. I'll go in and do it with her. Get on a program."

("We think her heart may be slightly enlarged, but this would be expected given other factors, and does not concern us overly at this time.")

"I want to hear more about what's happening with the antibiotics."

"Now, Ann, the doctors know what they're doing."

"I know they know what they're doing. I want to know what they're doing, too. I want to know what they think might help her improve."

"Well, I'm sure they'll tell us what all we need to know. She just got dehydrated is all, and wasn't taking care of herself."

("If we cannot find the cause of her illness, we cannot treat it. She has no time to spend in an undiagnosed condition if she is to recover.")

"She just has to get through this medication, is all, and get the fluids back in her body until her kidneys are working better, and then she can go home. Norman, do you think LaNita would sell us that hospital bed?"

("I strongly suggest you do not tell your parents all these things. They do not seem to comprehend the complexity or seriousness of Joyce's condition. Unless they begin to want these discussions, we think it would not be wise to distress them with various diagnostic possibilities. And for now, these are only possibilities. You must understand this also.")

"I don't know," Daddy said. "We'll cross that bridge when we get there."

("I understand," I told him. "Thank you, Doctor.")

1975

I want to stay somewhere dark and lonely, but the summer afternoon beats through the windows. I pillbug in the cavelike hallway, arms around knees, chest heaving, shirt sleeves damp with tears. I love Johnny Cartwright, the boldest boy in third grade. "I don't want to go," I say. "I'll never see him again. He's moving away and I'm moving away and I'll never see him again."

Joyce, twelve, kneels and folds her arms around me. She tips my head back onto her shoulder and strokes the wispy hair from my forehead as if for fever. "Don't cry too much," she says. Her voice and skin are soft and cool as milk. "It won't always hurt."

We're moving to Oklahoma, jettisoning from the capsule within which we have become ourselves. We are irremediably Texan, lovingly brainwashed by state history books since kindergarten. We know Stephen F. Austin and Jim Bowie and Ima Hogg and Bob Wills and Roger Staubach. We know the great limestone hall at Fair Park, its fossil slabs looming upward like the walls of the Red Sea around the Israelites. We love, because we know them, the dizzying twists and lane shifts of freeways, the spiked glitter of downtown Dallas. We know what the six flags are. We know to never pick bluebonnets. We belt the songs out, "The Eyes of Texas" and "Texas Our Texas" and "You're From Big D," our back-seat anthems on car trips. We wonder whether we'll still sing them, whether we've the right. We know all the words to "Oklahoma," but we falter after "Brand new state! Brand new state! Gonna treat you great!" We don't mean it.

We look back, thinking of Granny laughing at one or another of her grandchildren and of Granddaddy in overalls and beaten felt hat in a front yard lawn chair, playing solitaire on his lap board, waiting for neighbor fellows to come jaw and dip snuff. We think of Granny's mop-headed dog, Muffin, running circles in the back yard, looking for us; we think of jars of sun tea and the branch of the mimosa tree we'd never managed to climb to and the way the Texan sun shines white in a sky as big and clear as an afternoon nap, making everything it shines on look large and open. Into the hollow bellyache of leaving we run a siphon from Texas. We carry Texas everywhere, sloshing in the invisible cavity. But we pull on Oklahoma like coveralls and boots over our street clothes.

"Your daddy needs to be close to his parents," Mama tells us. "They're getting older and he needs to be there with them."

"Do we have to say we're from Oklahoma?" Joyce asks.

"No, I don't guess. If you want to be Texan you can still be Texan."

"When can we move back?" I ask.

Mama presses down a suitcase lid and snaps shut its two silver clips. "When you get grown you can move anywhere you want," she says. She swipes her black lacquer bangs from her forehead, the other hand on a beveled hip as she surveys the pile of clothes and coats yet to be packed. "Now get on and make sure all y'all's toys are out so we can get them in the boxes."

Muskogee, low-slung, brick-clad, two-laned, is small enough that the blue endpaper of the sky is always visible over the rooftops, small enough that the streets named with letters don't use the whole alphabet. The weekend tour of our world, public library and grocery store and church and both grandmothers' houses, can be accomplished in a single morning and afternoon, sometimes hitting no more than two traffic lights. For the weekday circuit, we don't even need a car. Every morning, Joyce gathers books and sack lunch and sets out across a misty field of vacant lots for the junior high school four blocks away. She joins the pep squad, earning with fervid yells her maroon sweatshirt, two limp maroon-and-gold pompons, and a cluster of friends whom she dares not invite home. They're black, and she won't subject them, or Grandma Hester, to Grandma Hester's discomfort. "They're my friends," she says. "I don't think anybody would treat them bad, but I don't want to hear them get talked about."

As Joyce's short figure recedes across the field, her long, brown hair bouncing on her back, Hunter and I each take one of Grandpa's square, tool-burred hands to walk the maze of alleyways and residential streets to Whittier Elementary. Before and after school and during recess, the schoolyard is a fenced reservation of tribal conflict, a beaten expanse of dirt and concrete and dry, struggling fescue. Children clump and knock against each other like marbles. We assert dominance or pliability by choosing sides for Red Rover, by claiming and keeping the swing with the longest chains. Hunter, six, finds boys who will race, shove, yell. I'm afraid to climb the slide, afraid to cross the monkey bars, afraid to broach the cross-legged circle of girls who guard their pit of fashion dolls and fashion doll accessories.

After school, Joyce and Hunter and I reconvene in Grandma Hester's tidy white tract house. At three in the afternoon, Grandpa snores in his deep, upholstered rocker, his bald head and square jaw lax, his open scrapbook on his lap and closed paste pot on the TV tray. Grandma, angularly plump and stooped at an angle that makes her look solicitous rather than frail, greets us in her house dress, rolled brown hose, and her perfect beret of gray hair. She marshalls us into kitchen chairs around a plate of warm chocolate cookies and glasses of watery milk. We mustn't dawdle. With ladylike modulations of her firm, waterfall soprano, Grandma snugs her timetable over our afternoon like a fitted sheet on a fat mattress. Soon we must spread homework over the vinyl tablecloth, and homework must be finished long before time to set the table.

In Grandma Hester's house, the trash cans are always empty. Nothing accumulates. Sometimes, Joyce and I wad a Kleenex and throw it away so we can spy on the empty trash can later. Meals are on time. Laundry is folded promptly upon removal from the dryer. But the house overflows with us, with our noise and child sweat and our need to eat and find places to sleep, guest rooms and living room and rollaway bed. Careless, we turn blindly and bump Grandma's rules: Sit up straight. Practice your penmanship. Wipe your fingers. Don't run. Don't laugh too loudly. Don't leave the refrigerator door open. Don't lie on your stomach to watch television. Don't talk back. When Grandma corrects us, pointedly not looking at Mama, Mama's forty-year-old, lipsticked mouth is steamrolled as thin as Grandma Hester's seventy-year-old lily-frond lips.

"Y'all mind your grandma," she says, flicking her eyes upward from the inked ovals she has swirled on tiny newsprint blocks of house and job ads.

"Now, calm down," Mama tells Joyce when Grandma irons the puckers out of Joyce's seersucker, a flowing cornflower blouse that made Joyce's eyes look like blue puddings. "She didn't mean to hurt anything."

"She ruined it," Joyce cries, behind the closed door of the guest room where we sleep.

"I know it," Mama says. "But it's just a shirt, and that's your grandma. She was so proud of getting those wrinkles out for you. Huh. Now all this time she must have thought I let you wear that thing all wrinkled."

"I don't want to make her feel bad," Joyce says, snuffling. This is, after all, Grandma, who never sends us away, Grandma who teaches us dominoes and card games, whose shivering, naughty giggle chases a surprise escapee joke. "Did you hear about the man who got on the bus? He told the driver he wanted to get off at 3rd and P."

But it's also Grandma who wags her finger at us when we sit at the kitchen table making faces at each other, making up nonsense names to call each other, seeing who will crack and laugh first. "Now, I never," she says. "Young ladies ought not behave this way. It's about time you were learning to be young ladies. And those shorts you have on are too short. That's just indecent at your age. Now straighten up and get your homework done and then think about changing your clothes." She seizes the round laundry basket heaped with towels and pads down the hallway.

Joyce fumes, her shoulders back, her front teeth lightly gritted, and her drooped eyes shifted, cold, gray-blue globes trailing white contrails. "Young ladies ought not behave this way," she whines and minces. "You need to be young laaaaadies."

The laughter slams like popcorn in my chest. "Stop! Wait!" I say, and keen in a nasal drawl, "I never. Your shorts are so short. I never. Now straighten up!" We relax like melting snow into our laughter, untying each other's fading snickers like boot laces. We warm against each other's giggles. And into this bath of hilarity Mama slaps her hands hard on the table.

"Your Grandma is down there in her room right now crying her eyes out. How could you? I'm ashamed of both of you right now! Now you are going to apologize to her though I don't know how you're going to make it up to her. I'm just ashamed."

Joyce and I stare at each other as though loading our thoughts onto opposite sides of a scale. We register the exact weights of shock, regret, and unrepentance, and won't need later to compare and balance our conclusions.

"Goodnight," I whisper to Joyce that night as she burrows warm beside me under the heavy, chenille spread. I think she may be sleeping, but the bed's silence grows heavy, like a square pan with rising cake.

"I miss Texas," she whispers back.

The first time she loses fifty pounds, she wants to win the heart and body of a young man who dates slender, active girls. She spends her student loan for membership in a plan that provides a regular weigh-in and measurements, a

weekly supply of boxed and bagged food, and a counselor who smiles but dispenses little information. She lifts weights at a gym three times a week, trudges dutifully on the treadmill.

She eats only her small daily ration, bolstered with fresh vegetables, and loses fifty pounds in five months. The young man whose affection she craves is still not attracted to her. She doesn't care anymore. She feels powerful, impudent, free.

She stops buying the prepackaged food when she travels out of the country for summer work. She thinks, I can do it myself. I don't need the plan. How hard can it be to eat sensibly on my own?

She gains the fifty pounds again, over a year. She feels hollow and nauseated at the thought of the lost money. She can't afford to replace the clothes. She shops at garage sales, discount stores—accepts holes and small, mendable rips in garments. She can hardly remember her thinner self. She only remembers failing, feeling fat and awkward.

She consoles herself with food. She can afford a full grocery cart. She orders pizzas. While she eats, alone at home, life feels dreamlike and pleasant. Whenever she stops eating, fear and guilt crash on her, like a sand castle on a small, stranded fish.

Time moves differently inside a hospital, where after only a few hours you no longer feel yourself move through time. You move toward or away from the patient's white sheets, the dormitory cinder blocks, the cafeteria clatter; we moved toward Joyce's tests, her naps, her feedings, the jagged puzzle-pieces of her conversations. We lost our appetites for time, and others took care of time for us. So rather than beat our hearts against time, we relaxed and slipped from medication to water cup, electrode to readout, empty to slightly less empty urine bag. Events repeated themselves like the line on an electrocardiogram readout. Hypnotized by routine, we stopped watching time. Yet time crawled toward us like some prehistoric, predatory tortoise.

Around us, objects of metal, rubber, or sterile plastic became pre-dictable yet remained utterly foreign. We couldn't pretend to translate the telegraphic flashes and beeps of equipment, yet their rhythms pressed into our lungs, into our sleep. Fascination sat like a heavy child in our laps. We shifted it aside to accommodate the hospital as normal, nothing to be frightened of—naturally, one might always lie down to eat one's food from a plastic tray, sip milk through a straw dipped in a paper carton. One might always in the course of a day hike up one's gown for an unnamed nurse to smear lotion over the white moonscape of one's belly. One might hear the hue of one's urine discussed in front of one's father. One might gasp for breath and quickly be fitted with the clear cup of a flexible oxygen mask. To blink at life is to invite life's trammeling. We pretended that hospital time was the only sort of time, and that none of the hospital's accoutre-ments or incidents bewildered us.

Amidst our pretense, Joyce lay ponderous and sullen. New nurses gulped, first seeing her. Two nurses struggled to lift Joyce when the sheets were soiled; two nurses braced and hoisted her when she slid and couldn't wiggle upward to straighten her spine. Beside her bed, a blue curtain on an oval track fell in its quiet drape against the wall. Like a trophied spear against the sky, a bag of blood hung atop a pole beside the curtain.

"Why is she losing blood?" I asked Dr. Abu. In our poses near the nurse's station, we greeted one another with mirthless smiles of comfort and with the usual audit: I held still so he could gauge my balance of worry and detachment; he let me watch him mask his exhaustion, pull a scarf of strength across his face. His dark eyes were like closed boxes, his voice, deep and floating as if toward shore, from a boat on the ocean at night.

"We're not sure," he said. "She doesn't show the signs of someone who is bleeding internally. We cannot run the tests that we need to do. We cannot give her one type of medicine, for it will interfere with the other problems." A shadow of frustration and pain like the black blade of a cir-cular saw passed across his face. "Her white count is still elevated. She still has not produced urine. We simply cannot perform a diagnosis."

He gripped the lip of the station desk with both reluctant hands, braced his arms as if for a hamstring stretch. He watched his hands as though for signals, answers coded in their thousand-times bloodied, soaped, and rinsed planes and lines. He turned his head. His eyes were cold but comforting, like a friend's hand reaching for mine in a power failure, in a stopped and blackened elevator. "The amount of fat on her body," he said, choosing his words slowly, "prevents us from learning what damage has already occurred within her body."

In a hospital room fifteen steps away, Joyce squinted, petulant and bored, over the high dune of her gowned stomach, at a relentless television. Fifteen steps away, my father, who had sat bedside with his father and years later his mother as they died, swung a sports section page in its flimsy arc past the features to the box scores, and my mother, who had been far away when the news came that her father and years later her mother had died, gently snored, her hands folded on her stomach and her head tipped forward onto her breast. And next to me, Dr. Abu straightened his spine, looked me in the eye, and allowed himself the dream of a deep sigh. He said, "This is a nightmare."

❖ **1976** ❖

Joyce and Hunter and I map the three acres of rolling woods and rugged grass atop which perches our new brick house in the countryside. We scrutinize the ravine where pokeweed grows, the clumps of black locust, the ramshackle pond, filled yet with fetid mud and the previous owner's discarded kitchen appliances. We scout the ruts where cows once grazed, the pasture's barbed-wire profile, the dim, corrugated tin barn, its ancient straw heaps cobwebbed. In the dank, rusted recesses, a honeybee menaces in loops around my nose and scalp, then buries its barbed stinger flush in my left arm. I bite down on silence, more frightened of the extraction, of sharp tweezers stirring the wound, than of the burning toxin. I shudder in Daddy's wing chair with an ice cube up my T-shirt sleeve and the Bee and Venom volumes of the *World Book* on my lap. I wait for fever, swelling, choking. I have been caught out; the shoe has dropped. I might die now as I deserve for the formidable sin with its roots spread in my heart.

The sin started when I was six. I peered over Joyce's elbow at her hymnal, following the quarter-notes of the stately pledge, "Oh, lamb of God! I come." We sang the second verse. "Just as I am and waiting not to rid my soul of one dark blot—" And I pictured my mother.

She's my dark blot. The prayer was swift: God, take my mother. Then I sang on, wicked and wrong and horribly sincere. I want a mellifluous, dreamy mother, who gazes into my eyes, enamored of me, enrapt in silly games and secrets—and I have gotten a sharp, plainspoken mother who never dallies and for whom I seem not a miracle but an odd inheritance, one that must against all reason be reminded nightly to brush its teeth. Yet hasn't she with calm labor quilted my blanket, each square the embroidered portrait of a different state flower? Hasn't she with masking tape galleried my drawings and stories along the hallway? How is this not enough? Could she love me if she knew my ingratitude, my longing for relief from her scowl, her weariness of my need for attention?

We sing this song nearly every Sunday. It feels like crossing a rotted suspension bridge. A weak plank cracks underfoot; I feel the wish again. I can't unthink it or forget I meant it. Just as I am! One dark blot! I think of it when Mama slides a second pork chop onto her plate and Daddy winces and groans, "Toppy, no"; she nearly cries with the dual inabilities of putting the food back, obedient to his distaste, or of now relishing the fat-crust creaminess. In Daddy's frown I feel wanting her gone. In Mama's squinted, lowered eyes and slow, defiant chewing I feel wanting to be worth her love again. In church, when the song's five somber verses have passed, I slip my hand into Daddy's suit pocket. I hunt, as for a rare medicinal herb, the limp sliver of yellow paper, the inked eyelets of Mama's cursive "I love you," inserted there after she sewed the last hem of the suit. He never removed it from the pocket.

When I'm nine, the sin, weekly and secretly examined and memorized, is part of me like the freckle on my wrist, the pumpkin strings of my voice. I've kept it dark. So I'm gratified when Joyce credits me with sin; she doesn't laugh when I suggest salvation.

We change from our church clothes. The tender, tomato-clay aroma of Sunday pot roast drifts through the house's heating ducts. "Joyce," I say. By such preludes we introduce any conversations never to be repeated beyond our door.

"What."

"Can I ask you something?"

"I guess."

"Do you want to get baptized with me tonight?" I ask, and hold my breath while she stares, her blue eyes steady and inscrutable as the moon.

The church curriculum doesn't introduce the death and resurrection until seventh grade, near a more predictable age of accountability for one's sins. But every week the sermon's exhortation, the desire to pledge my life to Jesus, has pulled me like a kite string, like a hand encircling and squeezing. I want to seal a covenant with the God of wrath and love. I don't fear a lake of fire as I do the hell of the Book of Jude, where sinners are wandering stars for whom the nether gloom of darkness has been reserved for ever. I don't fear hell. I fear losing heaven. I fear that black rot in my own heart will sever me from God, from home.

I wait for Joyce's judgment. Joyce—who recites scriptures looking out the corner of her eye, fascinated, as though God were muttering to her, who sings hymns as though they were feast platters lifted with both hands, who prays aloud, quiet and firm, as though God lived in a kind of cottage workshop in her ribcage—Joyce hops off her bed with her dress undone in the back and jumps across the room to hug me. Her voice swells from deep in her breast like a waterfowl's.

"I was waiting for you," she said. "I've been thinking about it a long time. I wanted to do it together."

"Joyce," I say. A brilliant alloy of joy and shock swirls. I pry my arms from the band of her hug. "You didn't, really."

She nods and shrugs, the one-shoulder, eyelid-lowered shrug of refusal to explain. She means it. Almost fourteen, certainly accountable, she has imperiled her soul to wait for my baptism. I vine my arms around the oaken curves of her ribs.

The evening service seems short and light, a gauze scarf floating over our family in the pew. Grandma and Grandpa in their time-softened clothes and skins flank Hunter, who squirms, his burr haircut bobbing forward over paper and pencil. Daddy dives for the ebony reef of bass notes along the bottom staff of the hymnal, while Mama's unabashed squeak barrel-races around the written tunes. Joyce trains the finely engineered tension of her rounded-pecan face and Greek-column body toward the pulpit. She sits still as forcefully as others might play tennis. She nudges me and with a quick glare, a traffic-signal blink of reproof, directs my eyes toward the preacher when my attention drifts.

When most of the congregation has slammed car doors and driven away, a few remain to sing and pray, to witness a moment as discrete and definite as an ice cube in a tray. Joyce and I stand at the front pew, looking up at the elders. "I believe that Jesus Christ is the Son of God," Joyce says, "and I come to be baptized for the remission of my sins." I repeat the good confession after her, my mouth dry.

"I'm afraid to have my head under water," I whisper to Mama in the dressing room as she wrangles the white cotton gown over my head. It swirls, falls cool around my skin and panties.

"That's not what you're supposed to be thinking about," Mama says. "If that's what you're worried about you might want to wait a while to do this."

I shake my head no. I'd never heard of anyone going straight to heaven being drowned by a preacher. Besides, Joyce has already descended the steps. The water sloshes; the curtains of the puppet-stage baptistry gasp open, revealing her in profile. The preacher's hand cups the air over her head, and he invokes the Father and Son and Holy Ghost. Joyce presses a washcloth to her nose, leans back in the hook of the preacher's arm. The water dovetails and closes over her forehead and round chin. She drips with the amens of the faithful. She turns, a jubilant torque inside the clinging, opaque gown, her clownish smile nearly a laugh, looking for me. "It's okay," she says. "Go ahead." As she sidles past on the baptistry stair, I descend into the water, the rough tile gripping my feet, and think, look, I'm as tall as her now.

While we dress, the tiny remnant of the congregation sings. Daddy, grinning and easy, shakes hands and banters with the elders. Joyce hugs Mama. Mama waits quietly, patting her purse, a smile waltzing on and off her lips and a thought fidgeting in her eyes as she watches Daddy. She looks at me as if I were a wild fawn that might run. "Y'all sounded so grown-up," she says. I cross to her and hug her waist, pressing my head to her breast. She pats my shoulder. "Okay, there," she says, "I'm real proud of you. That's enough, now. That's enough."

Joyce and I in bed that night, as every night, spin words like a wheel toward our goodnights. In our tiny bedroom, crowded with furniture like a mouth with unpulled teeth, we have installed the fiction that one side of the room is hers and one is mine. But we have no room for secrets. She knows the toys I stuff under my bed; I know the scraps of paper she gleans from school. Our thoughts and silences are public. Lying in bed, we know each other's breathing the way we know our blankets' warmth.

I can't sleep until Joyce returns my goodnight. She says goodnight and the world is at balance: an advent calendar opens; a hand closes around a hand; a butterfly hides, then spreads its cafeteria of color. "Are you going to tell people at school that we got baptized?" I ask.

"My friends. Are you?"

"It's not a secret," I say. "It's big news, right?"

"Don't expect those kids to care," she says.

"Goodnight," I say, and wait for the butterfly wings to beat.

"Goodnight," she says, and as I fall asleep, I listen to her breathe.

A bubble of happiness bobs in her chest. She has eaten only 800 calories so far today and has cleared lunchtime's hurdle, and now she craves something sweet. She wants to choose something healthy, as though the health were in the food and not in the choosing. Grapes, she thinks. Or half a cookie, a gluey splash of brown sugar and chocolate . . .

She thinks ahead to dinner, and recalls the refrigerator shelves. Pasta, she thinks. How many calories in pasta? Two hundred a cup? A cup is nothing. If she only eats a cup she'll still be hungry. Four hundred then; two cups is plenty. But there, that's 1200 calories and she still wants the grapes and cookie now. She can lose weight at 1500 calories. Wait—she forgot the sauce. And she'll serve bread for her husband, and eat some herself. And can she have something sweet after dinner? If she eats the grapes now she won't have any fruit left after dinner. She sighs, a sharp burst, and feels her chest tighten and her head tense. Well, she'll lumber across that bridge later. Right now she knows she can have the grapes. She opens the refrigerator, and sees bread and jam and leftover meatballs and a pitcher of lemonade. In a few seconds she'll be eating, and she feels like a student deciding to cheat off a friend's paper. She wants a meatball. No one will know if she takes one meatball. Its taste, the deep tang of garlic and tomato, spackles her tongue. No one will know if she takes two. But now, her health. She turns on the TV. Her smile disappears into the blank receptacle of her face. She eats to the bottom of the bag of grapes, swallowing almost without chewing, filling the quota.

"Some good news," said Dr. Bemeka. She flashed a smile as sudden and ephemeral as a clap of hands. She ran a finger down Joyce's chart. Mama and Daddy straightened in the bedside chairs. "Joyce is producing urine now."

"When?" I asked.

"Since last night. This would indicate that the medicines for her kidneys have started to work and that her kidneys are beginning to stabilize."

"Oh, good—good," Mama said.

"That's great," I said. I smiled, and Joyce smiled back a rubbery smile. She hadn't eaten breakfast that morning. Her toast had tilted cold and papery over a loaf of scrambled egg. Lunch, a sandwich and chips, sat untouched now. I followed Dr. Bemeka into the hallway, then saw Dr. Kamath leaning in her white coat, like a leafless, snow-covered branch, over papers on the nurses' station. She favored me with a calligraphic smile, an unambiguous stroke of encouragement across the fresh parchment of her face. Yes, she had a moment for charts and questions.

"Dr. Bemeka told us about the increased output. Have the BUN and creatinine levels dropped as well?"

"Not yet as we would like, but we would expect to see that next."

"How long," I asked, "before the kidneys are stable enough to begin antibiotics to fight the infection?"

"We are giving her antibiotics now," Dr. Kamath said. "But to aggressively treat the infection, and to find out its cause . . . I'm sorry. I just can't say."

"Is the improvement to her kidneys likely to last?"

"You must understand," she said, spider-legging her fingertips on the desktop and then placing her hands together as if for a blessing, or prayer. "So much is wrong in your sister's body. Any improvement is a sign of hope. But she is fighting high odds of recovery."

Dr. Kamath had found more ways than anyone else to tell me that Joyce was likely to die. Hearing it felt like an accidental, shallow stabbing in the kitchen, when just before the stinging pain, I'd stand awash in blood and denial of my clumsiness. Oh, that didn't just happen. I didn't just hear her say it.

"I don't want to lose you," her bridegroom tells her. "I don't want to lose you to a heart attack at forty. Please. Please do something. Please try."

"Your daddy and I are going to go for a walk and see some of the fall foliage hereabout the hospital," Mama said. "We'll be back but we'll probably leave before suppertime."

"Are you coming back tomorrow?" She mustn't be left alone.

"You're still going home tomorrow?" Daddy asked.

"I need to get back to work," I said. "Since she's a little better. . . but still, do you think—"

"Somebody ought to be here with her, yes," Mama said. "The nurses don't always come when she calls. We thought maybe we could take that dormitory room you've been staying in."

"We'll set it up," I said.

"Norman," Mama mused. "I ought to call Hunter. He was asking if he needed to come up here, and with his car throwing smoke the way he says, it doesn't sound like there's any need."

Exercise is punishment for being fat: something unpleasant she must mete out upon herself, a consequence of her lack of discipline. Exercise makes her confront her body, reminds her she feels bad about her long physical lapse. So to reward herself for restrained behavior, or to console herself for slip-ups, she skips exercise. You've been good today, she tells herself. I won't make you go to the gym.

Movement feels awkward. She doesn't look like the other women in the aerobics class. She doesn't wear the clinging outfits that leaner women wear. She wears baggy sweats and long, loose T-shirts to hide her tummy roll and panty line. The baggy clothes set her apart. She feels marked, stiff and ungainly. She feels she will not be picked first for the team.

She resents wearing clothes that make her look lumpy. She hates to feel lumpy and slow. Movements she needs to do precisely, effectively, quickly, make her lumpiness and slowness more obvious. She can't bend—her abdomen is stuffed in the way. The insides of her thighs jiggle. She doesn't like the fins under her arms squashing against the machine pad when she does the tricep pull. She doesn't like her boobs bouncing, even in a sports bra. They feel like two fifteen-ounce cans of tomato paste hammocked to her ribcage. Except her boobs weigh more than that, and the hammock is her own skin, and it pulls and hurts.

But she knows the only remedy is the very exercise in which her body feels so intensely uncomfortable. She knows she feels powerful and energized after exercise. But she doesn't like to go. She is embarrassed by her body. How does she make the step from embarrassment to joy in movement? She wants to find a way to move that causes her joy, that causes her to forget her body and others' bodies around her.

Visitors inch into a hospital room, looking for a place to knock, far enough within the door so that their bedridden friend hears them, but far enough away to preserve the mirage of courtesy and also to escape if necessary from the vulnerability of nudity, vomit, sleep. Hospital staff stride in and out unannounced, prepared, perfunctory.

The counselor, a tall woman in brown trousers, brown cardigan, and graying brown ponytail in a brown barrette, entered without preamble. She paused at the foot of Joyce's bed, a fan of fine smile wrinkles opening like a safety net. "Joyce?" she said. "I'm Susan. Hello. We have an appointment?"

"I'll go now," I said. "Joyce, I'll be back after dinner. Do you want me to bring you anything? Something to read?"

"No," Joyce said, gazing at Counselor Susan as if at a present from Santa she dare not believe is really meant for her. "Thanks."

I waited outside the elevator bank amidst a silent crowd watching the down arrow. At last there's help, I thought. Would Joyce tell the counselor how it felt to live in a body she could hardly hoist up a staircase, could not buckle a seat belt around? Would she ask for hope, a way to believe she could live healthy again? Would she dissolve her defenses, admit the pain of being fat, the pain of not asking for help? What would it do to her to ask, to say these things? Could this conversation turn her, open her?

At the cafeteria entrance I stopped, patted my pockets senselessly, put my hand over my eyes, and sighed. The elevator going up stopped at every floor except for surgery. On the tenth floor, I stepped as softly as I could back into the room. Neither Joyce nor the counselor noticed me. Counselor Susan leaned forward in the chair, both hands clasped atop her clipboard, asking a question. Joyce answered with a smile and monosyllable. Counselor Susan tried again, this time laying one hand flat, palm up, as she craned her chin slightly forward. Joyce answered with a smile, a shrug and nod.

She looks so happy, I thought. Somebody cares. It's all she wants— not to have her leash slipped, but only to be petted. I backed out of the room, out of Joyce's privacy. I'd get my purse later.

 **1977**

Joyce wields her birthright, her full lexicon of wordless speech. With a relaxed eyebrow she bestows regard; with a feinted squint she showers anger. Powerful at fifteen, she lifts and lowers her eyelids to an astonishing array of positions and shapes, framing the mystery of expression in her blue-gray eyes. With nothing but the intent to blink she can repel, or command me to follow. With a suppressed twitch of the lip she can raise our mother's voice a half octave. Her gaze, heavy as concrete blocks or light as soap froth, pilots our afternoons.

She laughs with mouth wide but smiles with closed lips, a quick curve like the rim of a pink china teacup. Her lower lip is a taut puff like a child's bicep; the top of her mouth the angle and curve of a quarter-rest mark. She never looks at a camera. She always looks at the photographer, her eyes full of pointed remarks, her lips teasing, as though her smile might split into approval, welcome.

From Joyce's dictionary of expressions: Aggravation. Blue dice eyes thrown to the side. Lips like a pink umbrella rolled on the desk of the square jaw, the teeth lightly gritted like a locked drawer.

"Stop looking at me." Joyce whisks a round brush down the thick underside of her hair and stares into her own eyes. Between us stretch the long bathroom vanity and the high, silver wall of the bathroom mirror. We crowd each other for the sink, for the drawer where we dump combs and brushes. Joyce slicks a pale pink gloss over her lower lip. The bus comes in ten minutes. I haven't combed my hair.

"I'm not looking at you," I say.

"Yes you are. Stop it."

"It's just your hair's doing this flippy thing in the back."

"So?"

"I don't know. So it looks funny." I lean forward on the counter and bat my eyelashes at myself. I picture the layered geology of bathroom flotsam below the counter, the hair curlers and Epsom salts and half-used perfumes and stacks of Mama's romance novels. Joyce forces through her nose a breath halfway between sigh and growl; her pupils narrow. I shouldn't have said her hair looks funny. The bus is coming; she can't do anything about it.

"It doesn't look bad," I say. "Just funny. Are you mad?"

"Why would I be mad?" she says, and slams the comb and brush drawer closed.

From the dictionary of expressions: Patience. Hands laid on thighs like houseshoes by the bed. Temples and jaw quiet, as though the skin itself were drinking the wait. Eyes flashing suddenly—then lidded and silent again.

Daddy leaves for work first. He drives forty-five minutes through winding hillside roads, treacherous in winter and miserable in the broken air conditioning of the summer. He's an accountant for a regional tree nursery. The growl and pinch of unemployment have finally vanished from his eyes, his shoulders; he'd quit the auto shop after they asked him to cook the books. The recession ate at him and his new mortgage crushed him. He sat angry and unapproachable. Then he got the nursery job. In the winter, he laid plans, and in the spring, began to bring home trees, at cost.

Mama works at Bacone Junior College. A secretary in the registrar's office, she files and sorts enrollment paperwork and learns the college catalog and college politics. She keeps a jar of candy on her desk for the students. She works through migraine headaches when she can stand it, to save her sick days. In the summertime, Joyce and I alphabetize student records, tri-fold letters into envelopes. When we help, we applaud ourselves; Mama can work fewer hours on the weekends.

Mama's and Daddy's money pays for the mortgage, the cars, the household bills, reduced-cost school lunches, school supplies, and the collection plate. Mama's wardrobe, its tailored lines and linen blends straining around her hips and bust, dissolves into a mix of single-knits, busy prints, blousy gathers. Daddy's shirt collar threads fuzz where they will later fray, but new shirts don't appear in the ironing. Joyce and I don't ask for clothes. When Mama has ten unspent dollars, she takes us to the college thrift store, where the proprietress has checked the T-shirts, pantsuits, dresses. They are clean. They have no rips or holes.

From the dictionary of expressions: Fantasy. Eyelids drooped over a bright gaze. Walking as though her spine were floating, levitated above her pelvis. Smiles floating on and off; arms limp in a loss of need for time.

Joyce and I descend the bus steps at the country town's single-story, rock-walled school building. Joyce enters the main door with the other high schoolers, and I wander toward the elementary wing, where everything seems smaller, less significant. We keep our books in desks, not lockers, and we can't mill in the hallways between classes. The stories Joyce brings home are from a free, less frightening world, where teachers are not grouchy spirits hovering over the room, but, as Joyce describes, are more like accomplices, like guides along blind precipices. In Joyce's stories, classmates are not competitors but colleagues.

David is in Joyce's class, a tall boy with a lean grin, thick-rimmed glasses, crinkly hair. "David came up behind me today and swatted me on the head and said 'Joycie, little Joycie.' He's so smart. But we're just friends. And Susie's mom, when she takes us to see *Close Encounters*, said were there any boys we wanted to ask to go with us! But Susie said no it was just the girls."

Susie, short, plump, and strong, lives as though her fantastic daydreams were trampolines—her lion's mane bounces, she dances, spins, encircles her blazing fireplace voice with wide arm gestures. Joyce stays at Susie's house after piano lessons on Tuesdays until Mama comes from work. "I wish Lorena could go but she's supposed to help her mom with something, I don't know what."

Lorena's is a farm family. Lorena has moroccan-olive eyes that she casts to the side as she twists her naturally crimped hair around a finger. She has no fear of boys, and when she sings, her voice hangs on the air like fallen leaves upon each other. "That reminds me. When Leah Ann comes over next time could you stay out of the room? Go play games with Hunter or something? We want to talk and do our stuff."

Susie, Lorena, and Leah Ann are Joyce's best friends. All three study the Bible. All three laugh, uninhibited, and never slur or tease other girls. "Last time you hung around with us the whole time and Leah Ann talked to you the whole time. It makes me so mad I can't even see. Just let me be with my friends when they come over."

Leah Ann is slender like a peach tree switch and has a voice as soothing as cold cream. "I wish Leah Ann was in English class with me," Joyce says. "I wish we didn't have P.E. right before that class. I sit next to

David and my hair is always sweaty. But he never says anything or treats me any different. He's a good friend."

From the dictionary of expressions: Betrayal. Hot, flat tears squeezed from quarter-moon eyes. Pout like a snapped handbag. Sidelong glances thin as tenpenny nails.

After school, our small, parentless house feels empty, and we break open its secrets. We unshelve Daddy's photo albums, discover and read his letters home from Korea. We finger Mama's brooches and strings of beads. We inventory closets and cabinets and cedar chest, learning where all the things we loved from Dallas have been crammed, folded, forgotten. We rifle the kitchen pantry before we divide the snack cakes or fried pies, our after-school treat allotment.

Joyce, the convenient babysitter, balances the benefits and burdens. She can play any of her records without Daddy's wince and Mama's commentary. But Hunter and I, shrill with excess energy and craving attention, hound her, pick at her. In sullen fits, she locks us out of the house on warm afternoons.

"Go away!" she yells through the door. "I hate having a brother and sister! Don't come back! And don't you dare tell on me, don't you dare!"

From the dictionary of expressions: Moral certitude. Chin raised. Eyes lowered, gaze patrician, sliding down the blunt nose. In each phrase a held sniff, a pulling up of the skirts from the mud, a pulling on of gloves.

"What do you want to practice first, sign language or piano?" Joyce squares her prim, indomitable teacher's posture.

"You go first on piano," I say. "Then let's do sign language, then I'll play piano."

Joyce folds the hinged case back from the bone-colored keys. We left the upright behind, in Dallas; Mama and Daddy have found used a glossy walnut spinet with a delicately carved music stand. Joyce plays popular music now, rippling the chords of the satiny, romantic songs grooved in her stack of 45s.

But I want to play the classical pieces she used to play, feel that world shaking my skin. I've learned the C and G major scales and can sight read the inhumanly gleeful ditty, "Crunchy Flakes!" Joyce works me through her beginner's books, page by page erasing her old worksheet answers and checking mine.

"Wrists up," she says. "Back straight. Ann! Back straight! Now. Play the left-hand part. This time, go slow and even."

"I want to play it fast," I grumble, "like it's supposed to be played."

"If you don't go slow and even now, you'll go fast and sloppy later and it'll sound terrible every time and you'll give up. So left hand only." She perches on the piano bench end, watching the music and my hands. I press the keys one after another, and no matter how slowly I go, it feels like magic, the vibrations in fingers and ears and emotions in long, synchronized parabolas.

From the dictionary of expressions: Learning. Eyes focused as if through pinhole toward eclipse; lips in catering-napkin precision. Aggressive levering forward from the waist. Hand on pencil as if tensed on a balance beam. Listening as if in a clench, as if to seize and swallow small prey.

Joyce draws her thumb from cheek to chin.

"Girl," I say.

She swipes her knuckles forward on her cheekbone.

"Tomorrow."

She repeats the motion, brushing her hand back and forth.

"Every day. My turn! My turn!"

Before Sunday evening services, Brother Cole teaches sign language to teenagers and young adults. After some practice, we sign prayers and songs for a small group who attend our church and who cannot hear. Joyce, diligent and adept, interprets shorter sermons and scripture readings, with cubits and lepers and covenants. I choke on simple prayers and resort to a limp, fabricated string of thank-you-God-fors. The brothers and sisters, isolated with us behind the glass wall of the cry room, nod at me, tired and indulgent. But they follow the manicured semaphore of Joyce's fingers, and in response riffle the gossamer pages of their Bibles. Joyce's hands swoop and dip in a clean beat; she captures and releases the sermon's sentences with her body. Her face glows like white jade; her glance stays fixed on a corner of the room, and she smiles.

"It's not your turn. You give me words and I'll do the signs. Give me something hard."

"Fine," I say. "Greedy."

"Funny," she says, and pulls a frown, and with her right hand scratches her upturned left palm.

From the dictionary of expressions: Love. Into the sleeping-kitten calm of lowered eyelids and folded hands sneaks a smile. The smile breaks open like an orange peel around an orange; white teeth interrupt. Short, plump arms curve out, a shell cracking free from the body, a newborn hug, which shames refusal.

Joyce wouldn't eat. The nurses cajoled her, chided her not to feel guilty, cautioned that starvation wouldn't help her. They slid loaded plates of oatmeal, cold cereal, noodle soups, fruit cups, pudding, and Jell-O onto the tray, over the wheel of her belly. Joyce dutifully dipped a spoon and raised it to lips that squirmed with revulsion. She smudged food onto her tongue, closing her thinned mouth daintily around the utensil. Two bites, three, no more. "I can't stand this stuff they bring me," she whispered to me, her eyes wedge-shaped and pleading. "Nothing has any flavor to it. It's just . . ." We frowned at her plate together. "Yuck," she said.

"I'm glad you're here," the charge nurse said when I approached the embattled fort of the floor station on Saturday. Behind the rounded curb with its towering vase of flowers, the nurses were a hive of small, cool, precise movements, non-straying hair and eyes. The nurses had clean, white teeth, low voices, and perpetually busy hands; they gave short answers that brooked no further questions. The nurses never stopped working. They were like rocks in a stream, like a moving stream around rocks. "We were all wondering. Do you know what we might bring her to eat that she would like? We're concerned she's not eating. If she doesn't start eating soon we'll have to feed her intravenously. Any ideas?"

Intravenously. Strength ebbing. Picky, petty taste buds, wanting salt "You might try a hamburger. And french fries. Could she have that?"

"She just needs to start eating. We'll try it. Um. Was there something you needed?"

"I'm going home today," I said. "My parents will be staying here in the dormitory, but Dr. Abu suggested I give you my home and work numbers to keep with her chart."

"Fine," said the nurse, and sped the digits onto a Post-it note. "Do you know your parents' room number, so we can find them? Are there any other numbers? A cell phone?"

"My husband's," I said, and she wrote that number, too, large and assertive, on the file.

"And what else?" she asked.

"There's one thing," I said. "I never asked. Can you tell me—how much does she weigh?"

"We don't know," the nurse said, shrugging. "She wasn't weighed when she was brought in. We don't have a scale here that goes heavy enough to weigh her."

I nodded. Too obese for the MRI, too massive for the CT scan, too heavy for the scale. Too incomprehensible to my unprofessional eyes to seize on a guess. Three hundred eighty, four hundred? Four fifty? I only knew that every time I entered her room, my brain, even with its store-house of memories, refused to categorize as human the conical deposit of flesh transmitted as an image by my optic nerve. A first glance didn't compute a woman, my sister, but perceived, as a shock, human eyes blinking astride a thick, human nose, atop a vast, cotton-tented form. Then, the brain would process: Joyce, my sister. Quick jolts of anger, fear, and sadness followed, and settled at last into an equilibrium from which could be born loose strands of conversation. If I, who loved her, were unsettled, unable to see her, what could I expect of the nurses, with their howling, leaking, aching caseloads?

Here it is: She has to love herself enough to heal, but dislike herself enough to want to change. She has to believe she deserves good things, to treat her own obesity. But her obesity persuades her she's not worth good things. She has to believe in herself as a person with healthy habits, though it's not yet true.

Her life obese is a tense, internal contradiction, a continual tug of war. To function in society, to hold a job, and to keep friends, she must project a positive attitude. To do this while feeling miserable about herself is a draining labor. And she's reminded by every physical and social activity, small and large, that she's obese, and she must stiffen the fragile lace of her outward pleasantness against this jackhammering thought.

She presents herself as a person who is not constantly thinking about food, but to control her unpredictable desire, she constantly plans her response to food. She presents herself as confident, capable, happy, but she questions and doubts every choice as futile. She constantly fights to accept herself, to know she's worth saving. She constantly fights not to accept herself, not to become complacent toward her destructive habits.

She has to forget herself, but she has to watch herself. She must maintain constant control, but must maintain the appearance of not needing control. She must hide her struggle with weight to function in society, yet to resolve her struggle with weight it must be paramount in her mind.

It's not the obesity that exhausts and saddens her, but this conflict. She wakes with it and sleeps with it; she carries it like a sick and crying infant, every minute of her day.

I read a novel while Joyce slept. Between paragraphs I looked up at her, hoping she'd wake and want to talk, hoping she'd sleep so I could gaze on her face. In sleep she wore a perplexed look, her eyebrows furrowed and her lips plumped forward. A plastic oxygen mask capped her nose, the elastic strap a white fissure through her brown hair. I didn't want to leave her. I wanted Mama and Daddy to arrive so I could put to an end the terrible feeling of knowing I would leave her soon. My leather-trimmed bag, jammed with the week's rumpled clothing, waited in the car.

Dr. Abu passed Joyce's room, leaned backward in the hallway to catch my glance. I nodded and followed him to the nurses' station. "She's sleeping," I said.

"That's good," he said.

"Is it the medicine or the illness that makes her sleep so much? I mean, I haven't asked about any side effects of the kidney treatments."

Dr. Abu smiled gently as if at a child confused by multiplication tables. In the depth of his dark eyes, a door closed and his eyes darkened further still. "Remember, she is fighting a serious infection and a loss of function in her kidneys. You can expect her to be very tired. As for side effects—let us say that none of them are consequential in the face of what she already is battling." He leaned, the long architecture of his body angled sideways toward the desk, announcing with silent balance that he did not intend to walk away from me.

"I'm returning home today," I said. "My parents will be here."

"Home is where again? Not near Tulsa?"

"Kansas City. Five hours, a little more. I can be here that quickly if I'm needed. How do I stay in touch? And what should I ask when I call? What will give me the most information in the shortest phone call? Because I know the nurses don't have time for phones."

"You should be able to call this desk and find out her condition at any time," Dr. Abu said. "When you call, the things to ask for are tests performed, test results, changes in treatment, measures of the kidney function. Don't rely on the white count to gauge her status."

"Dr. Abu," I said. "I hate to mention . . . But sometimes the nurses don't tell me the results of tests or how she's doing. They say they don't know, or can't tell me. And my parents wouldn't know until too late . . ."

"No," he agreed. "Look. Just in case." He rummaged in his coat for a slip of paper, and unclipped his pen from his shirt pocket. "Here. This is my number. Don't hesitate using it. No, seriously. I wouldn't offer if I didn't mean it. If you can't find out Joyce's status, call me. I'm not always immediately available, you understand. But I will always call you."

I folded the slip of paper into my notebook. I looked up into his near-smile, into the hushed theater of his eyes. "I don't know how to thank you," I said. In his eyes, the stage curtain tugged. He put out his hand, and I shook it.

I carried my purse and my notebook and Dr. Abu's phone number and a headful of emergency knowledge to my car. I knew where to sleep, eat, or find solitude in the hospital; I knew the bathrooms and phones on every floor. I knew what time the nurses' shifts changed and which nurses relayed her charts most faithfully. I knew now how to tell when Joyce was thirsty, uncomfortable, in pain; I knew when she wanted company and when she wanted to be alone. I feared my parents' limit of understanding but could not begin to measure their readiness for compassion. They wouldn't know what to ask, but they wouldn't leave Joyce now.

I drove back to Kansas City, unrelieved to crawl from the hospital's shell and soak up the salt water and bitter ash of daily routine and nightly news. I'd missed work; we'd hired a new writer to train; my own assignments sat forgotten and tardy. Everyone's work had buckled around the craters smoking in New York, Pennsylvania, the capital. But I couldn't slough off the hospital. It too was now my life; she was still there. I spent the weekend filing the edited copy from old projects, outlining new documents, and thinking of Joyce's forced, gap-toothed smile as she'd waved goodbye and told me to get out, go home.

I'd been at St. John with her three and a half days.

PART THREE: SEARCH TERMS

 1978

Joyce's driver's permit lies inside her pink suede thrift-shop wallet, a barricade between Joyce and Daddy on the truck seat. The pickup jolts down the mile of potholes between our house and Highway 16. Joyce hasn't driven on the highway before. Today she graduates from passenger to chauffeur, the most important person in the car, the one we mustn't bother or distract. She trembles.

"Come with us," she'd said in our room. "Daddy said as long as you don't ride in the middle." I'd hesitated. The invitation leaks need and adventure. "Please," she'd said. "He doesn't mean to but he makes me nervous. I get so I can't think. Maybe if you're there it won't be so much like that. Please come on."

Daddy rides between us on the bench seat. The knobs of his knuckles twitch as Joyce's hands slide on the wheel. "Check your mirror," he says. "Now on this hill move toward the right. A car can come fast over the top." I peek around Daddy's shirt buttons at Joyce's clenched jaw. She steers without a hiccup, her acceleration even and confident. The pickup surfs off the tall, blind hills and into the flat quarter-mile before the highway. Fencelines and foliage blur by.

Our road, on postal rural route one, doesn't have a name. Mama teaches us to say we live on the old river road if we ever have to call an ambulance. That's how people know it. Our house is a mile down the old river road. If you go around the curve toward Three Rivers cemetery, where mossy incisions two centuries old fade from gravestones, you've gone too far.

Along the last flat quarter-mile of old river road before the highway, gold and green fields spill out of the oaks. Bay horses dip sateen heads, clip the pasture idly with hard hooves. To the west, El Caminos and Mercury Cougars and Ford pickups bead the top-stitched gray seam of the highway. Ahead, the road hockey-sticks in a rising left toward a stop sign. "Okay," says Daddy, "slow down now. Get ready to brake."

We hurtle forward. "Joyce!" Daddy says, his voice like a shovel blade. "Slow down! Put on the brake!" We lunge onward toward the curve—"Joyce!" Daddy yells, "Brake! Brake! Brake!" We plunge toward the drop-off and the waving clumps of foxtail and johnsongrass, and Joyce sucks a loud breath and wrenches the wheel and we curve with the road and leap past the stop sign, and Joyce's face freezes in disbelief as Daddy looses an upward cry, a duck-and-cover "Ohhh," and from the left the motorcycle disappears under the gently turning wheel.

Daddy pops my seatbelt and jumps from the truck. Joyce looks down through her window and shudders. Tears fluff over her cheeks. Daddy holds the boy under the arms; the boy sits in the roadside gravel, helmet at hip, his head in his red, raw hands.

"Are you all right?" Daddy leans toward Joyce in the open truck door. "Joyce," he says. She nods. "You all stay here," he says. He pats Joyce's motionless hand. "It's okay," Daddy says, his voice soft as calamine lotion, his blue eyes watery as a birdbath. "It's over now. Nobody's hurt. Joyce," he says. She jerks her chin sideways and from the slits of her eyes accuses him wordlessly. "Nobody's hurt," he says again.

Daddy shuts the truck door. The boy stands, and he and Daddy drag the bike frame free of the wheel well. We wait for the highway patrol.

Silence presses the truck cab windows. Joyce's lowered eyes are like the last minutes of candles, when the flame drowns in the melted wax. Expressionless, she recedes into her body, suddenly a stranger—a sullen, blue-eyed brunette. Dumpling hips, belly, and breasts corrugate her five-foot-two, gymnast's posture. Her thighs are plump like songbirds. My body is unlike hers. I am newly lanky, hunched and slouched, my arms and legs shot long and quavering like a flowering hedge's spring stems. My face is whittled of its baby chins.

"You okay?" she says, misery powdered on her rasping voice.

"I'm okay. You okay?"

"No, I don't guess so," she says. She gulps twice, as though swallowing a vitamin's chalky lump. She blots the fresh bulbs of teardrops with her stiffened fingers. "I didn't mean to," she says. "Ann, I tried to brake. It just—I got slowed down, like that—why do I freeze? Why do I do it? What if . . ." Her questions run like pancake syrup, then soak into their own unanswerability and are gone.

I have only one comfort to offer. "Do you want me to sit between you and Daddy on the way back home?" Joyce blinks, nods, and tries to tame the swell of her lower lip.

Home, I hurry to the bedroom. I don't want to hear the retelling or watch Joyce's face contort. But voices in our house arrow through the drywall, through the air ducts, down the short boot of the hallway.

"Oh my," Mama says, the words ringing inside the galvanized tub of her soprano.

Daddy's voice rumbles. "That old patrolman had a hard time not laughing when he found out they were going in the same driver's ed class." Through the drywall and the closed doors I feel Joyce's swollen embarrassment, her explosive need for an escape route. There's nowhere to go to get out of her way. Her throaty complaint oozes through the air ducts. I sneak to the bathroom and lock the door. When she's in our room, I'll go sit outside behind the giant bois d'arc tree.

"I don't want to drive," Joyce says. "I'll wait for driver's ed."

"You'll drive over the back road to church tomorrow," Mama says, her voice rough and worked as her cherry-vanilla dishpan hands. "We'll take two cars and you can drive with me on the way there and with your daddy on the way back. You're not about to sit home dwelling on this. And I don't need you making that face at me either. That's about enough. You can go to your room and pout if you have to. Dinner's in an hour."

"I don't want dinner," Joyce says.

"I cut up a whole chicken on account of you wanted fried chicken," Mama says, "and that's what there is, and you're going to eat with the rest of us."

She tells her spouse, "If my weight goes above 175 I'll get help." But she doesn't believe the scale as its numbers roll to 180, then 185, then 190. Her point of utter misery is at two hundred pounds. Her body torments her; her habits disgust her; she has begun to fade toward social invisibility. She stares in the mirror at her naked body, incontrovertibly obese. She wants to scream. She must change the way she lives, starting right that minute. She feels she's blindly drawn close to the edge of a pit, to a new depth of fatness, from which recovery is even less likely.

She starts a program she's read about. On this plan, carbohydrates are restricted but not forbidden. She feels wonderful after the first week. I'm not thinking about food the whole time, she realizes. She eats what's allowed, when it's allowed, and having made the one decision to follow the plan, is less able to make harmful decisions.

She rides a stationary bike and lifts light weights. She wants to be more like her husband, who thrives on his workouts, craves them. The fifty pounds slide off in five months. She buys new jeans, a thin white tank top, a silk suit.

She and her husband move across the country to start new jobs. She feels depressed and foolish explaining her dietary guardrails to co-workers who invite her out. And she's tired of thinking about food—of what she will be allowed and when she will be allowed it. She looks for loopholes. She starts to fall on her food ravenously, gobbles what she gives herself so that she can have more food in the time allotted for her carbohydrate intake.

This is sick, she tells herself. I don't want to live this way. I can't follow this plan anymore. I'll just eat sensibly.

And the pounds return, like old customers.

Monday, September 17. I swiped my entry card and threaded through quiet hallways. The office Kerri and I had shared was bare and dark; we and all the software developers had been relocated. Our new offices smelled like wet wallpaper glue, stiff carpets, and acoustic tile dust, and were oddly vacant of office smells—coffeepots, microwaved macaroni, printer toner dappled across miles of paper on dozens of desks. In my absence, colleagues had packed and reassembled my computer, had carefully transplanted my files and papers like tender vines.

I returned to this garden of daily troubles, from which most co-workers had not noticed me gone. Like office workers everywhere, they carried the whirl of their lives—the disagreement with a spouse, the children's soccer schedules, the household repair budget—silently in and out of their offices and cubes. Like most small companies, ours encompassed the staff as a spinning galaxy of routine buffeted by customer forces. Like hundreds of thousands of other social and economic bodies, we swirled flat and nameless that September in an vast, dark cosmos of terrorist jubilation, media shock, and body count. Microscopic in this universe, I fell back into my orbit, but with Joyce lodged in my mind. I drafted text, attended meetings, began to train the newly hired writer. I chatted with office mates but told Kerri the truth.

"Wow, it's nice," Kerri said, leaning against the door frame of my new, narrow office. She nodded at the desk's heavy cherry lid.

"The quiet's good," I said. "Better for phone calls."

"How are your parents?" Kerri wiped a bolt of blond hair back from her forehead. "Are your parents okay?"

"I don't know. About the same. They haven't slept much. They never have anything to report. Joyce is fine, nothing's changed; I should stop worrying."

"And what do the doctors say?"

"The opposite. When nothing's changed, it's cause for alarm. Her kidneys aren't improving. What am I going to do if she needs a kidney?"

"Do they think that's a possibility?"

"The one doctor talked with Joyce about dialysis. They told me she wouldn't be a good candidate, which makes me think they're closer to a last resort. But transplant, mm, they haven't said it. It's my imagination. I'm a victim of it, imagination. All the possibilities, all the time. Yet . . ."

"It's worse not to imagine what might happen next." Kerri tipped her head behind the disappearing garnish of a sympathetic smile.

"I've been imagining the possibilities for so long. It was hard to see her in the bed, but not unimaginable. She's so large, she can't even move. For months—years? Months? Her weight, it was—the hospital bed seemed inevitable. So I'm not surprised."

"But stunned?" She nodded.

"Thanks," I said, "that's it. Horrified. And stunned."

"So how are you dealing with that?" Kerri waited, leaning into the coming answer. There, I thought—that's what you ask a friend to make sure she's stunned, not paralyzed.

"It's weird," I said. "I have a whole new routine. Morning, I call the hospital for the night's test results. Late morning, I call my parents to find out what the doctors said—or at least, what they heard. Evening, I call the hospital to see how she responded in the day, whether her symptoms changed. And whenever I hear a new word—some condition they're looking at, some indicator—I'm online looking it up."

"That doesn't sound so weird."

"Yeah, well, the thing is, sometimes it's like I've been doing these things forever, like tracking my sister's health is a natural part of the day. Then other times, it's like a dream. Where you know you're supposed to do something, but you can't remember why you, or why now, or why that thing. But you go ahead and do it and it leads to the next part of the dream. It's like this little routine of calls and research is what I know to do, but I have no clue why I'm doing it. The routine makes sense, but the reason I'm in it doesn't make any sense, and I get shocked with it over and over. She's sick, and it's needless."

Kerri's blond hair cupped against her shoulder. Between two slow blinks, her eyes held steady, and her smile was like the cocoon of a smile, like a receiving blanket cozying a smile. There, I thought—that's how you smile at someone who doesn't know what makes sense.

She squints at the simple math of her sandwich. Bread 160 calories fat-free mayonnaise nothing turkey slices 100 calories lettuce and tomato nothing. It's not enough for lunch. What else can she have?

She isn't hungry now—but what if lunch isn't on time, or she has to work late? What if she gets hungry? She doesn't fear the hunger. She fears the want to eat. She fears exposing the want in public. She fears others seeing how desperate she becomes, how unable to concentrate, how panicked and prone to tears.

Hunger's scary. If she gets hungry, then she has to eat in front of people when she's least likely to control what she eats. She can't eat in front of people. If they were to see how she can eat! They'll know she deserves to be fat. She can't let it happen—let herself get hungry and lose control in front of people. It's disgusting to see fat people eat. Fat people shouldn't eat. Fat people don't deserve to be hungry. We ought to just live off the stores.

She can't take the chance that the want will grin from her eyes. She eats an extra half-bagel, an extra banana. Quietly, she wakes the want.

A technical writer makes sense of information. She collects and expels information as though the brain were a lung for the reformulation of facts. She is trained to gulp huge amounts of data and exhale the few molecules her readers need. She sifts to answer questions, to mark the shortest paths to understanding. She immerses herself in many voices to distill a single phrase. She feels her reader's confusion; she is compelled to answer questions, especially the ones her readers don't know how to ask. What can I expect to happen next to Joyce? My parents didn't ask.

It didn't seem a diversion to switch from a search through computer programming concepts to a different search for terms I'd heard the doctors say: Kidney failure. Acidosis. Enlarged heart. I followed the words through the interlinked chambers of archived biological knowledge. Edema. White cells. Infection. It was the way I knew to fight panic, to keep breathing. Breathe in the information. Breathe out the answers.

For instance, a search term: kidney function.

The kidneys cup the spine like mitten potholders. They scrub our blood clean of natural wastes and the toxins we funnel into our bodies. The kidneys juice four hundred gallons of blood every day to drip out the daily half-gallon of urine. The kidneys stand watch over our blood, its salts and acids; they salvage water when we're dehydrated, and they guard us when excess water in the blood might flood our hearts.

When the kidneys aren't working, waste clogs the blood and poisons the body; excess water strains the pump. The kidneys are as vital as the heart or lungs. When they don't work, if you can't have dialysis, you die.

Next search term: BUN.

BUN stands for blood urea nitrogen, which our body normally produces but does not need to keep. BUN forms when we digest food, and it breaks down into energy we need and acids we don't. If the kidneys aren't working properly, the blood's load of acids grows heavy, and the blood will contain too much BUN. Too much BUN might mean congestive heart failure is looming or that your intestines are quietly bleeding, or that your kidneys are failing. A healthy adult can expect 7 to 20 milligrams of BUN in every one-tenth liter of blood. Joyce's BUN hovered at 100 milligrams.

Next search term: creatinine.

The body's muscle produces a waste protein called creatinine. People with a little more muscle produce a little more creatinine, but the amount you produce every day stays about the same. When kidneys are damaged, the amount of creatinine in the blood doesn't rise right away. It goes up after the kidneys have been struggling for some time. The normal reading of creatinine is around one for an average adult. Joyce's serum creatinine level was 6.2.

I sat back and closed the browser window. No matter how much I read, there was more to the body than I could learn. However compelled to search for the facts of Joyce's illness, I mustn't let myself believe I knew the truth. The body has a multitude of truths on its unmapped path toward death. I had been foolish to believe I was learning how to predict Joyce's path. Yet I was still closed in the dark box of fears, and I wanted to claw my way into the harsh, pure air of information. I typed in the next search term, and I checked my watch—three hours until I could call the hospital again.

1979

A glassy capsule, adolescence bobbles deceptively from the spidery arm of the fairground ride. Adolescence tantalizes you with three-dimensional adventures superior to childhood's flat merry-go-rounds. Adults far below you nod and smile, seeing your life as a ride they have gotten off. From their distance, you appear safely belted into the predictable whirl of a gently bobbling box. But inside the capsule, heavy forces disorient you, nauseate you, press you forward, back, up, down, spin you on one axis and then another; you're pushed and pulled until your body begins to stretch and lump. If you throw up or cry you'll be mocked until you graduate high school. Yet you haven't learned to giggle and preen, pretending to enjoy the buffeting. You grow angrier still at the adults, who dismiss this stomach-churning, mind-whipping trial as something trite and known, something they can turn in a hand and remember, like a paperweight.

Joyce is sixteen, firmly seated in her adolescence, and I am twelve, falling into mine as down a stairwell, as into an embarrassing dream. Blossoming like thunderheads in our tiny bedroom, our adolescences shove for space, as we do on this summer trip.

We ride, crammed shoulder to shoulder in our female adolescence and in the back seat of the Biscayne. Hunter sleeps, his ash-blond burr head lolled sideways like a kitten curled on a windowsill.

"Girls, if I see one more elbow or hear one more whine from back there we're going to stop the car," Mama says. "Y'all aren't too big to get a swat. Or do I have to come back there and sit between you?"

Joyce and I compress our sidelong glares: see what you did. The back seat is already crowded, and Mama, undeniably and unhappily, has grown past plump, with soft loaf arms and a jellyroll bosom and a collection of cottage cheese-based diet plans.

A gooey blob of sweat dislodges and rolls down the side of Joyce's red, blotched face. "No, ma'am," she says.

"It's just crowded and hot," I volunteer.

"Enough!" Daddy's faint hysteria sounds like brakes' prolonged screeching before a crash. "If I hear one more complaint!" He grits his teeth, unappeased by suddenly silent progress through the grasslands. Maybe he'd like a lemon drop or a can of soda from the cooler. Sweat soaks Joyce's long brown hair. She folds her hot, itching arms across her waistband. Her tense chin and pinched eyes are like the crowd noise from a stifling tent. To break her restraint, I need but to glance at her. I don't mention the lemon drop. I don't mention the soda.

We're driving away from the typical summer. Behind us lie long afternoons in Great-Grandma Roberts's front porch swing. Hunter races his scale model cars down her sloped concrete driveway. I wander through the darkened rooms of Great-Grandma Roberts's house and into the back yard, through the roses and bachelor's buttons and daisies in the strip of garden that points like an arm to a giant pecan tree. On the porch swing, Joyce leans against Great-Grandma Roberts and hears stories about Great-Grandma Roberts's youth and Daddy's boyhood. Joyce's creamy arm presses against the long white wrinkles of Grandma's bicep, and Grandma pats Joyce's knee. But we are far away from that now.

We rocket around the curve of the planet, two scowling girls beside their sleeping brother. Behind us a blur of asphalt and yellow stripe tethers us to the tiny brick house, its parklike acreage, its summer Saturday routines: Daddy rises first, before dawn. Under the canopy of pale light, oak leaves, and robins singing, he marches out to the pasture pit he inherited from the previous owners—a farm pond half-dug, filled with garbage and discarded appliances, even the rusted hood and fenders of a junked Chevy. Daddy dreams of the pond he'll carve into the land, how it will sparkle and how he will stock it with fish. He clambers into the twenty-by-twelve-foot quarry, its muddy slopes studded with metal debris. While he chops the morning's first shovelful of red clay and tosses it over the lip of the hole, Mama wakes and plods in her housedress toward the ritual of coffee and a hot skillet. She blankets a plate with spongy pancakes for Daddy, and then she calls us, her voice like hands clapping near our ears. We stumble into a day of household chores, of yard games that end in a chase over soft lawns and thorny pastures, a day that smells of clipped grass and macaroni and cheese, a day that ends in the sisters-only Saturday evening basketball game.

The white net hangs stiffly from the basketball goal's orange rim, and Joyce heaves the rough orange ball from her shoulder. "Jerry Don!" she shouts. Or: "David!" If you make the basket, the boy you've named will love and marry you. The ball trampolines from the back of the rim and plummets through the net. "Whoooo-aaaa!" Joyce yells, waving her arms as if flagging a plane, her wide-legged jeans flapping around her short, leaping legs. "I'm getting married! I'm getting married!" I fall on the juicy grass and can't stop laughing. Joyce whoops it up in the dusk, a pale, delirious moth. She's taught me an unassailable rule of sisterhood: about boys, we never tease; we never tell. People are ready to pounce and shrivel your dreams. We do not help those people, not even in the moments when we hate each together.

Those moments of hatred, residual, evaporate now when we pass under the Plano water tower's blue saucer. Joyce drops me a grin like a shiny coin. The urban scenery thickens and we forget the heat. No longer a blur, the drive becomes a kinescope of thrilling landmarks, our memories reanimated, the city's name a defibrillator.

Dallas! Under the Texas sky's high sheet metal, mirrored skyscrapers shoot like lily stalks from a low, thick bed of brick warehouses. Sunny Dallas suburbs dust-ruffle the raised freeways, and green and white signs cheer our progress: Richardson, Garland, Mesquite. We descend into the fabric of frame houses and mimosa trees, the street signs familiar as forks and knives—there, Wadlington Avenue, a lawnmower growling and a dog barking, and Granddaddy in faded, denim overalls unfolding himself from the lawnchair and Granny, her soft mob cap of white hair brushed back from the dark seed eyes in her apple-shaped face. "Y'all have gotten so big," she says, hugging each child. "I'm just so proud to see you. But now you kids look hot. Go on and fix y'all a glass of ice tea."

Joyce grabs my hand. "Let's go out back," she says. Her smile stretches. For this trip, we forget our ages. Like hobo provisions in kerchief bundles, we hoard vacation souvenirs, family details: the sunbitten faces and billowing drawl of the aunts and uncles; Mama's relaxed helpfulness in the breeze of Granny's kitchen chatter; the objects in Granny's house, unmoved, unchanged—overstuffed bags of quilt scraps, Michener novels, school photographs of Granny and Granddaddy's nine children.

At night, lonesome and nostalgic, Joyce and I knock together like two tiny dolls in the grip of a fist. "Don't hog the sheet," she whispers.

"It's not big enough. Sleep closer to the middle. The air conditioner's loud."

"Not for me," Joyce says. "It sounds like when we used to take naps on the floor. I wish I could stay here all summer. Granny's going to let me drive her car tomorrow."

I won't go, I realize. She hasn't asked me. Instead, Daddy and I are left alone in the house—Hunter is with an old playmate; Joyce has driven Mama and Granny to a cousin's house. Granddaddy snores. "Come for a ride," Daddy says.

The cemetery spills like green sauce. White stones fleck the clipped expanse. I try to match Daddy's loose stride down the gravel paths. He wears a baseball cap now whenever he goes out in the sun, to protect his balding, rectangular head. "Did you know that your mama and me had another baby once?" he says, his voice low like a clarinet.

"Robert," I say. Like a desert, the cemetery spreads around me; Daddy is my nomad chief and Robert the oasis, lying hidden nearby. "Joyce told me about him when I was real little."

"She did?" Daddy sucks on this peppermint drop of information. I've seen the church bulletin in Grandpa's scrapbook: The family requests that instead of cards or flowers, books should be donated in Robert's name to the Military Parkway Church of Christ library. Did you know this about your mama and daddy? Grandpa had asked. Did you?

"Is this where Robert is?" I ask. Daddy retraces a line segment among the stones.

"Supposed to be," he says. Freckled hands on slim hips, he looks left and right, searching for the name of his son. "His grave used to be right here." The cotton shirt droops from his shoulders; his chest deflates. Under the cap brim, his eyes dull as they do when in a store he realizes he can't afford the things he planned to buy.

"They've let it grow over," he says slowly. The words sink like a hook in a fish.

"Sometimes they do that," Daddy tells me at the car, "if you don't come back and take care of the grave yourself." I shove his sadness deep into the middle of my hobo bundle, where Joyce won't notice. She doesn't tell me about her drive, either. We pack these souvenirs for the long journey back to the adolescent fairground. The latch snaps on our whirling capsule. We ride together.

Each telephone call to the hospital was like a train ride at night, in which one travels blindly; neither the world left behind nor the unfamiliar destination seems as real and secure as the train. With the warm cradle of plastic between my hair and ear, I imagined the tenth floor hallway, felt myself leaning against the nurses' countertop, felt the waxed tile under my sneakers. After I dialed, I imagined the nurse's hand closing on the receiver, lifting it. I listened, and the surfaces around me lost their meaning and solidity. The room around me was less real. Not even the pen in my hand, scribbling dictated numbers and words, was as real as the nurse's voice, her hurried obligation, and the sanitized, cream-colored hospital building from which she spoke.

"She's resting comfortably this evening," the night nurse said. "Her urine output is still low. Her medications haven't been changed today."

"It's all about the same," Mama said. "They say she's not any better but I'm listening to what they're not saying. They're not saying she's getting any worse, either. So if I were you I wouldn't worry. There's nothing different than you knew before."

"Her BUN and creatinine levels are slightly increased," the morning nurse said. "We're seeing some fluctuations in those numbers, so a slight increase isn't necessarily meaningful. Her white count is slightly down. She's on a course of antibiotics to help fight the infection."

"She doesn't look good, Ann," Aunt LaNita said. "She's having to keep her oxygen mask on a lot more of the time. I just don't have a good feeling toward it."

"Your Aunt LaNita worries a lot," Mama said.

"I don't know all what the doctors said," Daddy said, "except her breathing's not as good. Your mother's here; did you want to talk to her?"

"I don't really feel like talking," Joyce said, her voice creaking like a branch in the autumn night wind. I pictured her face rising like yeast bread from the thick pillow's depression.

"Do you want me to call you again?" I asked her.

"It doesn't matter," she said.

"You know, I'm going to give you Virginia Hollie's number," the morning nurse said, when I called again. "She's the patient care coordinator. She supervises the nurses, and she has all the patient information from day to day. You're much more likely to find her available when you call, and able to give you fuller details. You could call her instead of the desk. Would that be okay?"

I imagined the nurse straightening her back, flexing shoulder blades and calves to address her tired muscles. The edges of her voice grew raw, like torn paper. She knew answers she couldn't tell me. I pictured the long hallway of darkened rooms, the gush of pain and fluids, the day's dizzying kaleidoscope of needles and tubes and bags and pills, the faces pleading from pillows, the cramped and faltering hands on call buzzers.

"Thanks," I said, stretching the word's soft middle to warm it. "Tomorrow, I'll call—it's Virginia?"

"Virginia Hollie."

Will it ever stop? Will she ever be enough of a different person to never become obese again? She has no idea what she's fighting, what enemies coil within her own mind and body. She only knows she wants to eat. And she does it even though she's had success, has seen herself lose weight. She does it even though she wants to be healthy.

She has a weight consequence, not a weight problem. She feels angry and depressed so much of the time. She uses food to feel better. Food feels good, and she doesn't want to deny herself relief. And this has consequences.

She feels bad about herself and then eats. Then, because she ate for the wrong reasons, she feels worse. So she eats. And then she feels miserable about herself. So she eats more. And she thinks, maybe it won't show up on the scale this week. Maybe she has exercised enough, maybe she can eat lightly on the other days. But she knows there are no other days, that there is only today over and over again, and that she has no proof that she will make today a different day, and that even if she does, that she'll keep it up the rest of her life.

Consequences: she gains weight. She doesn't look good in her clothes. Her face is puffy. She doesn't sleep well. She dwells on the weight gain and on her habits and feels guilty, and because she judges herself not worth much, and to feel better, she eats again. With terrible efficiency, she punishes herself and makes herself feel better in one stroke.

"Yes," Virginia Hollie said. "Yes, I can go over Joyce's chart with you. But tell me—your parents are here with your sister, is that right? Would it be easier to give information to them?"

Virginia's voice sounded like sweetened sun tea, like forty-year-old wisteria bushes, like checked homework, like a soft yellow ruler reinforced with a slip of steel. I pictured her in her first gentle wrinkles, her short hair dyed its natural brown, wiry as the bristles of the rollers it had been twirled around. I pictured her in a blue linen business suit, with trim legs in sheer fawn stockings and feet in matching blue pumps. I pictured her toying with silver-rimmed glasses on a chain.

"I talked with the doctors about this," I said, "or I wouldn't say it."

"Mmm."

"My parents are having a hard time. They don't ask enough questions to find out what's going on. They don't believe it's as serious as it is. The doctors haven't told them very much. But they've told me. I know what's happening to Joyce."

"I see," said Virginia.

"I live five hours away," I said. "I need to know when to get in my car and drive down there. I know there's not much I can do for Joyce—just be there with her—but for my parents, I need to know what information they're going to be dealing with. Five hours of driving is enough time to get myself ready to help them."

My imaginary Virginia nodded in sympathy. I pictured her with a smile that didn't leak into her sympathetic voice. "I see," she said. "I'm here every day, and you're welcome to call. I'll help you as much as I can. What did you want to know today?"

"First—is it okay if I still call the nurses' station in the evenings? My parents aren't very—descriptive, and they don't remember the details from the doctors."

"Try not to call within an hour of shift change. Be aware that the nurses' availability is second to patient care."

"I'll keep those calls brief."

"That's fine."

"But it's okay that I call them. Find out how she's doing in the evening?"

"Of course, of course," Virginia said, her voice like aloe. "Now, let's go over Joyce's status this morning."

"That'd be—I really appreciate this," I said. "If I can, I'm hoping—if it's all right, I'd be grateful, too, if you can tell me whether I'm asking the right questions. Whether there's anything else I need to be asking."

"I can do that," Virginia said, with her dignified, unleaked smile. "So let's first run down the latest tests. I have your sister's file open here. Yes. Oh. My. Mm. This is—speaking of numbers, before we get off the phone, let's make sure I have all your contact numbers. Right?"

The nurses had been careful collecting phone numbers, diligent in gleaning the list of places where Joyce's family slept, where we loitered by day. Cell phones, home phones, spouses' phones, work phones, other family members' phones, the phone numbers of dormitory and hotel rooms as we checked in and out. "That's good they do that," Mama said, "though I can't think why they'd need all those numbers. There's almost always one of us been up here so far."

I could think why. The nurses' pack of phone numbers reinforced the truth even when I wished the lies were right. The hospital needed those numbers because Joyce was in danger. Each phone number was an arrow in a quiver, waiting to cleave a coming morning from life afterward. Joyce's condition could turn. The causes of her bleeding, the lack of oxygen, the infection, could be discovered and could be more monstrous than any certainties so far.

So although the nurses had the phone numbers, I recited them again for Virginia. Her voice sounded like a crisp linen stationery sheet, like a trimly labeled, open file cabinet drawer. If there were need, Virginia would call. I folded that assurance in my heart like a air bag under a car dash, and Tulsa, like a hypothetical car wreck, seemed farther away.

—————————————— ❖ **1980** ❖ ——————————————

The secondary teachers have materialized from legend into flesh. They bark, glower, pace, interrogate exactly as Joyce described. She has created each of them for me, the bent heads over gradeless papers, the parabola of voice volume from assignment to discipline. For instance, other algebra students squirm, but Joyce has trained in my imagination Mr. Hughes's impatient growl, his rugged, detailed scrutiny of chalked solutions. Just do the work, she said, never say you don't know an answer, and don't be afraid of him. "Mr. Hughes asked if you were my sister," Joyce says. Punishment rides her voice like pollen on a bee's legs.

"So? What did you say?"

"What do you think, dummy?"

"Why did he want to know?"

"They all ask," Joyce says.

Joyce battles her homework for the prize of her teachers' respect. She grits her teeth and overpowers dates and formulas. Before a test, she looks worn, as though study has left bruises under her clothes.

But after school, in the music room, she heals. I wait in the hallway while Joyce's chords and harmonies glow like bottle rockets. Pop songs rise from Joyce's hands and float. "Joyce is a natural accompanist," Mama says. "Ann's a performer. Joyce knows how to play without taking over the vocals. That takes a real skill."

Lessons end. We promenade the dogleg of the empty hallway. The janitor swishes his mop in arcs. Clock hands hiss and click. After school the building is a soft, dry sponge—sex has vacated its pores until the next day. Then, girls with flaring hips in tight jeans will flounce past boys who scrawl cartoon breasts in their notebook margins; classmates will sort themselves into desks by last week's bleacher liaisons; yet another junior will encapsule her pregnancy and abortion in harsh murmurs and hand it to her friend in the girls' room like a quarter tampon; and Joyce will arrive home breathless with Lorena's proof of adulthood.

"Married!" Mama says. "Oh, my. It's not—"

"No, it's not that," Joyce says, between crumbling bites of a chocolate snack cake. "They just decided to get married."

"Well, it's smart of their mamas and daddys, too. You girls listen, it's better you get married than get in a situation."

The portent crawls up my back. The body's itches and tingles are like privately owned art, safe from the voyeurism of language. Thought about sex is a locked casket, a vault of germs that can't be closed once opened. The word "sex" is a key kept hidden and unlabeled. "Lorena would never," I say. Mama and Joyce exchange a look, a duet of signals.

"Don't be surprised. Good girls have strong feelings, too," Mama says.

"But Lorena wouldn't." I stutter at the violation. Not Lorena, pure and dedicated, with her merry, guiltless laugh. "It's just she's in love. People in love get married, right?"

Mama and Joyce trade a second look, agreeing over my head. In rare collusion, they know something about sex that I don't, and furthermore see some reason that my ignorance is beneath correction. Joyce rolls her eyes at my teary pout.

Sex wakes in us and drives us to our mirrors. We check the swath of jeans from buttock to heel; Joyce tugs at the back hooks of her bra to lift her breasts, two cupcake lids on her ribcage. My thirteen-year-old chest is flat as soap. I slouch; my butt droops. My upper arms jiggle, but Joyce's look firm as foam baseball bats. Is Joyce fat? Is she fatter than me? I can't run in gym like the other girls. My thighs aren't fendered with muscle. My tummy bulges forward over my crotch. But I'm not the fat one. I can't be the fat one. Joyce is plumper than me. I lie in bed, my hand crawling over the curves, trying to decide what parts of me are fatter than the other girls at school.

"I don't like my name," I say in the dark. "It's plain. You have a good name."

"I do," she says. "Joyce Marie. Joyce, joy, joyful. I pretend they're singing to me, you know, in youth group? Rejoice! Rejoice! And again I say rejoice! The guys at school call me Joycie," she says.

"They don't call me anything," I say.

"Just wait." She rolls in her twin bed toward the wall. "Wait 'til they grow up."

"When's that?"

"Who knows. College maybe."

"You'll go to college in a year."

"I'm not staying here."

Here, our parents, distorted mirrors, reflect who we aren't. Mama's weight has settled on her like ripe peaches in bushel baskets. She keelhauls herself on new diets, disappointment contorting her face. Stresses swarm her like wasps, the unpaid work hours, the late-night computer and business courses, the dirt in the woodwork and grouting of her home. "You girls need to help out more," she says. So while a stack of Joyce's 45s drips down onto the turntable, Joyce and I heat breaded meat patties and oven-baked french fries. Joyce carves the lid from canned corn and dumps the kernels in a pan. We scout the crisper drawer, but save the lettuce and tomato for tomorrow night's hamburgers, red lumps fried in the cast iron skillet. Daddy likes meat with his dinner.

As autumn creeps past, Daddy more often sits in the wing chair, watching TV or looking out the window. His face is hidden by the chair's curved fin. The TV blares and jars, program after program. Daddy lives in a feast of weariness: the long commute to office fluorescence, the relentless calculator; the impossible stretch of inelastic budget across food, clothing, fuel, collection plate; and the welcome fatigue of driving the shovel into the planet's wall, the unyielding clay of the pond or the tilled garden bed. He stripes his three acres with grids of saplings from the nursery—pears and apples, plums, peaches. Around each mounded rootball he digs a moat, then fills the muddy cup with water. At sunset he leans on the shovel or pitchfork handle and sighs through his sweat.

When Daddy sits looking out the window, he rests his chin in his right hand and searches the green and black summer evening. His pale blue eyes are alert and humble, nearly sad, as though he were watching for an old friend who isn't showing up. Weather drifts across his face; he is unreachable. He gazes at the trimmed, lush lawn and the loft of white clouds over the oaks, at the robins probing the grass for insects. He looks at his yard as though he were looking at the face of his mother, wondering whatever he is supposed to do with his love once she has passed.

"Dinner's ready." Joyce peeks around the wing chair. "I made cornbread to go with the beans."

"Well, I can hardly wait," Daddy drawls. With a last, piercing look toward the window, he hauls his tired body forward and up, his knees cracking as he stands.

She doesn't know how to eat. That's the only logical conclusion; she can't eat sensibly on her own. She feels deficient. Eating is so basic. How hard can it be to get it right? She's smart. She's read since she was fifteen everything she could find about nutrition, diet, behavioral change. Yet she doesn't know how to make herself do what she knows is right. She wishes she could stop eating entirely. It's not like alcoholism — she has to eat to live. But to keep herself alive and healthy, she has to do it right, and she doesn't know how. She's tired of failing.

She slides a wedge of lemon cake from the buffet, and as she eyes the dishes of chocolate pudding, she feels a bolt of ignominy like a suppressed cough. Other people can have a slice of cake and not overeat, she thinks. Other people know how to eat without gorging. Other people get this right. Why can't she? She feels stupid, and wants to feel anything good, and the cake's there, in her hand.

Search term: kidney failure.

When your kidneys fail, you will feel a burning sensation when you pee, and you will look down to see bloody or coffee-colored urine. Pain may shoot through your lower back. Your blood pressure will rise. Your kidneys are refusing to release the water from your blood, and your face and ankles may swell while your heart fights the onslaught of fluid. You will feel tired; you will turn away from food; you may vomit. You will not be able to catch your breath. Your canvas of skin may begin to itch. You might need either to urinate frequently or not at all. And you will become anemic as your kidneys stop producing the trigger chemical that makes your bones create red blood cells. Your heart will pump harder to distribute oxygen; it may enlarge under the strain; you may feel an irregular heartbeat. Without enough red blood cells, your heart and brain won't get enough oxygen. You won't think clearly; you'll feel cold, light-headed, depressed. Your behavior might become strange.

Also, your failing kidneys will release albumin faster than your liver can produce it. Most of your plasma is albumin. Albumin moves hormones and drugs in the blood, and it keeps the blood's fluids from leaking into tissues. If you don't have enough albumin, your ankles, abdomen, and lungs will start to swell with this leaked fluid. If your kidney failure isn't treated, you may be jolted with seizures, or feel your body choke in congestive heart failure, or fall into the sleep your family will call coma.

Not everybody has all the symptoms, or the same symptoms. How kidney failure feels to you will differ depending on whether your kidney failure was sudden or has been a long time coming. Chronic failure might not show symptoms until as much as 80 percent of the kidney has been damaged. And if your kidneys have been progressively failing, new medicine that you take for other conditions can cause them to fail suddenly.

The desk phone rang while I cursed five pages of notes I'd forgotten to include in the user manual. I patted the desk to find my pen under the paper drifts and glanced at the phone display. It was an outside call.

"This is Virginia, from St. John."

Busy Virginia, honest Virginia—her melting bitter-chocolate voice and obelisk pauses created a safe room of time, a tornado shelter of time. She never hurried my questions or truncated her answers. This leisure gave the impression that whatever was happening to Joyce was happening at a pace that allowed reflection, absorption. But Virginia had never called me. Her voice was a warm kernel inside the chill of the call.

"Hello, Virginia. Has something happened?"

"There's been a downturn. I'm so sorry to tell you. Joyce is in bad shape this morning. Her kidney function is worse. She's no longer in stable condition."

Silence and words crawled like crabgrass, a chokehold of roots. Grab, uproot, speak, I told myself. Say something. "What do I do, Virginia?"

"Oh, honey," she said. "I can't tell you what you ought to do. I don't feel that's my place."

"No, what I mean is, I'm coming to be with her if it's serious. I have a five-hour drive ahead of me. I'll leave right now to be with her. But I need to know how serious this is, whether we're watching her slide or watching her recover."

Virginia cleared her throat, a soft scrape like gift wrap around a parcel. "If it were my sister, I would be here," she said. "It's very serious. Five hours might not be enough time."

"She could die?" I asked. Virginia faltered over my lapse of comprehension. "Please," I said. "Whatever else, I need to know how to help my parents."

"Yes," she said. "She could die. You should be prepared for that."

"Thank you for telling me," I said. "Thank you, Virginia."

"Good luck, dear," she said.

―――――――――――――― ❖ **1981** ❖ ――――――――――――――

Memory books, glossy black padded slabs, float down the hallway crooked in seniors' elbows. Black gowns folded in square plastic packets flop in lockers atop ragged piles of spiral notebooks, stapled mimeographed handouts. Orange and black nylon tassels, twisted around the buttons of mortarboard caps, swish against the cheeks of girls plotting how to feather bangs and bobby-pin the cap, to salvage their hairstyles for post-commencement parties.

At our kitchen counter, Joyce opens her memory book to a page emblazoned with a curvaceous gray headline: "Myself . . ." The book prompts the senior in chirping asides. "Here's your chance to identify yourself with vital statistics and a photo. How about listing your special interests?"

"It's rude to read over somebody's shoulder," Joyce says, radiating annoyance like a shove and slap. I rattle my after-school cornflakes into a chipped bowl.

"I wasn't," I say, pouring the milk. "Anyway, you didn't write anything yet. Can I read it when you finish?"

Joyce shrugs the shrug of superior complacency, the shoulders hoisted high for a long beat. "Whatever," she says. "Just leave me alone." She bites the tip of her tongue. The neat pitched roofs and Dutch wooden shoe curves of Joyce's oversized penmanship swell across the page. Between sentences she lifts her pen and gazes up at the cabinetry, the next phrase forming clear as ice in her black-flecked blue eyes. She leaves no hatch marks of revision, no scars through her words.

"I like to listen to good music," she writes. "If the television isn't going, music has to be. My main group is the Commodores but I like all kinds of music. I like to read also. But the one thing I do best is watch TV. My favorite show is M*A*S*H. The TV can drive me from almost anything. I also like the Australian group Air Supply. If I'm not watching TV, reading, listening to the radio, I'm watching guys. Mainly good looking ones like David H. I like to go on walks, watch football (Dallas and Houston), basketball (Philadelphia), and baseball (Texas)."

She pastes her senior picture alongside these confessions: a sheer gloss shines on her pale pink lips. Everything shines except her skin, as smooth as eggshell. She sits with shoulders square and head high, a crowned monarch. The soft, thin gathers of her pink calico dress fall from a lace-edged seam across her breasts. Her brown hair rests in wings on either side of her broad cheekbones. Amusement, indulgence, and pride glow in the blue eyes. She looks like rose quartz, like a white candy heart with pink lettering. I'm a friend, her demure eyes say to the camera—are you ready for that?

It's a fair question. The air is never neutral between us now. What we feel deeply and hide most from others, we slice open and hurl at each other in the tiny, suffocating bedroom.

"I can't wait until she's gone," I'd told Mama. It was bedtime, and Joyce's anger had filled the room like a swollen river after heavy rains. What had I been doing this time—swallowing too loudly? Fidgeting in her peripheral vision? "She gets mad at every little thing, and it makes me feel bad. I get scared when she's like that, and she won't stop being mad."

Mama had frowned over the top of her bifocals, then glanced down to mark her place. A brown paper grocery sack by her rocking chair bulged with romance novels. Mama and Joyce fight, too. Resentment and hatred fan from Joyce like blasting waves of heat, and Mama absorbs her daughter's misery, returns it screeching and scolding. Daddy, in his wing chair, sinks his chin in his hand and stares out at the black trees against the night sky, or at his own reflection in the storm window.

"I know," Mama'd said. She'd reached for her sewing scissors to chop a loose thread at the wrist of my nightgown. "I'd have thought she'd grow out of it by now. Just put up with it as best you can and try to be nice."

In our dark room, I'd pulled the sheet and the fraying blanket binding over me. "You know I can hear every word you all say down there," Joyce had grumbled toward the wall.

I couldn't take anything back. "Goodnight," I'd said, queasy, her anger in my stomach. She'd made no sound, the way a hot stove is soundless. "Goodnight," I'd whispered. "Joyce. Goodnight."

"You spoil everything," she'd said. "Goodnight." Even a snarl was a benediction, just as long as she talked to me.

"I'll be so happy when I'm gone and I don't have to babysit you anymore," Joyce says now, closing the memory book. "I hate it. I hate being stuck with you. I have to listen to you and everybody else say how smart you are. But you're a big baby and a know-it-all. If you don't get your way all you do is cry. If I have to spend one more month with you I'll scream the whole house down. I'm so glad I'm getting away from you."

"Me too," I say. "I won't have to listen to you gripe, and I won't have to listen to your sorry old music. I won't have to sit with you in the car or see you at ball games. And if I decide to walk to town I won't have to ask you. And if I decide to walk down the tracks I will. I don't care what you say."

The rails run a scant three-quarters of a mile from our house. At night we hear the haunting bellow of the whistle, the coal train relentlessly bumping north to south. In the summer, I like to walk as far as the tracks, then follow the adjacent road, the only sounds the slap of sandals on clay and gravel and the buzz of bees and locusts in the berry brambles.

"I'm not going to be here to stop you," she says, slow with realization. I think she's given in, but her venom has changed to ice. "Ann," she says. "You have to be in charge now. So I'll tell you this one more time. Never, never walk on those train tracks. Don't walk along them. Don't stand and wait when you cross them."

"I know." I squirm away as if she's grabbed my shoulder.

"I want to tell you something," Joyce says.

"Okay, I know," I say, "leave me alone."

"Shut up a minute," she says. "Look. When I was little I saw a baby get hit by a train."

Through my chest, my head, a memory migrates, of flailing on the edge of a stopped breath. The last cornflakes in the milk look like something that will make me sick.

"Mama was driving. We were leaving the grocery store and everybody was stopped at the tracks and the train hit them. The baby flew out and got killed. I saw the whole thing. I saw that baby die," she says, her hands humping into loose fists, her eyes wide with threat. I see the down-covered skull, the bright puddle of blood, the receiving blanket hung on the windshield shards, and Joyce's blue eyes not covered by her pudgy hands. The baby stops skidding on the pavement. Joyce can't even scream.

"You can't ever, ever tell Mama and Daddy," she says. "When it happened, Mama asked if I saw it. I told her no because it scared her so bad. I didn't want her to worry. So I told her I didn't see it, but I did. The baby was so tiny. All the blood.

"You think nothing is going to happen to you," she says, "but it can. Your foot can get stuck or you can fall down or the train can just come so much faster than you think it is. If I ever hear you were playing around on the tracks I'll tell Daddy and you'll get in so much trouble you'll find out what it means that you don't know what hit you."

"Wow," I say. "Okay. I promise."

"Don't even joke about it," she says. "And don't tell. I don't want her to know."

"Joyce, I promise," I say.

She shoots me a mean squint. A cold chill runs its light fingers under my clothes. I don't want her to leave me. "Honest," I say. "I promise."

We do not willfully disbelieve. Denial is a paralysis of belief. A monster looms over us, or inside us. If we could perceive it as a threat, our bodies would react in familiar fight or flight—but the monster looks like nonsense. Our brains can't accept that anything like it exists. It's insane to react to a threat that doesn't exist. So we walk into the monster's teeth, dismissing the danger as a silly hallucination.

I wandered up and down the hallway at work, looking for Dean to tell him I'd be leaving. He was in a meeting. I couldn't think what to do. Mustn't leave until I tell the boss. Maybe don't need to leave at all. If I go and it's not serious, what then? Need to go. Must take work? What happens to work if I go? Maybe no hurry. Mustn't leave until I figure it out. Mustn't do anything until it makes sense.

"Hey, are you all right?" Jeff was, like all the senior software developers at the company, articulate, competent, and generous, his kindness tempered with cynical wit, with caustic, verbal precision. The company hired for these traits. He walked toward me. His question was one that we always answer, professionally, with misdirection, pleasant babble. How are you? Fine. Am I all right? Jeff was only a little taller than me, blond as pine. He craned his head forward slightly, his eyes peering at mine as if under a lid.

I shook my head. "No."

"No, you're not all right," he agreed, standing close to me. The other developers needn't hear the explanation.

"The hospital called. I have to go. My sister might be dying. That is, now. She might be dying now." The tears hung in my eyes and would not fall.

And in the midst of our colleagues, Jeff stepped forward and clasped his arms around me. A hug can be something other than affection. It can be a transfer of strength. It can be an obeisance to pain, and the paradise for words that die of futility.

There, I thought. That's what you do when your colleague is not all right. That's how you hold someone whose beloved is dying.

"I'd known there was an illness in your family," he said. "Will it help to tell me?" So I told him: Kidney failure. Infection. Morbidly obese. And the clinical recitation clamped denial to me like armor. "I'm waiting for Dean, to talk to Dean before I go."

Dean returned from his morning meetings. He listened to my story. "Why are you waiting?" he said. A compact man with brown hair and a meticulous brown beard that appeared to weather rather than gray, Dean was my boss, a vice-president of the company. Our team trusted him. He walked with a boatsman's balance and sat with the ease of an eighteen-year-old who knows he's going to ace the final, who already has summer plans. He walked me to the door, each word a soft step down the oak planks of his voice. "Look, if it makes you feel better, carry work with you. Then work, or ignore the work. Look," he said. "None of this is important."

"I know," I said. As I spoke, I began to recognize denial, and felt sick. I would not have known I was paralyzed, except that I wanted to run. "I know, and yet. It's like I don't know what I should do. If I get there, and she's all right, and then later she needs me . . ."

"Here's what you should do," Dean said, his eyes dark, rum in a cask. "You should go. What you should do is go. I'll tell you this: I had the same thing once—I had to make the same decision, and I waited . . . Go. Be where you need to be. Your work's not going anywhere; it'll be here when you get back. Just stay in touch." His smile was like paper cuts reopening. "Don't waste a chance to be with your sister," he said. "This is not something you want to regret."

That's how you talk to someone in denial. That's how you make a paralyzed woman run. That's how you help her speed to Tulsa, stopping only once for fuel, the leather-trimmed bag in the trunk stuffed with black knit funeral clothes and warm sweaters for the frigid hospital hallways.

She had stabilized again by the time I arrived, and she was alone in the room. My heart pounded; adrenaline lurched. Joyce smiled, her eyebrows raised in a shallow pagoda arch. Her glance slid sidelong toward me, her lips slick and shaky below the oxygen mask, her head immobile in the pillow, and her body, like an untouched burial mound, holding her captive, its high globe a heavy earthen blanket on her heart.

At the gym, she waits by the water fountain. A slender woman in a sweaty tank top fills a water bottle. Look at that back, those long and permanent thigh muscles. She's had those muscles since her teens. A tape measure tight on her waist would push no bulge above or below. That woman has never known what it's like to be fat.

She despises the slender woman. Then she despises herself. Would she really want a healthy person to feel fat? No, that's not it. She wants the slender woman to smile at her. She wants the slender woman not to avoid her eyes, not to look away, embarrassed. She wants to know she belongs at the gym, just as much as the slender woman does.

Search term: white blood cell.

A white blood cell has a short and beautiful life in our bodies, like a rainbow after a storm. The white blood cells fight our diseases. They can produce antibodies, or can consume invading viruses or bacteria. We need more white cells when an infection fights back, or when we are under great emotional or physical stress, or when the tissue of our bodies has been burned or traumatized. Then, our bone marrow, which is the blood hatchery inside our bones, makes more white cells. A high number of white cells in the blood means that a battle is being fought. When all is calm in our bodies, a microliter of our blood contains 4,500 to 10,000 white cells.

Search term: infection.

Your body is a continent. Tribes of bacteria multiply peacefully here—the enterococci in your intestines, the staphylococcus on your skin. But bacteria that are harmless in their normal breeding ground, if allowed to travel or spread to a new location, become invaders, marauders, destroying in order to multiply, leaving behind the scorched earth of their host, your body. Your body's immune system fights to regain its ground; it manufactures the special type of white blood cells that ingest bacteria. But sometimes the fight is beyond the body's strength, and only the surgeon's scalpel can stop the infection by removing the infested tissue. An infection loosed in a sterile space, like your abdominal cavity, can multiply rapidly and unchecked—to thrive, it kills its host.

Sometimes a size fourteen fits her. Maybe these fourteens. Just in case, the sixteens. Won't need them, but just in case. And this shirt, the red that always gets compliments—it has a long hem; will it cover her belly? She'll try two pairs of jeans and the red shirt with flowing sleeves. So pretty. Will look like vivacious adventurer.

Fourteens first. Ouch. Legs too tight. Can't even get the butt pulled up. No way. Okay, truth now, been a while since the last fourteens. Maybe cut small, these.

Sixteens. Denim tourniquets around her thighs, butt squashed tight and flat. Oh, God, what is that, a five inch gap? The pants v'd out across the white cotton jelly bowl, her belly bulged forward between the zipper teeth. How can sixteens not fit? Any sixteen should fit! Sixteens should be huge! She's—she's huge . . .

She can stand here as long as she wants and the pants won't get any bigger. Can't be right. Turn around. Look again. Maybe if she lies down to zip them. One pair at home like that already, torture in the morning, flesh pinched in the waistband, breath tight and stunted from a compressed tummy, fat rolls flopping over. But if she loses weight they'll fit. Shouldn't she think positively? Shouldn't she buy them and lose into them? So cute, the flare. No flared ones in eighteen.

Eighteen. She has to try on the eighteens. Should she get the twenties also? They're not even on the same rack! You have to go under the plus size sign to get the twenties! What if the eighteens don't fit? Oh God. They have to. They make the belly so big in eighteens that the legs are always loose and pouched around the tops of the thighs. First will try the red shirt. Dashing red shirt makes eighteens not so horrid.

Standing in panties and bra, she doesn't look so fat. Looks like she should fit the sixteens anyway. Doesn't look bad, just womanly, in panties and bra. After all, her husband loves her, does not look away when in bra and panties she stands near him.

Oh no. Oh, oh no. Moron. Fool. Don't cry. Under the collar, top three buttons fasten, but none of the others will button over the belly. Maybe wear it tucked in? Right! Tucked into what, the jeans she has to lie down to zip up? Tucked into the belly rolls flopping over the top of the jeans? Sure! Stupid. Why did she think she could fit this? Sleeves so tight she can't reach her big, flappy arms forward. So tight it's hard to take off. Just want to get out of here. Want to get out of here and not cry.

Oh, but. She can't leave until she buys a pair of jeans. She can't wear her old jeans on casual day anymore because the zipper will break. Okay. It doesn't matter. Go get the damned eighteens. Fat. Ugly. Idiot. Okay. Calm down. If they fit, buy them and celebrate. What will make her feel better after this?

Milkshake. Cold, creamy. She's breathing more easily now just thinking of pants that fit and being out of the store, treating herself. It's okay, she says. You're okay. Breathe. Breathe. You're almost through this now. You're almost done.

Search term: cellulitis.

Cellulitis is an infection. Its hot soreness can spread in a flash from your swollen, red skin to the layer of tissue under your skin. From there, it can creep like a safecracker past the vault door into your blood and your lymph nodes. If you don't treat it, cellulitis can kill you. It can spread to the deep layer of tissue under your skin and find destiny as a flesh-eating bacteria, or as sepsis or gangrene. If you have cellulitis, you likely are shaking with bitter fever, and you feel nauseated and fatigued. Your muscles ache. You need antibiotics.

"Her white cell count is still quite high, over 50,000," said Dr. Abu, "though I would again caution you not to attach so much importance to that number. It's only one indicator." I scuttled next to him like a hermit crab in the shadow of a protective tidepool boulder.

"Yet the infection is still—"

"Unknown. Yes."

"The cellulitis? Had it spread into the fascial lining?" The infection could sink deep, into the thin margin between skin and organs. Had it?

"We don't believe so," Dr. Abu said. "The cellulitis, in fact, appears to be clearing. The kidneys are still the main problem, though we are increasingly concerned about the infection." He watched my face as though watching a videotape of a difficult birth.

He'd wait for me while I gathered scraps of fact and confusion into words. He'd let me work my voice through the strange filters of duty and insanity. How could it feel natural to be in the hospital again? How could its hallways have become homelike, its rhythms comfortable and easy? How could I feel anything but revulsion and fear? Why did I feel, instead, relieved to be back in the hospital with Joyce and the nurses and Dr. Abu?

To be understood, even a little, by a highly intelligent person is to find refuge. I felt Dr. Abu's gaze like the watch of a sentinel over a sleeping village: Dr. Abu watched over Joyce. Though her enormous body and its abnormal fat repulsed the world, he watched her, a charge in his care, and he understood she was someone to be loved, safeguarded. I gave him a tiny, tight nod and the short stitch of a smile.

"About the kidneys," I said, "I have the serum creatinine numbers, but not the creatinine clearance numbers. Would the clearance numbers indicate anything different from what I know?"

"Not significantly," Dr. Abu said. "Let's go through the latest test results." I nodded and swiftly lettered down my notebook margin: BUN. Creat. WBC. ABGs. Dr. Abu read the bold capitals as they leaked onto the page. A question formed in his dark eyes like a water droplet pulled into a sphere. "What is it that you do? Something related to the medical field?" he said.

"I'm a technical writer," I said.

"Ah," he said. "And that is?"

"I research and explain things," I said. I shrugged, embarrassed. "I write software manuals."

"Ah," he said.

"Mostly I learn how much I don't know," I said.

Dr. Abu put his hand on my forearm. I felt my pulse rock once, under his palm. "It's fine," he said. "It's good you and your family are with your sister."

1982

Freshman year: Joyce's diary.

February 2. It hasn't stopped raining since Friday night. I think if it had kept raining like that the college might not be here anymore. I would have loved to pull off my shoes and wade through the water but right now I can't afford to risk getting pneumonia. As it was I was pretty wet. The water came up ankle deep in some places and I couldn't resist splashing through it.

It's funny how people act differently toward the water from rain. Here you have your basic tippy-toer. He or she tries to walk where there isn't any water puddles. When they realize they have to walk in the water they make a face and stick their toes down in the water. All the while saying, "This is going to ruin my shoes."

February 9. I'm getting sick and tired of hearing people put other people down. It seems that I can't go anywhere here on campus without hearing someone say something bad about somebody else.

I went to get change in C-Dorm last night and a girl was talking on the phone about one of the basketball players. She said he cussed all the time and talked about some famous player like he knew him. Maybe he did know that famous player. What makes her so sure he didn't and what right does she have to talk about him like that anyway? I was afraid to turn around and look at her for fear I might hit her.

I get behind someone on the way to class and they start talking about someone I know and like. Maybe it's ME. Maybe I'm taking everything too seriously, but I don't think so.

February 27. My roommate is sick. She is homesick. She is making me go crazy. She is constantly analyzing everything I do. She cuts me down for studying! She also does self-analyzation which drives me even more crazy. She thinks she has to explain everything that she does or says. She smacks her food all the time while we are in the room because "I can't help it" but she seems to be able to control it in the cafeteria. Amazing isn't it?

She calls me mean and a tyrant because of some of the ways I feel toward people. She won't even give her teachers a chance. Maybe she needs to quit school. She can't find anything but bad in it and she never studies. She just sleeps all the time or reads horror stories. I always have to leave the room if she wants to listen to the radio (loud!) and I need to study. But when she does study she turns off the radio whether I listen to it or not. She says it's impossible to study with the radio on. Don't I know it! Yet when I leave she always acts like I'm being a baby and that I don't have to study. Once I felt like telling her, "Get behind me, Satan." I might not be alive if I had said that.

April 14. One of my favorite forms of exercise is walking. I love to walk. I try to walk at least twice a week. Usually I walk on Saturdays during the day and sometimes I walk on Tuesday or Thursday night. I walk down to Wal-Mart or TG&Y. Walking to TG&Y is much more fun and it takes longer to get there so you get more exercise. It takes about an hour to walk down to TG&Y. Then my roommate and I stay at TG&Y. for an hour or two. Then it takes another hour to walk home.

Walking along the road can bring some good times too. One time a guy stopped and asked us if we wanted a ride. He was real cute and he had a nice car, but he was smoking a joint so we let him go. Several people stop and ask us directions which we seldom know but we help them as much as we can.

Sometimes people we know will drive by and honk sometimes scaring us half out of our gourds. Most of the time it's people we don't know who will honk. Usually they holler something at us like "hey" or "yeah" or something to that effect or worse. Two guys in a little sports car hollered "Oh yeah, uh huh," and my roommate hollered "Unhuh" then "Maybe."

It's fun at night. A lot of cars see us and turn on their brights. We are blinded. They see us plain as day and we don't have the slightest idea who they are. But the greatest thing about being out at night is looking up at the stars and the moon. It gives you a feeling of security to look up there and realize if God took that kind of attention with them, how much more he is watching over us.

May 22. Today seems pretty exciting for some reason. So far I've done laundry, watched TV, and picked Hunter up from baseball practice. Maybe it's the game tonight. I don't think so. I was supposed to get new shoes this week. I didn't. Maybe I won't. I did hit a few balls to Hunter this afternoon. But that wasn't too exciting. I think I hit pretty good considering how long it's been since I've done that.

Hunter's been surprising me lately. He says the most grown-up things. He's only 13. I guess he is growing up. He has also been reading books. That's the biggest surprise of all . . . I don't think I'll ask him about any more books. Maybe he'll ask me.

August 8. These days seem so boring. Everytime I think about boredom I remember what our ladies' class teacher said, "Christians should never be bored." It makes me feel real guilty when I get bored.

Today was one of those days. There just didn't seem to be anything to do. I finally decided to catch up on some reading. I was reading *The Screwtape Letters* by C. S. Lewis and I was on the chapter about the love of God.

He brought home the fact that Satan doesn't understand God's love. How can Satan understand the love that erases all wrong doing when a person asks God? Satan has evil intent in everything so he probably thinks God's love is a disguise for something God wants.

In chapter seventeen, Lewis talks about gluttony. He says gluttony is not always excess. Gluttony can be wanting something that causes you to go to extra trouble, just to show for instance you only want a little glass of ice cold water and a piece of toast just so. This caused me to think a lot about gluttony. If what he says is true than Satan has infiltrated our lives sneakily again. How many people ask for less just to prove they aren't gluttons?

She watches a woman across the food court and thinks, That woman is fatter than me. She feels she's dodged a public embarrassment—at least she didn't order a fried hamburger and onion rings like that woman did. She only had a small nachos. The woman is huge. It must be miserable. Look at her, she thinks. That woman can hardly look up from her food, and she can't smile. She wonders if the woman shops for clothes in this mall. She wonders what it would be like to be that size. Where does she find panties large enough? Who sells them? How does she feel buying them, how does she feel putting them down on the checkout counter? Is it the same way she feels when she sees jokes on television about fat women? Terrible to have your panties a joke, then have to wear them, unfurl, step in, worming the elastic over your undulating folds, humiliated. She's glad she hasn't let herself get that big.

How much fat does it take on a body before others see it as ruin? Before it is ruin?

Her gaze is seized by a second woman, a size four, she guesses, in a peppermint-striped sleeveless top. The size-four woman pushes a stroller, where her plum-cheeked baby sleeps. The size-four woman nibbles a pretzel and sips a large drink.

She watches the size-four woman look at the fat woman, a brief, disconcerted twist of revulsion like a fog passing across the size-four woman's face.

Why should anyone care what a size-four woman thinks? Still, she's suddenly offended and angered by the shreds of nacho cheese congealing in their grease-spotted cardboard boat, as though the food had been dumped into her like garbage by hands not her own. She's glad she finished the nachos before the size-four woman saw her eating them. She's glad the size-four woman hasn't looked her way.

Joyce no longer actively lay in the hospital bed, wriggling with discomfort. Passive, inert, she waited for her aches to surface in a tense ripple over her cheekbones or arrow back from the fine muscles around her eyes. Below the oxygen mask, her lips pursed and relaxed as though she were blowing bubbles in a swimming pool.

"This is a different ventilator," a woman in her room was telling Mama and Daddy. The three stood around Joyce's bed like shepherds at the nativity. "Oh, hello—you must be Ann. I'm pleased to finally meet you."

"Virginia," I said. Our introductory smiles resonated briefly, like the tick of a clock pendulum.

"I was just explaining to your parents about the change in Joyce's equipment," Virginia said. With her rose-petal-and-thorn voice, her unwrinkled dress suit, she slipped into my image of her like a puzzle piece into a gap. Her face trim, her chin firm, Virginia was not grandmotherly, but administratorly. "This ventilator is adjustable. It can do a little more of the work of Joyce's breathing for her. You'll see nurses adjust its controls."

"Is she going to have to keep the mask on all the time?" Mama asked.

"No," Virginia said, looking down at Joyce like Madonna on the child. "Only when she's having trouble breathing, and when she's asleep. When she's awake, as long as she's breathing fine on her own she can have the mask off."

"It looks uncomfortable," Mama said.

Joyce widened her eyes in agreement and then blinked at me, You don't say.

"Joyce, are you okay in the mask?" Virginia asked. She mittened her mother-of-pearl fingers around Joyce's bed rail.

Joyce's eyes flashed, a panicky two-step left and right. "Feels good to breathe," she said at last. Her voice was like the stress groan of a wooden window sash.

"That's right," Virginia said, and tilted honeyed curls again. "If you need anything," she said to Mama and Daddy and me, "let us know." Her parting smile was like the final signature on a contract: her availability might continue, but as long as I was at the hospital, I no longer needed her as an intermediary. We watched Virginia clip out of the room on square pump heels, on her way to other patients, other families.

"Well, she seems real nice." Mama dumped herself into the low, upholstered chair and propped her left foot over her right knee. She pulled off her canvas slipper and began to massage her ankle and the arch of her foot. "Don't mind this here. I can't stand for very long, my feet get to hurting so bad. Is that the woman you talk to on the phone every day?"

"She's in charge of the adult ward nurses," I said. I watched Joyce, her eyes nearly closed in—what, boredom? Sleepiness?—and her lips pursing, blowing—bubbles? Kisses? Unvoiced objections? Without the accompaniment of her eyes I couldn't hear her thoughts. "I get the idea she follows all the patient cases pretty closely."

"Somebody needs to." Daddy's complaint bloomed, a rare flower, a rumble from below his lowered cap brim.

"What do you mean?"

"It's just terrible," Daddy said. He looked at Joyce's body in the bed. The sheeted vault of her stomach rose and fell; she had closed her eyes. A vertical line shadowed the smooth span between her eyebrows. "I don't think we can leave her alone. She had to call our room in the middle of the night. She was ringing and ringing her buzzer and the nurses didn't come."

"What was wrong?"

"Her bag there was getting empty and the needle was hurting her." Daddy shook his head slowly. "I don't know what they do, not answering like that. What would she have done if we weren't here to go get the nurses?"

"I just don't think they're paying all that much attention," Mama said, defiance rippling like flame along gas jets. "They just come in and do their little swab here and there and take things in and out and hardly give her a second look. I don't think much of them."

Powerlessness is like the fluid that swells around an ankle sprain. It signals that searing pain waits any pressure, any forward footstep. It warns you not to move, for fear of ripping the ligaments further. Could I step into Mama's blind protectiveness, Daddy's sudden and misdirected grasp of Joyce's tenuous hold on health, their narrow demands of our allies, the nurses? Powerless against their powerlessness, powerless against the march of hours, the drip of drugs . . . I ought to be here, sitting with Joyce, to retrieve the nurses or a drink of water, help adjust her limbs, watch for the catheter bag filling, check her prescriptions and doses. What game was I playing, far away from her, scribbling vocabulary words? Impotent, foppish, foolish. What good did it do? Who did it help? Powerless, I pulled her chart from the wall and readied the spiral notebook. A new prescription flowed into Joyce's arm as part of the bagged, intravenous cocktail that relieved her pain and fought her multiple, mysterious infections. Vancomycin, I wrote.

I miss Joyce while she's away at college, as I would a favorite sweater that's been locked in a trunk. In the emptiness of our house, I shiver, but my sweater is at the bottom of the trunk, and the trunk is locked.

Joyce's summer holiday growl is like rust on hinges. "Why do you care what I want to do? We do what you want anyway. Friends at school? Why should I tell you? You don't listen." Her plump face wrinkles in a cringe of irritation. Our eating, speech, and movement grate on her. She grinds her teeth and walks away. After dinner, when dishes tilt in the sink, she retreats to our room with cassette player and headphones. Mama tightens her lips and Daddy scowls and sighs, but Joyce simply folds the leaping, marine wonderland of her eyes into a sharp, hunched shrug.

Then one morning, after weeks of this frostbite, I wake as with a breaking fever. The lost sweater blankets me. Across the room, the heavy trunk stands open, the padlock hanging by its long iron hook from the latch loop.

"Good, you're finally up." Joyce's chin is lifted, her hair brushed back from her eyes. "It's not so hot outside today. I thought we might go out to Honor Heights. I feel like taking pictures."

Honor Heights Park, built as a tribute to returning World War I soldiers, rises and dives over a high hilltop on the west side of Muskogee. Its hairpin road descends past rock trails and rose gardens to loop around picnic grounds, a fountained pond, and a small lake truffled with pintail ducks and fat-breasted white geese.

"Wow. I'm getting dressed. Do I have time for breakfast?"

"Good grief. Just don't piddle around all morning or I'll change my mind. Why don't you call Karen and see if she wants to go? I'll take some pictures of you together."

We cruise in Joyce's Chevy Malibu wagon, the windows open, the oldies station loud. My friend Karen, thin as bone china in a jade spaghetti-strapped tank top, leans forward from the back seat. The rugged waves of her dark hair pummel her sharp cheekbones. She opens her smile like a child's coin purse for Joyce, whose silken, round face looks twelve years old. The wind tosses their jabbering voices.

"And I had this one class, American History, and Dr. Wilson, he re-enacts the entire Hamilton-Burr duel. It's great!"

"My brother Jim lives in Florida. He got me into bodybuilding. Not competition, though. It's crazy what they do to their bodies to win."

"He's Hamilton, and then he's Burr. He runs back and forth and then pretends to be shot and fall on the floor dead."

"I want to be a choreographer. You know, a dancer and a choreographer? Maybe for a professional cheerleading squad."

"And next year in one of the elementary ed classes I have to learn to juggle. Dr. Vincent says you can't teach unless you can hold a classroom's attention. So you can't pass the class unless you juggle."

From the park's iron entrance arch, switchbacks wind in a tunnel of oaks and redbuds. Honor Heights drops its emerald skirts down the hillside. Layered banks of green azalea bushes bolster the terraced beds; fat roses bloom in a grid of gravel walkways. A warm June wind slaps the lake, and a goose crank-calls from far out on the water.

A mulch and sandstone trail stairsteps beside the downward course of clear water. Waterfalls splash and sparkle in basins of granite boulders. Footbridges cross shallow pools. Karen leads us up the trail, her long thighs and calves flexing beneath the white denim cutoffs. Joyce and I follow, our shorter legs straining in their blue jean casings. Joyce braces her feet at shoulder width. Her fingers bracket the snapshot camera. She holds the camera as though it were a stack of money. At the summit, she walks to the overlook's edge and shoots a leisurely panorama of the farmland far below. With her fingertips, she mops bubbles of sweat from her forehead. Then the three of us sit on a stone bench, hip to hip, quiet. A landslide of treetops cascades into flat meadows, hay fields bright as leaf lettuce, long, green threads of treeline boundaries. A breeze jerks the redbud leaves; a waterfall gargles over a rock lip; a blue jay spits its rusty yell into the woods.

My Other Body ◆ 153

It's nearly noon. The sun's hot hand on our heads forces our gaze back to the shady trail.

"Pizza?" Joyce says.

"Buffet," Karen and I say together, and laugh to mask our logic. We can finish a large pizza together. We might not leave anything for Joyce. We pick our way down the trail, pausing behind Joyce as she frames a begonia bed or a stray creek rivulet in her lens.

A week later, Joyce and I sit cross-legged, dealing prints like solitaire cards on the living room carpet. Tom and Jerry pounce and shimmy on the television. Mama won't be home from work for an hour. "That was fun that day," Joyce says.

In a glossy square, Karen tilts against a bridge railing, her collarbone a ceramic ribbon under the white, freckled skin. "Karen's so pretty," I say.

"You're pretty," Joyce says. She pops up a searching look like a button through a buttonhole.

I push away a picture of a girl I half-recognize. The girl balances in the crotch of a tree trunk, reclining on the bark column. Her fluffy perm falls, a light brown feather duster, past dark eyes and a toothy smile. "I'm funny-looking. I look fat. My neck is fat. That shirt's the only one that fits right and doesn't look stupid."

"Ann," Joyce says, her eyes wide and drooping with surprise and pity. "You care too much what people think." She taps the girl laughing in the tree. "You look pretty in this picture."

I don't look like that. I don't look that good. "It's a good picture you took," I tell her.

"Yes, it is," she says, with trim pride. "Now me, I look te-e-e-r-rible in pictures. That's why I take them. The camera doesn't point at me."

"You have no goals," says her spouse. "You lose a pound and gain a pound, lose a pound and gain two pounds. What are your goals?"

To get you off my back, she thinks. "Look," she says. "I've been setting weight loss goals, the daydreamy kind you're talking about, since I was fourteen. Sometimes I find old notebooks where I charted them out, dates and goal weights. It makes me so sad to find this stuff in my own handwriting—meaningless goals and failures. I'm tired of goals. I want a plan. I want my goal to be to follow the plan."

"But—how will you know what you achieve unless you have a goal?"

"How can the number on a scale be my goal? I don't know how to get there. I agree with you about goals—but somehow health has to be my goal, not a target weight or an amount of weight lost by a certain date. I can't set myself up to fail again. I have to find a different way. A different goal."

The late September sky draped rich and cloudless. A sidewalk hugged by emerald St. Augustine blades outlined the colossus of the hospital. I scurried next to Daddy's easy infielder's lope as we walked toward the throb of traffic. Ahead, a few late-morning shoppers pulled in and out of parking spaces near a brick village of specialty stores. A breeze raked the tree-peppered shops, and neither Daddy nor I hurried toward the eventual first question.

"Daddy, where's Hunter?"

"He's home, looking for a job."

"Does he know how sick Joyce is?"

"He'll come up if she's here much longer. He doesn't like hospitals."

I said a prayer for forgiveness as quick as a curse: I hadn't remembered because it hadn't altered my life. Four years ago, Johns Hopkins surgeons had put saw and drill to Hunter's skull, removing the cancerous tumor stuffed in the sinus cavity. Hunter had lain weak and speechless, claustrophobic inside his white mummification. Sedated, he endured his claustrophobia through later MRI scans. The cancer had not returned. My fear for him had dissipated to a hiccup whenever his checkups were due. But for Mama and Daddy, who had sat at his sterile bedside, the images of their son's motionless six-foot-five frame, with yards of cotton packing inside his head, would not have faded.

We strolled past the storefronts—card shops, florists, children's pleated fashions. In these tranquilly forbidding establishments, well-hemmed and precisely moussed Tulsa shopped for wine, chocolates, diamonds, tufted ottomans. At the corner where we decided to turn back, Daddy and I stopped like pilgrims at an unexpected shrine. Behind a vast glass pane, metallic bunting hung in scalloped fans. Patriotic confetti swirled in glossy heaps around the mannequins' sequined high heels. Red and blue spangles and white bugle beads gowned the mannequins' shoulders; the dolls' dull eyes aimed upward under the red, white, and blue ruffles and quills of satin hats and headpieces. Around the figures, platter-sized lollipops spun, red, white, and blue metallic pinwheels: America celebrates her siege with the merchandise at hand.

"My word," I finally said.

"Sure is something," he said, wide-eyed at the gaudy, festooned enormity.

I'd called him three weeks ago. Joyce's health stalked my mind, as it had since her springtime visit, when she could barely climb the stairs. Though Joyce would never be cajoled into treatment, she lived under their roof. Maybe they could force her.

"Daddy, how's Joyce?" I'd asked him.

"She's having trouble finding a job," he'd said. "It really has got her down. She goes around to the schools and puts in applications. She's not even getting on as a substitute."

I'd swallowed, rocking toward the hilltop in the roller-coaster car, just before the plunge. "Daddy, you know the reason they don't hire her is because she isn't in good health."

"No, she's healthy," he'd said, with dark, melodious reproof. "She's just big, and slow."

The coaster slammed down the rickety rails. Healthy? He could think that Joyce, who couldn't breathe lying down and who no longer walked but wobbled on swollen feet, was healthy?

"Daddy—how do you know she's healthy?" Don't screech. Keep the voice even, logical, detached. "Has she been to a doctor?"

He'd paused. "No," he'd said, disarmed, thoughtful.

"I know she doesn't want to go to a doctor," I'd said. "But she needs to go soon. It's been more than a year since she saw that doctor in Dallas. It's so—I just worry about her."

"I know," he'd said, comforting me. "It's okay. I know." And together, to belittle the specter of Joyce's fat, we'd recategorized our worry as our own regrettable flaw. We'd changed the subject.

She's just big, and slow. An anchor sank, heavier than denial—the painful surprise at feeling so much love. This is my daughter, beautiful and vibrant and willful. When I look at her, I see a thousand memories of her, hear her voice echo forward from birth. Big, slow, precious; how proud of her I've been. She can't be sick. Nothing's wrong with her. It's hard for her—I see it now, I understand she struggles. The bigness and the slowness, torture enough, can't have taken her health if they haven't robbed her of my love.

"Your mama and I plan to stay up here at the hospital," Daddy said as we walked toward St. John. "We can go home to wash clothes and such but we'll come right back. If we go anywhere, it'll be to LaNita's house."

"How's Troy?" At LaNita's house, forty-five minutes from St. John, Uncle Troy lay in a hospital bed in the converted guest room. His minutely calibrated engineer's mind ticked inside the valiant remains of destroyed nerves and wasted muscle.

"You know he went back in the hospital this week."

"No, I didn't know."

"The doctors say he might live two days or he might live thirty. If he gets to be stable again she'll bring him home from the hospital. She can't let him go. I don't know how she stands to watch him like that."

"She loves him. Maybe she doesn't see the disease—she just sees him. I can't imagine how hard it would be, to let go of somebody you love that much."

Daddy sighed and nodded and measured the height of the hospital with a long look. "I guess that's right," he said.

 1984

Great-Grandma Roberts's white frame house stands empty. Joyce unlocks the front door, and we walk through to the silent kitchen as if through a cleaned and darkened church. The Thanksgiving turkey thaws in a black enamel roasting pan in Great-Grandma Roberts's refrigerator. We are to prepare it, the centerpiece of the meal, the meaty tinder for tradition's hearth fire.

Over the ziggurat of carved turkey, Grandma Hester will ask Daddy to say the blessing. Daddy doesn't lead prayers at church. The congregation unnerves him. Even amidst family, Daddy's holiday address to the Lord God is an annual tremble over ham platters and yeast rolls, a deep quaver that binds his verbatim recital in our bowed heads: "Heavenly Father, we come before you to thank you for all your many blessings and for bringing us here today. We ask you to bless this food for the nourishment of our bodies and bless the ones that prepared it. We ask that you forgive us our sins and go with us this day and throughout our lives. We ask it in Christ's name. Amen."

Joyce and I have never cooked a turkey. "There's nothing to it," Mama scolds. "The directions are right there on the package. Y'all are old enough to cook a turkey, surely."

At twenty-two, Joyce is less my elder than before, our ages immaterial. I've slid toward her like a bead on an abacus: one gap closes, and one opens. We're both in college now, survivors of a shared and finished journey, escaped from anyone's continual knowledge of our whereabouts. But our distance is immense. We know some of the names but none of the voices of each other's friends. Neither of us knows where the other goes at night, what movies she has watched, what books she reads. We attend different churches. We sit far apart in chapel. We have each begun to smuggle our old belongings from home, to devoid the bedroom of our individual memories.

Sometimes I see Joyce across the red clay campus. She hugs her books to the peanut shell of her torso and climbs the steps toward the elementary education classrooms. Or she kneels, troweling the hosta beds in her job with the landscape crew. Or alone, she carries her tray across the cafeteria. From her apartment a mile across campus, she sends me greeting cards. "Just saying hello," they say.

Joyce studies the turkey's plastic casing. "I don't know what Mama's thinking," she says. "According to this the turkey won't be done until 2 o'clock."

"Can we cook it hotter?"

"No, we're going to follow the directions exactly how they're printed. I don't want to be for the next ten years the one who messed up the turkey. So. You take the wrapper off. I'll see if I can find a rack that'll fit in the pan. Then we need to rub it down with oil. No, not the rack. The turkey."

"You're the turkey."

"You are."

After the blessing we'll carry plates past the fragrant mosaic—snowy mashed potatoes, jellied beets, juicy turkey scallops. I'll sit near Joyce to secretively watch her eat. She has accumulated rituals like barnacles. They're spellbinding. She starts with a finicky inspection of the bite on the fork, followed by a careful carving of the bite into two smaller tidbits on the plate. After a small, self-conscious head-thrust forward and a last dubious glance at the bite, the tongue flickers out to accept the fork tines. The lips protrude, capture the food. Another inspection of the fork. Chewing, forward in the mouth. Swallowing and two gentle smacks of lips. The licking of the fork. Then, after a wait bordering on neglect, the next bite. Deliberate. Watchful. Dainty. She tips her iced tea glass between both hands and stares into the tea as if she suspects it has made fun of her. She gulps hard, her lower lip working at the rim of the glass. She clears the moisture from her mouth with a quick overlap of her lips.

"Did Mama tell you what happened in Grandma Roberts's surgery?" Great-Grandma Roberts, the white floss of her hair bulging in a cap, her driftwood limbs arranged on the gurney, had loosed a cavalcade of curse words and obscenities, railing at the doctors and nurses and every family member she'd seen that week. ("I can't imagine where she learned some of those words," Mama'd said.)

"Uh-huh. Mama said people do funny things under anesthetic. Did Daddy tell you about taking Grandma Roberts for a drive?" ("I know where you're a-taking me, she'd pouted to him. You're taking me to a home. Well, you can just stop the car and let me out." So Daddy had decelerated onto the shoulder, then gallantly opened her door. "Get out and walk," he'd told her. Grandma Roberts's jaw dropped, he'd said, and she'd huffed at him to get back in and drive. "I'm eighty-one," she'd told him. "Old enough to know better," he'd said.)

"Yeah," Joyce said.

"You know when I was little I would look at the blue veins in Grandma's legs and my knees would feel like jelly."

"That's silly."

"She was old. It scared me."

"That's even sillier. Did I ever tell you how she learned to drive?"

"No. How?"

"Grandpa Roberts had come out here from Arkansas. He was building the house, this house. He didn't want to bring her here until she had a house. So while he was gone, she decided to learn to drive. She asked some workmen to teach her. They said they would do it for a kiss. She never told Grandpa Roberts, but that's how she got her driving lessons." Joyce turns the oven knob, and the gas whooshes, splitting into flame. "That's good," she says. "I never have lit a pilot light."

"Do you think Grandma Roberts will get to come home again, or will she really have to go to a nursing home?" I dig the tip of a paring knife through the turkey's thick plastic wrapper and twist the blade to slice a ragged line toward the thigh.

"I don't know. Probably a nursing home. Let's don't talk about Grandma in the hospital." Joyce lines an orange rosary of sweet potatoes on the tabletop, then sits with the trash can between her knees and the peeler in her squat right hand.

Grandma Roberts lies across town sedated and unhappy in her hospital bed but surrounds us in the form of her house. Every inch of threadbare carpet, every shined mirror, every embroidered hem on every hand-sewn dishtowel conforms to her scent, her smile. She has lived in the house sixty years, turned its doorknobs, washed its dishes, rocked in its chairs, turned off its lamps above the heads of sleeping children.

("It sure is hard to be in the hospital at holiday time," I'd said to Daddy, when we saw Grandma slack and frail, asleep.

"It's hard to be in the hospital anytime," he'd said to me.)

I peel the thick, beige shell from the bony arc of the turkey breast. The clammy, dimpled turkey skin slides against the slick, pink meat.

"What's that?" Joyce nods at the turkey.

From beneath the peeled wrapper, a black speck emerges and forms a black bracket, an evil, arched eyebrow: an insect part. A shiny, armored cricket leg is pasted to the turkey breast. Inside the sealed package, the squashed, black, cryogenic cricket amputation gleams up at us. Its pronged, hairlike combs lie crushed against the white fat sail of turkey skin.

Do crickets live on dung, like flies? Will the crackling, roasted skin burn and melt disease away? Can we wash the turkey in hot water? Can we scissor away the tainted flap of skin? The words wither in my throat. "Joyce. What do we do?"

"You know what Mama's going to say if we don't cook this turkey because of a dinky little cricket leg?" Joyce's lips tighten, pink granite. She spreads fingers to shield her eyes. "Come on, please. I can't do it. It gives me the woozies."

Shuddering, I slide a butter knife against the turkey carcass. I shave the insect leg into a paper napkin. I bury the crumpled napkin in the trash can, under the sunset curls of sweet potato peel. Hot tap water scalds my shaking hands. The turkey sits dumb and dead in the ragged petals of ripped plastic wrap. "At least that's over," I say. I capsize the turkey in the enamel pan and strip the wrapper off in a single flourish.

A shining black parquet smothers the flattened tract between the drumstick hillocks, the fatty cowl of folds around the cavity—thawing, black cricket bodies mash in a sprawling mass, ebony-eyed heads jutting, antennae and legs protruding, thoraxes and wings crushed into a crunchy, black jelly. Dead crickets swell from the bird's hollows. A single cricket with half a head drips from the turkey and bounces to the floor. Joyce's scream fills the kitchen like milk in a glass. I splash myself into her scream like an ice cube. When we manage to stop shrieking, we look back at the jet-coated bird. Joyce grabs my hands and squeezes, and from our bellies we disgorge into each other's faces husky, straining screams of revulsion, frustration, anger, fear, until we spend our pent anxieties and panic and resentment on our adult excuse, a ruined turkey. Joyce slowly releases my hands from her squelching grip, and without a word, she pulls me into her short arms and presses the globe of her brown head against my shoulder.

Her husband's gone out. Listen. He might have forgotten something and come back. Garage door closing, section by section rattling downward, thunk. His car speeds away; he can't see through the front window as she opens the refrigerator door. More than a half loaf bread, turkey slices he doesn't like and won't miss, mayonnaise; with two slices gone it still looks like more than half a loaf. Want chips. A small handful, another handful. Finish making the sandwich; it's harder to hide than chips if he comes back. Pickles, no calories. Thirsty. More chips. If she closes the bag with this much air at the top it doesn't look changed. Want more. Healthy. Baby carrots? Six. Ten. Raisins. Sweet. Chocolate graham crackers. With chocolate syrup. Feels good, not getting caught. Feels so good, delicious food she's not supposed to have. It creams and crunches and salts and soothes the inside of her mouth. She can do this if she wants, eat what she wants, no one can stop her. Glass of milk, baby carrots. One more sandwich still looks like half a loaf, reasonable, maybe she had toast

for breakfast. No punishment. If the garage door opens she can hide the sand-wich inside her shirt and go upstairs. Better wrap it in a paper towel. Hate eating near the toilet. Could stand in the tub, draw the curtain. More like a room that way. No chance of interruption. Can take also granola bar, diet cola, left-over pizza slice.

She can't remember, after, what she ate. She can't list it. In her memory, the binge turns to a slop trough. She calls herself stupid. She calls herself crazy. But, she thinks, at least I've gotten away with it this time.

Search term: Vancomycin.

Vancomycin is a powerful antibiotic, more powerful than the bacteria that have, in their war to survive and dominate, resisted penicillin, methicillin, and other antibiotic drugs. Vancomycin is the fission bomb of antibiotics, used when the armies of bacteria swarm past other medicines once thought powerful enough.

Vancomycin works like too much sand in a cement mix. It prevents the material in the bacteria's cell walls from bonding. The bacteria cell needs its strong mesh armor to stay alive. With cell walls breached, the bacteria disintegrate and die. Hooray for vancomycin.

The doctors' litany carved a smooth, unvarying groove. Antibiotics to fight the infection could strain her kidney until it failed, which would kill her. If an unknown infection were allowed to spread, it could kill her. The daily recital of things that could kill her hypnotized me into thinking nothing would. We would simply go on this way, charting BUN and creatinine and white cells and fever and repeating the same ghoulish tune. She will not fit in an MRI; we cannot read through the masses on the X-rays; these are the only tests that could tell us what might kill her.

What does it mean to know that someone is dying? Who can know such a thing? How do you understand probable death? How do you stop preparing as though it were certain?

"I waited until we were by ourselves," Joyce said. Her voice was dry. The beige hospital room curled around us like a hand, its sterile metal accoutrements like rings cutting into motionless fingers. Joyce tapped the mattress and squinted, a threat against inattention, a short leash pulling me to the bedside.

"'Just As I Am,'" she said. "My favorite hymn." She closed her eyes and drank a deep breath, then another, her chest rising and falling like a wave against a cliff. Her eyes opened around the dark panels of dilated pupils. "You have to remember."

Just as I am, without one plea, but that thy blood was shed for me, and that thou bidst me come to thee—O Lamb of God, I come, I come . . .

She winced at my mute nod and hefted her right hand a few inches, waved it in flimsy circles. The pasty inner forearm skin was tracked violet and black with needle marks. "'Just As I Am.' You know what I mean," she said.

"It's okay you told me," I said. "I won't forget anything. I promise."

Just as I am, and waiting not, to rid my soul of one dark blot—to thee, whose blood can cleanse each spot, O Lamb of God, I come, I come . . .

"Don't worry. It doesn't mean anything. Not that I give up, I mean. I'm fighting." Her words floated light as a crinoline over her wheezing breath. "I know I have to."

"Well. You've got a lot to fight. It's really hard, isn't it?" She nodded, her head barrelling up and down. "I know you can do it."

"Ann, I want to get well. I want to get out of here again."

"Yeah. I love you." I've said that more often in two weeks than in ten years. You keep letting me say it.

"Don't go away."

"If I have to go home, I'll come back. I won't leave you."

"This is too much," she said.

"I won't leave you," I said.

Just as I am! tho' tossed about, with many a conflict, many a doubt, with fears within, and foes without, O Lamb of God, I come, I come . . .

"Except . . ." she said.

"What is it? Anything."

"Well, right now you can leave if you want to. I kind of feel like sleeping. Kind of boring to stay and watch me sleep."

"Does it bother you when people are here while you sleep?"

"No, I sleep however," she said. "I don't like to wake up by myself. But I know it's hard to sit around with me. I'd rather you go off and do stuff while I'm asleep and show up again when I'm awake." She pulled an innocent face, an expectant smile tweaking her lips: I'm in a hospital bed. Humor me.

I grinned and tickled the back of her hand with the back of my hand, then squeezed her fingers. "So sleep already. I'll keep checking in."

One night, she works late. She resents the hour. Want scrapes her throat like fingernails. From her purse, she scavenges coins for the vending machine. She indulges, buys a chocolate bar, a handsome slab in a foil wrap. A colleague, a thoughtful and intelligent man whom she respects, stops by her desk. He talks with her, both of them glancing at the unopened candy. Neither of them mentions it. Shame and self-disgust heat in her stomach; her appetite turns sour on her tongue. What must he think of her? What must she think of herself? At last, he smiles and goes. She feels hollow as the eye of a needle, as fat as the camel not getting through. She eats the candy bar. It's too much chocolate. It takes a long time to eat it all.

Search term: sleep apnea.

You fall asleep. You don't know that through the night you stop breathing for ten—twenty—thirty seconds before your body jolts itself barely awake. Many times in the night, you stop breathing. This happens because your throat's muscle walls relax and collapse, shutting off the airway. Your brain senses the oxygen level dropping in your body. You gasp a couple of deep breaths as your throat muscles tighten, and without ever fully waking, you fall back into the relaxation of sleep. You'll feel tired and your head will hurt in the morning.

If you gain weight, your apnea gets worse. The folds of flesh around your throat fall heavily and compress your airway when you lie down and dream. If you need surgery, sleep apnea is more serious. Under anesthesia, you may stop breathing more times, and for more seconds every time. Your blood oxygen levels will drop more than usual, putting more pressure on your heart. If your airway is blocked while you're sedated and flat on your back, you may need oxygen fed you from a ventilator, during your surgery and after.

She thinks, If you're obese, you know it. You know and you know and you know and you wish you could stop knowing about it but there it is. In your face. In your belly. In the way people don't look at you and in the way they stop to cushion or scissor their words before they talk about food with you.

She wonders whether there's some kind of trick to stop thinking about her fatness all the time. She's sick of knowing about her size. She's sick of thinking about food, sick of monitoring every bite, censoring and doubting every plate, trying to be acceptable to others and herself. But she cannot accept herself. And she can't stop thinking about that.

"You can see," said Dr. Kamath, "how the jaundice is no longer as apparent in her legs and arms." She tilted her head as though studying a floral arrangement. Joyce's hospital gown lay folded back from her belly. Dr. Kamath pointed to a red blossom across the creamy sacks of flesh. "Here, where the cellulosis is apparent, there is also some improvement."

I dared a peek at Joyce's face. Joyce wiggled her eyebrows up and down and mouthed a silent "whoopee." I snorted, and Dr. Kamath razored a cautioning glance across the bedside.

"However, because we are seeing this improvement it concerns us that the white blood cell count remains elevated. We also do not know what is causing her blood loss. And as the days go by, she is requiring more oxygen. Her acidosis remains elevated, and the X-rays, as we are able to read them, indicate pulmonary edema. All these things concern us."

No one had mentioned anything called elevated acidosis before. What was pulmonary edema? Yet Dr. Kamath mentioned the conditions casually; maybe they were simply more scientific terms for what I'd already been told. The unfamiliar phrases stirred adrenaline; new words could mean new turns of fate. "What happens next?" I asked.

"We continue testing. We were disappointed that we couldn't finish the sleep apnea test."

"Sleep apnea test?" With kidneys failing, why would it matter if she had sleep apnea? I didn't want the answer in front of Joyce.

"It was ordered yesterday. We attempted the test last night, but she couldn't breathe sufficiently in the position required. We cancelled the test after two hours. We'll continue to try to find the cause of the infection," Dr. Kamath said. "In the meantime the important thing is that the kidneys continue to improve and that she is able to breathe comfortably. Do you have any other questions? Joyce, do you understand what I am saying? Do you have any questions?"

"No," Joyce said. The clear alto syllable wafted, a soap bubble catching oily surface rainbows of politeness, sincerity, and grasp of fact.

Dr. Kamath nodded and left the room in a crisp swish of white jacket. I arched my eyebrows and blinked a question at Joyce. You feeling better?

"I forgot to mention about that test," Joyce said.

"That's okay," I said. "Did they do anything else?"

"How could they? I couldn't breathe. So they brought me back."

How did she get so fat? She doesn't remember looking any different. She looks from the scale to the mirror, and the numbers increase but the mirror stays the same. It's just her.

And then she sees herself in a store window reflection, next to a fat woman who's not as fat as her. And she wants to cry. Everybody but her can see how fat she is. I'm not fat, not fat, not fat, she cries, not fat and ugly; I can't see it! She wants the body that others see to look like the self she sees. She want to make it happen, bing! Just like a smile can change her face in a flash, she wants to change her body so that it matches who she knows herself to be.

But she can't make it happen in a flash. It can only happen so slowly that nobody will notice, not even her. But how will she see a positive change if she couldn't see a negative one? How can she feel better about a body that she couldn't ever really see? That's why it's so humiliating. She doesn't see herself as fat. But when she sees it in someone else's eyes, that she's fat and unseemly, she wants to disappear. She wants to hide somewhere until she can come out thin. And not have anybody comment. And not have anybody compare. Just be not fat and not worth any special attention.

But there is no hole for her to crawl into. She has to go to work and go— grocery shopping, my God, she has to purchase food in front of people. She feels useless and frustrated. She has no idea how to feed herself. And others can see it. An angry beast is tearing at her lungs like tissue paper. A band of muscly knots tightens between her temples. She hates her stomach. It feels full. She wants to make it feel empty. All she wants is to feel better.

I want to feel better, she thinks. Ice cream. No! No! Stupid! But she wants it, wants not to feel bad, wants something to put her hands on right this second to feel better—don't tell me I can't feel better! She screams. Who are you to tell me I can't feel better? She screams at herself.

Search term: acidosis elevated.

The kidneys expel extra acids from the body and they neutralize new acids. Elevated acidosis means that too much acid has stayed in the body. When this happens, the body tries to compensate. Cells work harder to buffer out the acids. If your acidosis rises, you may feel chest pain and headaches. Your eyesight can malfunction; you may become confused. You might feel like you're hyperventilating. You might feel like you need to throw up; your stomach and bones might hurt and your muscles will feel weak. Doctors use a test called arterial blood gas analysis, or ABG, to check acidosis.

Search term: ABGs.

The arterial blood gases test, in addition to showing the amount of acid in the body, tells how much oxygen and carbon dioxide are in the blood. The part of the test for acids has to do with how well the kidneys work. The part of the test for oxygen has to do with how much help you might need breathing.

She feels like a disappointment, like a shipwreck, like a careless house fire. Even if she lives today correctly, eats well, exercises, she will wake tomorrow the same disappointment, the same inadequacy. Even if she minds her nutrition and her activity for a week, for a month, she will still be fat.

She'll be fat for a long time after she stops living fat. She can change her entire life, and she'll still be fat, with all the approbation of the fat—the carefully masked glances, the unasked-for advice, the darted inspection of her plate in a restaurant, the ill-cut, cheaply made clothes. She braces herself for the desolate days ahead, the days when only she knows, with no reward, that a healthier person lives inside the visible, fat shell.

Search term: pulmonary edema.

Pulmonary edema happens when fluid builds up in the air spaces of the lungs. The lungs and heart are like fraternal twins; they look nothing alike, but what hurts one hurts the other. If the heart is weakened—for instance, when the kidneys fail and water floods it—then the heart calls for help, passes the deluge to the lungs. Pressure rises in the lung veins, and they push fluid into the lung's air sacs. With fluid in the lungs, oxygen can't fill those spaces. You can't breathe. You can't speak. It feels like drowning. You will need oxygen from a face mask or a ventilator. In extreme cases, you'll need a tube snaked through your nose down into your lungs and attached to a machine to help you breathe.

Search term: enlarged heart.

The enlarged heart is not itself a criminal in your body, but is like a glance between two criminals, the causes and consequences. The first shadowy culprit, the one that expanded your heart, might be any of a rogue's gallery—high blood pressure, inflammation of the heart muscle, thyroid malfunction, excess iron, anemia . . . but the felon nodding back at the other end of the glance has a weapon ready: congestive heart failure.

Search term: congestive heart failure.

The heart doesn't completely fail. But it fails to pump as well as it ought. It's weak after months of battling to pump the blood past a biological logjam—clogged arteries, perhaps, or high blood pressure, or some collapse or flaw in a heart valve or wall. When your heart feels weak, you feel weak. The vigor of your blood is sapped, leaving your energy thin and watery and your breath sharp and short. You know you ought to be able to climb the stairs. You feel so tired.

PART FOUR: ICU

 **1985**

Christmas passes. I plant the live Christmas tree just outside my bedroom window in the cold, red Oklahoma clay. I force the shovel blade through the matted, dormant grass. I sweat inside my coat and think of a boy, the blond, grinning artist who gestures palm up with his cigarette, who frightens me with intimate conversation. I am big; my hips are big, my breasts are suddenly big; I have grown long hair as camouflage, and can't believe I'm worth finding behind it. But those feelings are a long drive away. For now, I plant a tree, which requires no kisses nor crying for lack of them.

The shovel bites into the clay. Joyce trudges up, her long brown hair bulging from her coat collar. A wispy bib of steam escapes her lips. Who does she want to kiss? I think. She never says.

"What do you want?"

"Nothing," she says. "I didn't want to stay inside. Daddy's snoring and Hunter's playing with his video game and Mama's picking at the leftovers and trying to get me to play Scrabble."

"You want to help here?" The wet wall of orange clay splits with a sucking sound. Mud spatters up my jeans.

"Not particularly. I just came out to talk."

I jam the shovel blade deep. "Okay, I have a question for you," I say. The hole grows twice as broad, twice as deep as the burlap root ball. A fluted clay pie crust lumps around the rim. "Did Mama and Daddy ever make you get your thyroid tested?"

"Same as you, first or second summer in college."

"How did yours turn out?"

"Same as yours. All normal. The doctor gave me a diet sheet."

"With meals and food lists?"

"Uh-huh."

"Of stuff we never have here in the house?"

"Uh-huh."

"And nothing like what's in the cafeteria at school?"

"Exactly. And he didn't give Mama a copy of it, either. Just me."

"Joyce? Am I really all that fat?"

"I wouldn't worry," she says. "Like me. Probably more fat than you need to be but as long as you exercise and try not to overeat you'll stay healthy." She edges forward, kicks at the tree's root ball. "I might help here," she says.

"Now that I'm almost finished."

"If you don't want me to, I won't."

"I'm not mad. I'm almost done. Don't get all muddy."

"If there's another shovel I'll help fill in the dirt. And then let's drive around and look at Christmas lights." Her smile peaks like a pink ribbon bow.

"Yay!" I yell at her. I drop the shovel and grab two branches of the tree, a dance partner. "Yay! Yay!"

"Shut up," she says, "you'll have the neighbors calling. Hurry up and dig. It's cold out here."

Later, in wintry darkness, we shuttle the six-mile stretch of highway between our house and Muskogee. The car heater smells like scorched lint. "Have you seen the pond lately?" I ask.

"I didn't go up there."

"Daddy about got it cleaned out this summer. That rusted out car and everything. Now he burns trash and tree limbs up there. He's ready to dig it all out so he can have his fish pond."

"Take him a hundred years."

"You know what Mama does at home?"

"Reads romance novels."

"Yeah! They're all the same! I asked her, did she want to read some of the books I'm reading and she said no, she read all those books when she was young, and I said, what, you read all the books in the world? and she said yes and to leave her alone. She's smarter than that. I don't get it."

"That's because you think you know what's best for everybody else. Your friends are better, your music's better, your books are better. We all should be just like you. Ha."

We wind past the country club's ranch houses, then through the downtown neighborhood slopes, a century old. Plum-shaped light bulbs spot the rooflines; florets wink on lamp posts. A white internal glow illuminates a plastic creche or beaming Santa. Joyce steers us through the feast of effort, the jeweled net of color over flat, paint-chipped Muskogee. "Oh, holy night!" Joyce hefts her singing voice, a cast-iron plow. "The stars are brightly shining!" When we crest the hill at Honor Heights, her mouth opens in amazement.

Cars string down the hill, through a ribbed tunnel of white lights. We emerge into the sparkling, fiery garden of lights—masses of glowing pink and red azaleas, formed in Christmas lights, crowd terraces. Bouffant foliage flames juniper and scarlet atop tree-trunk exoskeletons of amber light. Roses and lilies of light glow along light-gridded pathways. I point and name the flowers. I exclaim—a boy fashioned from light tosses a brilliant ball in the air, a Christmas-light doe lifts her startled head while her fawn grazes. "It's so beautiful," I say. Joyce chuffs a hard sigh. Her hands tighten on the wheel. A frown's claw has fossilized between her eyebrows. "What?" I say. "What is it now?"

"Nothing," she says, mournful through gritted teeth.

"No, what?"

"Why can't you just see things and be quiet? Why do you have to ruin it talking? Why do you have to comment on everything?" she says.

Before I sleep, I peek out the bedroom window at the silhouette of the freshly planted tree. It tilts in its frozen clay bed. It won't live past the ice storm. That night, ice pelts the house and cars. Ice crusts the rooftops and porch posts, snaps tree branches, turns the barbed wire fencelines into diamond ropes. The tiny Christmas pine glitters, a crystalline ornament stuck in the earth, each needle green inside its sharp ice sheath.

When the roads clear that week, we pack the car, and Daddy salts the gravel driveway. No one sees us out the door. The house disappears behind the fog's laced fingers. Joyce has promised to stay on the interstate, not to explore side roads. Neither of us speaks for the first hour. The ice crawls over spiked white grasses to the highway shoulder. Ice glints on glass branches, a white clash of saber blades. White cakes groan under a thin white mist over the leaden chop of Lake Eufaula. The ice stills Oklahoma.

"It's so beautiful," I say.

Joyce's indulgent smile is like folded pink paper, a passed note. "It really is," she says, glancing over. "It really is."

Thursday, September 20. Nine days had disappeared into antiseptic hospital air. I slept in the bland hospital dormitory room as though I were a rolled bandage put away in a box. Routine evolved: a shivering exodus from scratchy blankets, a perfunctory slosh in the cold tile stall while network news oozed into single, dried blots of words. The tenth day of rescue and search efforts has begun in the towers' rubble. Afghanis have fled toward their borders.

The ringing phone drilled through the somber plaster of reportage. I anticipated Mama's voice—cheerful, practical, an East Texas, back forty acres of a voice. East Texas lifted Mama's voice like mattress springs.

"Ann?" My name in her mouth had three syllables, distinct as xylophone keys. A-uh-un, a simple sound converted to a song. "Good morning, now, listen," she says, "don't go to the tenth floor this morning. They moved Joyce into ICU in the middle of the night."

Fear and acceptance, two claws, rattled my spinal cord. "Why? What happened?"

"Now, nothing's wrong, nothing's happened. They just wanted her to have twenty-four-hour supervision on the ventilator. With her oxygen levels going up and down like they have been, those other nurses just couldn't keep up with checking on her. They're just making sure she stays monitored is all."

"I'll get up there as soon as I can." Fear and acceptance crabwalk, hooking talons on the vertebrae. Mama says ICU means nothing's wrong, I repeat to myself, and the claws scratch on the bone.

"There's no need to hurry. At any rate," a sigh sails through her voice like the wind through the thick east Texas pines, "visiting hours aren't 'til nine o'clock."

She's terrified. She weighs nearly two hundred pounds again, with fat soft and pillowing on her hips, her ribs, her face. She doesn't want to die. Her sister died because she wouldn't get help. But she should be smart enough to figure this out herself! She should be disciplined enough to figure out a plan and stick to it! She should be able to do this without a fuss, privately!

She looks up into her own eyes, in the mirror, and thinks, What would I tell her, if I could? I'd tell her it's okay to need help. You haven't failed if you ask for help. You'll be okay. I love you. That's what I want to tell her.

She needs help.

She thought she could lose weight by herself, but she can't. She thought she knew how. She's read so many books and articles; she's memorized fat con-

tent charts, swears by the FDA pyramid, and breathes and dreams the mantra of fewer calories, more exercise. None of it means she knows how to do this. She doesn't know how to make her body and mind work for health.

She doesn't know what success looks like. She's fooled herself twice, lost fifty pounds twice, and thought she had changed her life. She's gained fifty extra pounds three times. How did she fail? How did she forget what to do? If she forgot and failed before, won't she fail again?

The realization is like a hailstorm in a drought: She can't do this alone. She can't punish herself anymore for not being able to do it alone. Why does she think she needs to be perfect? Why does she think she's a failure if she can't lose weight without help? She's sick of thinking about it—her weight, her fat, her food! There are better things to think about! Why does she think she doesn't deserve those good things? That she doesn't deserve well-cut clothes until she has a trim form to put them on? That she doesn't deserve friends until she can have friends who want to be with fit people? That she doesn't deserve sex until she can bring a better body to a man? Why does she think she doesn't deserve to be healthy and happy?

She's not a failure, needing help. That's surely not true. If she wanted to learn yoga, she wouldn't think she was a failure if she needed an instructor. She'd be a fool to refuse a teacher and then hurt herself trying to do every movement correctly on her own, with no correction or observation.

But she's ashamed. She doesn't want anyone to know she needs help. She doesn't want to tell her husband she sneaks food. She doesn't want him to know she thinks about food all the time. He'll be disgusted by her. It disgusts even her. It's distasteful, like talking about defecation, to talk about eating. It's like talking about wiping yourself properly to talk about the difficulty of choosing food correctly. You are supposed to know how to do this and not to need to talk about it.

But what if you don't know how to do it?

The hardest thing to do is going to be to tell him.

Waiting rooms gobbed against the eighth-floor hallway like peas along a pea pod spine. The larger waiting room, insulated with downy couches and armchairs, was punctuated by a watercooler, a coffee pot, a vacated reception desk. In the smaller room next door, a white erasable board hung near the door. Plastic chairs half-circled a small table near a long, severe sofa. A beige telephone, focal and revered, adorned each room.

The medical intensive care unit, behind its heavy double doors at the end of the hall, was like a rare botanical specimen in its own glass hothouse. The patients' rooms, dimmed glass petals, encircled the white hum of the nurses' station.

In a tiny, curtained room, a visitor might never suspect the ward was full, never know that other endangered human bodies filled other glass rooms with their slow tragedies, slow victories. Only the ICU nurses could feel the fullness of the ward, feel the thread of each patient's breath woven into the ward's muffling scarf, feel each patient's need, a warning prickle on the back of a nurse's neck. Behind the high, horseshoe desk and in the trim, spartan rooms, the nurses moved like sailors on deck, a thousand adjustments controlling the pitch and yaw of fragile vessels, the sickness-borne bodies in the beds.

Tubes streamed away from Joyce. Antibiotics and painkillers dripped, saline floated through its long siphon, and a cloudy bag of liquid food supplemented an untouched tray of noodle soup. Joyce slept, a worry line pinched up her forehead. Prongs disappeared inside her nose, and new oxygen tubes strapped snugly around her ears and chin. She looked like a small, frail person fallen helpless under her body's voluminous white landslide. Beige cotton straps loosely bound her wrists to the bed frame.

Joyce's damp head rolled. Her opening eyes were like oil lamps, embers of consciousness brightening to low flame. "Chips?" she rasped.

"Chips? What chips?"

She forced the words out like loose teeth. "Ice chips," she said, and waved her bound right hand in a circle. "Let me loose," she said.

I edged to the doorway to catch a nurse's eye. "Can I take the straps off so she can have some ice chips?"

The nurse nodded. "We filled her cup a few minutes back," she said. "She can have all the ice chips she wants."

"Ah," I said to Joyce. "I see it." The tiny paper cup sat sweating on the plaster windowsill, on the far side of the bed. I untied Joyce's left wrist first, below the taped needles, then crossed to loosen her right wrist. Joyce scooped a miniscule white plastic spoon into the cup's cold crush. She slowly shoveled four cylindrical pills of ice inside her lower lip and sighed at the melting relief. She handed the paper cup back to me. I put it on the countertop near the sink, next to the cotton balls and swabs and her chart and a filled syringe.

I felt, as a child might, helpless and responsible. I waited as questions boiled silently away, until the most important one remained. "Joyce, are you hurting?"

She shook her head no. Her lips relaxed.

"Are you sleepy?"

She nodded and closed her eyes. "I'll come see you later," I say. She had fallen asleep already. I thought about sliding the beige cotton straps across her wrists again, loosely pulling the straps. Joyce slept, her face peaceful, trusting. She looked no older than eighteen. I left her hands free.

"I need to tell you something," she says to her husband. He hits the mute button, nods at her, watches the colors shift on screen as she talks. "I'm so afraid," she says.

"Afraid of what?"

It takes her a long time to answer. He waits. "I'm afraid you won't love me anymore," she says. "I have to tell you something about myself that's ugly and scary. I'm so afraid to tell you."

He nods, and watches TV. He hears her faltering. He knows that if he looks at her, she'll stop.

"I've been hurting myself," she says, hesitant. "I don't know how to stop. When you leave the house, I eat and eat. You don't know because I hide it really well. I hate—see, sometimes I feel so angry I can't . . . the only way to calm down, feel better, is to make it hurt really bad, or make it numb. When I eat I can do both. And the other pain all stops."

He nods, his eyes large, dark, and unsmiling.

"I don't want to live like this. I want to get help."

He nods, still not looking directly at her.

"I want to talk to a counselor."

"I can get you some phone numbers tomorrow," he says, simply. Later, as they fall asleep, he holds her. Though she says nothing, he says, "Sh, sh," and strokes her hair.

"We'll stay through the visiting hours this afternoon and then we'll get on our way to Bartlesville," Mama said. She chewed a bite of meatloaf. "Be nice to have some home cooking tonight instead of this old hospital food."

"Now she's up in ICU," Daddy said, "I don't know we all need to be here every night. The nurses are right there all the time and we don't have to check up and make sure she's getting her medicine on time."

"Them nurses down on the other floor just couldn't get there fast enough when Joyce stopped breathing," Mama said. "It's better now she's up in ICU. The machine she's on is better. And the nurses are right there watching that monitor the whole time."

"We'll be back from Bartlesville tomorrow by lunchtime," Daddy said. "LaNita keeps saying she's fine but she can probably use a night where she's not the only one there with Troy."

"I feel all right since you'll be here," Mama said. "It's hard to try to be both places. You have LaNita's number if anything happens. But I don't expect it will. It ought to calm down a lot now that she's up in the ICU. Now she can get rested and start to get well."

"I also counsel men whose spouses have eating disorders," the therapist tells her. "And to the last one, none of them is upset by the way their wives look. What bothers them is their wives' neurotic behavior."

Her husband winces when she concludes, jubilant, "I can have a cookie tonight!" or, "I'm allowed enough calories for two servings of mashed potatoes!" She doesn't understand his discomfort. She figures out at last that it must be faulty to eat because you're allowed it—aberrant to take food not because you want to, but because you can. She hopes someday her body will be able to tell the difference. It would help.

Her body is oblivious to the signals of fullness. Eating, she's like a deaf child playing in traffic. She must rely on other signals to know when to stop, when to get out of the way. Her body doesn't tell her to stop. For a long time, she relied on watching what others ate. If others had a second helping, she could, too. But she gained weight and others didn't. She knows the world will tempt her throat and pocketbook with food. She can't trust its guidance. So she counts calories and calculates by their limits what she can have to eat. She thinks how much more comfortable a life would be where she could trust her desires not to hurt her. I want that life, she thinks: to eat what I want, and stop when I want—because my body tells me what it wants, and because it wants health.

In ICU, the window's beige blinds striped the black September night. Joyce sat upright in the sharply angled bed. On her lap tray, a nibbled sandwich escorted a straw-skewered juice box. Joyce bounced the TV remote in her unbound right hand. The ceiling-mounted TV gargled a police drama. A small whiteboard was wedged between her sheeted thigh and the bed rail. Joyce's eyes were metallic with purpose, with her marshalled list of questions. She swallowed. "What's the weather doing?" she said. Her eyes narrowed with the cracked, dry effort of the sentence.

"Weather?" I say. "Let's see. Today was a clear day. High, skinny clouds. The sky was so bright and blue, I couldn't believe it was cold outside. There was a little breeze."

"Want to see," she whispered.

"I know you do," I said. "It might not be September by then, I won't lie. But you'll see it again."

"Mama and Daddy?" she asks.

"They went up to Aunt LaNita's tonight. They want to do laundry and see Troy and sleep in a regular bed."

"Me too," Joyce said. "Regular bed."

"What, and give up all this room service?"

"Service," she said. "Reminding you. Ice chips." She jabbed a thick finger. "Shape . . . up. Hunter?"

"Hunter's at Mama and Daddy's house," I said. "I think his car must be broken down or he would be here."

Outside Joyce's door, Nurse Carol caught my eye and bobbed her pointed nose and chin. She'd said, regardless of charge nurse duties, that she'd find time to talk with me. My chest felt heavy with the need to be trusted.

Nurse Rita, the afternoon charge nurse, had answered inquiries with polite but brusque protection of fact. She moved visitors aside as though we were badly placed furniture. But Nurse Carol, with her hay-harvest posture and her direct gaze, adopted family members as appendages to the patient's body, external organs to be nursed and healed.

She waited by a pillar that served as backsplash for the doctors' station. Slender, with square, strong shoulders and a boxy, heart-shaped face, Nurse Carol was in her middle thirties, about my age, and taller—when she looked down to talk to me, her chardonnay silk hair dripped forward. Her light blue eyes were kind and tireless. She motioned me away from Joyce's door.

"How is she?" I asked. "She doesn't say what's making her uncomfortable."

"The oxygen makes her throat dry. The ice chips help. I know it's not easy for her, but we'd rather she try to speak than use the whiteboard. She needs to speak using her voice as much as she can."

"But how is she?" I asked.

Nurse Carol paused, sorting her facts. Her voice was still and steady as a fishing line, the lead sinker dropped in the deep lake. "We've had to increase her oxygen. The levels have been precarious. At times she's needed more oxygen than we're truly comfortable with. Her kidney functions have stayed stable, and that's positive."

"I missed the doctors' rounds today. I'd appreciate anything you can tell me. Dr. Abu has been sharing her lab results with me."

"I see," Nurse Carol said. She pulled the threaded needle of her gaze, a stitch to hold us together. "I'll tell you all I can, but it would be best if you were here to see the doctors in the morning. Have your parents been following her lab results also?"

"No," I said. Disloyalty and smallness crept on me like an itch. "Whatever you can tell me is a help. My parents—the doctors have suggested I not share too many details with them. I don't know that my parents want to know all the details. They don't ask questions. They don't see where things lead." How could they calculate the probability from the facts? This was their daughter. The only possibility was that she live. You can't think of your child dying, even if you did it once before and know what it feels like.

"If it comes to it," Nurse Carol said, "your parents will be the ones to make some hard decisions for her." She didn't say, not you. She didn't say, It's wise, this secrecy?

"I know." My small smile was a capsule of regret, respect. "With the big decision—the big decisions," I said, "they won't hesitate. They'll be okay. But they don't want the daily information, the details. So they won't see their decisions coming. They'll have to be told it's time to make them. I want to be here when they have to understand too suddenly. I want to know what's happening to her. I live five hours away," I recited, "but if her condition changes, I want to be here with her, for my parents. So I've been tracking the indicators and the tentative prognosis as closely as I can. I know it's not completely possible. But I'm trying to learn what I can, to stay prepared."

The thread of Nurse Carol's gaze gave a sudden jerk. Her comprehension was like a touch of fingertips on my face, on the knotted stitch. "Five hours?" she asked. "You live that far away? Where are you staying tonight?"

The cinder blocks and cold mattress waited. "I'm in the hospital," I said. "I'm in the dormitory."

"I ought to have your room number," Nurse Carol said. "Let me make sure we have the phone number for your parents, where they are tonight. If you want to give us a list of phone numbers where you and your parents routinely stay, that would be a good idea. We'll keep it with her file. Mark the phone number where we can reach you," she said. She found my hand, an impulse discovery, and squeezed my fingers. "I'll make sure the doctors know that number."

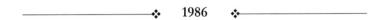

❖ **1986** ❖

College severs our adult lives, splits us like a machete blade. Fleshy, bulbed roots are sliced apart, and the flowers are transplanted to different plots, different neighborhoods, different states.

Joyce sorts books into cardboard boxes and teaching supplies into piles. Her campus apartment smells faintly of carpet deodorizer and monthly roach sprayings.

"See this?" Joyce holds up a construction paper booklet laced with yarn. "These are the pictures my kids drew for me to remember them with. What am I going to do with all this other stuff?"

"Yeah. What is all this stuff?" Brightly colored scallops of corrugated cardboard slide off a pile of laminated magazine pictures, paper plates, pipe cleaners.

"Well, there's different classroom decorations. This pile is lesson plans I wrote. The rest is stuff to go along with lesson plans. Flashcards, games I made up. I might be able to use it in Dallas. But who knows how long before I find a job." Secret plans sneak from her smile. Her long Oklahoma stopover is done; she's going home, to Dallas glass and concrete and wide sky and smog, to the aunts and uncles and their sunny back yards and their uncalibrated, boisterous welcome. The same sly smile at graduation had folded like an omelet around her excitement. Round and graceful in her gown's black pleats, the aqua lining of her hood belting the baby-fat double chin, Joyce had posed between Mama and Daddy, black mortarboard jaunty on her brown hair's loose, uneven layers. Neither Mama, bulky and beaming, nor Daddy, who wore his fifteen-year-old, homemade blue suit, the "I love you" still in the pocket, had much to say to me.

"There's something I've been meaning to ask you," I say, handing Joyce a book. "What was Grandma Roberts's funeral like?"

"Everybody cried a lot," Joyce said. "Daddy cried. Hunter cried. All the people from church were there. She looked so peaceful in the casket. All the hymns were the old-timey ones she liked to sing."

Great-Grandma Roberts's embrace is one remembered from childhood and lost five years ago. I can't imagine her either alive or dead. Instead, I picture Grandpa, ushered to the holiday table, the pap-filled spoon shuddering, Parkinson's like a tight glove on his hand.

"I feel funny. Like I don't have a right to ask."

"Mama and Daddy don't understand why you didn't come home," says Joyce. "Or why you didn't go home for Grandpa's funeral either. They stood around and talked about you. 'Doesn't Ann love the family?'" A wild, stubborn impulse, her sense of justice, rises like a wall cloud in the blue eyes. "I understand though."

I picture them, father and son. Grandpa waits in his bed, the room darkened. Daddy kneels and holds his father's hand. Grandpa's breath rasps. Then it doesn't.

"It's something wrong with me," I say slowly. "I don't feel the way I should. I didn't want to be with Mama and Daddy and the whole family. I felt like I would spend the whole time trying to get away from them. I don't understand funerals. I don't want Grandma not to be there."

"It's okay," Joyce says, soft as a receiving blanket. "Everybody faces things their own way. Just don't bring it up to Mama and Daddy to make yourself feel better. I'd let it go if I were you." She clears her throat. "There's something I've been meaning to ask you, too," she says. She drops her pink Jordan almond pout toward a box of history texts. "You don't have to say yes, but I really mean it."

"What?" In the quiet air-conditioned hum, the vacuum-cleaner smell of the apartment, the conversation feels charged with static electricity.

"Don't follow me to Dallas," she says. "I mean, don't move there, ever." She rakes a glance over my curiosity. "You know what happened the first week you were here? I mean the first week? Somebody walked up and said, 'Aren't you Ann's sister?' The first week! It was like church and school all over again. Every time you got promoted up the grades, to all the teachers, I was Ann's sister. And as soon as you got here, I was Ann's sister again and I have been for three whole years. It's not against you."

"I didn't know," I say.

"I know you didn't," she says. "You don't mean to crowd in on everything. That's why it has to be a whole city. It has to be a whole other state. I want Dallas for myself."

"It's not too much," I say, turning a light out in my voice. "But I can come visit you, right?"

She rolls her eyes. "You're so dramatic," she says. "Are all your friends so dramatic? How do they stand it?"

College has driven a blade between us. It flashes.

She wouldn't like my friends. Not their passionate obscenity, their messy experiments with sex and alcohol, and not their material attachment to icons, symbols, memories, subtle moments. My friends wouldn't like her. She wouldn't let them.

I'm embarrassed by her. I'm embarrassed by the meaty lump of her stomach and her flat, unexercised butt in jeans she wears too short, her socks exposed. I'm embarrassed by her blinking, noncommittal silence around other people, by the smiles that drain from their faces as she ignores them. I'm embarrassed by her celebrity worship, the confused swirl of reality and fantasy. I'm embarrassed that she has rejected grooming along with vanity—that she doesn't cut her hair, brush it smooth. Yet I'm proud of her irrelevance to makeup and fashion, proud of her integrity, her love for children. She insists on fairness, and she worships her God without politics or fashion. I'm upset that others don't see these things. I'm upset she thinks they do. I'm upset she's made herself difficult to know. And I'm ashamed of my embarrassment. It's a small, mean emotion; she deserves better. I'm embarrassed nonetheless. I imagine the pattern others see in us together—fat sisters, poorly dressed, one remote, one needy, both liabilities. I love her. I can't bear that others find her unlovable.

"Oh, you don't know my friends," I say. "Their drama's more a— what. What? Why you looking at me like that?"

"You didn't promise yet. I want to hear you promise."

"Good gravy, Joyce." I laugh. "Okay, I promise. I won't ever move to Dallas. I won't live in the same city as you. Ever."

"It means a lot to me," she says, shrugging. "It's all I ask."

She joins a weight loss program that emphasizes keeping records, drinking a lot of water, and educating herself about food, behavior, and her body. By this program's philosophy, she never has to diet again, but she has to live with food differently than before, and for the rest of her life. The program offers group support and discussion, weekly weigh-ins, a structure in which she can learn how much food and exercise make her body feel wonderful to live in.

It's not what she expected. She expected a room full of depressed women, whining about the causes of their overweight. She expected a room full of her at her worst. Instead she finds men and women with calm and cheerful attitudes, who have decided to learn different behaviors than the ones that had chained them to unhappiness. It's a room full of people in good humor, inventive, shar-

ing, making progress toward goals—a room full of people who don't think it's strange to need to talk about food and bodies. It's a room full of people who clap for each other's successes in a world that finds their predicament embarrassing and therefore the successes unmentionable. Yes, the room says. When nobody else wants to care about it, we can see what it cost you to gain even five pounds, and what you accomplished losing it.

The focus of her obsession becomes not her weight, not the scale, not even the fit of her clothes, but behaviors that she's happy with, positive thoughts about herself and pride in her behavior. A consequence is weight loss. She begins the slow return to a healthier body, a body carrying less excess fat.

ICU had demolished my sense of time. Time jolted and dragged with Joyce's waking and sleep. When visiting hours ended, time froze, purpose hibernated, reason fell unconscious. There was no time outside of Joyce, no stopwatch but her breathing. There was no North Star but her. In the waiting room, I followed a paisley of thoughts until the clock's black needles clicked into the nine-o'-clock angle. An ICU nurse pulled the laminated sign—Stop! Our patients are resting—from the double door. Inside, flapping white coats receded down the internal hallway to the separate cardiac intensive care unit. Dr. Patrick strode tall above the white flock, a glimpse of dark hair, an edge of profile turning the corner. Then they were gone.

Nurse Rita's hands dripped loops of beige cotton bandages. Her mouth was a rigid steel bar. "Excuse me, Nurse—were those the doctors leaving? Are they coming back?"

"Usually rounds are at ten. They were early today."

"I didn't see Dr. Abu there. Do you know how I can find him later?"

"Well, no," Nurse Rita said, "unless you're here for rounds you won't have much luck talking to doctors. You might see them in the hallway. But Dr. Abu's not with your sister's case now." The steel bar of her mouth was unbending, but her voice softened as she watched the confused, unstammered question purse on my lips. "The rotation changed," she said. "That whole team has gone off rotation."

So what will I do? I wanted to ask her, but her maple-syrup eyes hardened with purposes not mine. "Would you have time to go over Joyce's status?"

"Frankly, no, I'm sorry. I can tell you her medicines haven't changed and no different lab tests have been ordered for today. But more than that, I won't be able to go into it this morning. Understand, patient care is our priority."

"Thank you for that," I said. She smiled then, a surprising triumph of a toughened smile. She nodded and brushed past, her brown hair bouncing on the scrub top shoulders.

Dr. Abu, Dr. Kamath, Dr. Bemeka—gone to sleep, gone to study, gone from knowing. By the end of an hour's vigil, silent but for Joyce's labored sleep, defeat had percolated. What doctor was my accomplice now? Who would trust me with evidence, trust me not to get in the way? Who would forgive a daughter's assertion of her parents' incapacity to harvest facts?

Fat notebook broken to a blank page, I trolled the objects in Joyce's room. I wrote the names and percentage solutions of the medicines flowing from the hanging bags and bottles. I stared at cryptic digits and abbreviations on the monitor. I rifled back through the notebook. Pages were thick and black, medical entries interspersed with nighttime diary. In diary entries, I gathered twigs of words and heaped an ungainly altar on which to slay my fear. I wrote to sacrifice my fear of honesty and was rewarded with sleep. For the haphazard medical notations, perhaps the doctors would reward me with answers.

She's looking for a deeper change. Throughout her attempts to lose weight, she hasn't yet made it impossible for her to be a fat person. She wants to do that. She has to be a person for whom it is impossible to follow the habits that lead to weight gain, fat gain, poverty of body. Richness of body is what she wants.

By evening, Joyce wriggled, alert. "Hi," she croaked. Her left arm lay motionless in its puppet strings of tubes. The cotton restraining straps dangled from the bed frame. With her right hand trembling, Joyce dragged a sip through her water cup's straw, steeling herself. Her dilated eyes shone with announcement. She set the cup aside. She raised her right hand, three fingers spread.

"Three?" I said. "Three what? What is it?"

She lifted her eyes in mock appeal for patience and shook her head. She held up three fingers again, then arched them down to rest on the bridge of her thumb. She waited for recognition.

"E," I said. Goosebumps prickled up my arms. She had command. She was not trapped. "W. E. We what?"

Joyce coughed, a gruff growl. "Okay," I said. "Fine. What is it?"

Her hand formed letters, graceful and precise. W. E. A. T. H. E. R.

"Weather? You want to know what the weather's like?" Joyce nodded. Her head fell back onto the bed and her hand dropped to the mattress. "Warmer today," I said. "Not raining. The trees are starting to turn. A little orange, a little yellow."

Her right hand began to swoop and twist, words and phrases clutched and released in combinations of palm and fingers. "Wait, wait, slow down," I said. "Joyce, I don't remember any of the words anymore. Sorry. I think you're going to have to spell everything."

Her mouth dropped open, then she clapped it closed. She hadn't the strength to slap her palm to her forehead. "Look, I can't help it," I said. "It's been twenty years since anyone signed to me. I remember yes and no and maybe a couple of other simple things. How'd you remember all this stuff, anyway?"

She glared over the oxygen tubing that striped her face. Practice, she spelled slowly, shoving each letter toward me.

"Sorry," I said. She shrugged the shrug of lowered expectation and composed her patience toward the next attempt.

Ice chips, she spelled. She paused between each letter and waited for me to repeat it aloud. "Sure," I said, handing her the tiny, spoon-spiked cup. "They're right here."

Frowning, she spilled the ice chips down her gown's slope. A pout wobbled under the oxygen tubes.

"You want me to help you?"

The pout rocked out and in. She nodded without looking at me. "Excellent," I said. "So. Two for now, don't want your mouth full of ice." Her lower lip drooped and her tongue flicked to cup the tiny spoon. The ice chips slid into her mouth. She swished them from side to side, then nodded at me, her eyebrows raised. I funneled more ice over her lip. She waved her free right hand. Enough. Daddy, she spelled.

"Yeah, he's here. You want me to go get him?"

Daddy unfolded himself quickly from the waiting room couch. Joyce's eyes were eager, as if she were primed to jump. Hi, how are you, she spelled. "She just asked how you are," I said.

Daddy's jaw-dropped stare swiveled back and forth. "Look at that," he said. "Now I wouldn't have remembered that."

Joyce tapped the metal bed frame.

"Oh," said Daddy, grinning. "Yes, ma'am. I'm doing as well as could be expected. How are you?"

Joyce wiggled her right hand, pinky and index up, thumb out. Hopeful as a four-year-old who wants to cross the street, she waited for Daddy.

"I know what that means," he said. "I know that word." His voice tilted as though a grandchild were tickling him. "That means I love you. Doesn't it? I love you?"

She raised the sign again. She stretched the thin smile of teacher's approval, the gold star awarding smile.

"Well," Daddy said. He caressed awkward, arrhythmic pats on her smooth, still hand with his rough and freckled one. "I love you too. Do what the nurses say, now, and get some rest tonight." Leaving, he passed Nurse Carol, then turned back, his good ear inclined; Nurse Carol had called to him. Daddy steadied a mask of courtly respect. As he stepped near, Nurse Carol put her arms around his ribs and hugged him. A shard of surprise, like the spear of a cloud suddenly brilliant at sunset, shone in Daddy's face. His hands twitched, then he rested his arms around Nurse Carol's shoulders. She patted and rubbed his back. His shoulders straightened, and he smiled at her as if at a once-beloved babysitter.

"I spoke to your parents a while today," Nurse Carol told me an hour later. "Your mother seems to think we're waiting for Joyce's kidneys to heal. Your dad didn't say much but he couldn't take his eyes off your sister."

"I don't know what they think," I said.

"How much do you know?" Nurse Carol's stillness was like a sparrow's before flight. She wore her long, blonde hair in simple barrettes and her face without makeup. Her eyes, like careful injections, never darted aside.

"I know she's fighting more than one infection and that no one knows the cause of the major infection. I know the prescriptions could cause her kidneys to fail and that dialysis isn't possible. I know her heart is enlarged and I know that's all tied in with her ability to breathe. I know that people die from the kind of danger she's in."

"It's good you know that. But you need to remember, too, that she's a fighter. Her heart is strong. And the doctors are working every day to find out how to help her. Has anyone mentioned the free air to you?"

"No." Crucial terminology was now recognizable as a punch in the stomach. "Free air?"

"Ah." Nurse Carol looks through me as if preparing for a high dive. She gathers her decision at the edge of the board, and speaks. "The X-rays show that some air has escaped from her organs. It shows up on the X-rays in her abdomen—air where it shouldn't be. Now, everybody has a little free air. And a lot of things can cause free air, many of them not very serious. Punctures can cause it, a ruptured ulcer can cause it, that's common. But the doctors can't rule anything in or out. It could also be air escaping from her intestines, which is a much more serious situation. The unfortunate thing is that because of her size, the X-rays are difficult to read. So the only way to really know what's going on is to do an exploratory surgery. But exploratory surgery isn't a good option for her. She requires so much assistance breathing that even one surgery will be very dangerous for her. They couldn't do an exploratory surgery and close her up to schedule a later surgery. They would have to deal with whatever they found, right then."

I suspect she's not supposed to tell me this. "I'm glad you've told me," I said.

"What will you tell your parents?" she asked.

"That the doctors are considering more options to find out why she can't get over the infection. That there are surgical options. It would help them if that weren't a surprise. I don't want to hide anything from them. I hate crossing that line. But telling them guesses, telling them the worst case, yeah, it would be like telling them lies."

"Are you here in the hospital tonight?"

"With my husband. He'll be here by then."

"Your parents are sweet people," she said. Bittersweet, I thought, remembering Daddy's startled comfort in her arms.

"I won't ever lie to them if they start asking for the details," I said.

"I know," she said. Her honest voice both stung and cleaned, astringent.

"You'd have to stop telling me."

"I know," she said.

1987

Adulthood is a wall between us, like a dressing room curtain. On either side, captured in our individual mirrors, we change. Joyce's adulthood is different from mine. She has achieved her own life, her inheritance.

Joyce lives in Dallas among the aunts and uncles. She frequents their houses, arriving unannounced as they all do in each other's kitchens. Like them, she knows where keys are hidden. She thrives in Dallas sunshine, Dallas routine. On Sunday afternoons in Granny's clan-lumpy armchairs, she pokes bright floss through a cross-stitch pattern and trades truculent comments with Granddaddy about the Cowboys' forward passing game. She helps Granny cut up a fryer chicken. Uncle Harold might come over, his ruddy face beaming and greeting robust, or Cousin Brian might slip in, a foot taller than Joyce, holding words like mashed potatoes in his mouth, or Aunt Mickey might bring the kids.

(Mama says, "Joyce is the one good with babies and old people.")

Joyce rooms with Aunt Mickey, Mama's sharp-tongued, lazy-voiced, politically savvy younger sister. ("Wa-a-a-l," says Aunt Mickey, tapping blank voter registration cards like a poker deck, "nobody ever made life one day longer by wringing their hands worrying.") In the blue evening glow of television, Joyce marks her second-graders' papers with a waxy pencil, stickers them with stars and hearts. From her side of the wall of adulthood, Joyce sends me a class photograph. A ridiculous three seconds pass in which I cannot find her there, for her scrubbed, eager face blends perfectly with the beatific mischief of the seven-year-olds.

(Mama says, "Ann's the creative one. Joyce's the one good with people. Both of them taking after me at least one way, though, getting fat like they are.")

On my side of the wall I hunch quietly, try to let no sound of my life escape to her. Adulthood looms dark and narrow, a jail of bills. College is already slipping from my fingers. Why should she know how I've loved it? Loved the red dirt, the flat campus, the cubist days of classes and chapel prayers and walks to the park. Loved the library, the cloistered piano practice cells, the lye-soap smell of the newspaper darkroom, loved dressing in loose, punked costume, loved the spiral notebooks littered with handwritten poems, loved classes and skipping classes. Loved even the boredom. Loved even the loneliness. Why should she know? Why should she know that my plans are not an adventure, but a deferral—why should she know that next summer's mission trip abroad is not a mission for Christ, but an escape from adulthood into unpredictability? Why should she know my secret bruise, that I find no family in church, but only the makeshift sacraments of my own heart? Why should she know I'm falling?

On her side of the wall, in the Dallas church bustling with thousands of fabric-softened and fluoridated Christians, Joyce watches Skyler, a tall and doe-eyed ministry student. She angles her glance at him over the hymnal. After deep breaths, she approaches Skyler later, smiles up at him. He hugs her sidelong, asks after her week's happiness. On my side of the wall I hug myself at night, stroke my own hair away from my face, and imagine kisses to blot the ceaseless mirror memory, the flag of fat under my chin, the curdling on my thighs, the stuffed pouch of tummy.

(Daddy says, "You want to end up like your mama you just keep going back for more helpings the way you do.")

From her side of the wall, from a sunny Dallas day, Joyce launches written details of the day's meals, the evening's television programs, the comedic turmoils of the aunts and uncles. She butters the plain bread of her letters with the Oh, my! and Whoo-ee! and Good grief! of her speech. On my side of the wall, reading her letters makes me feel powerless and comforted, like a small child having clothes put on me. Her letters are unlike my friends' whimsical and poetic missives of dreams and plans. I bind packets of their letters in satin ribbons. Joyce's I forget, as a child forgets being dressed once the playclothes are on. Her letters are left layered with the fossil record of finished coursework and old bills, and are eventually discarded.

My husband pulled me from faintly liquored sleep accidentally, by walking on my feet. Our lumpy makeshift raft of twin bed and rollaway cot filled the dormitory room, squashed the other furniture to the walls. Nitin scrambled across the beds before the travel alarm buzzed. I yelped under the tangled lasagna of twin-size sheets and twin blankets.

"Next weekend we're getting a hotel room," he said. He'd tried in the night to hold me. The beds had slid apart and deposited him on the floor. Now the shower sizzled against the tile. I imagined how the cold ceramic felt against his feet, the hot water on his neck. Nitin's arrival was like a festival, a vacation from the lonesome hospital routine, this new job I went to every morning.

He sang in the shower. His voice had heat and depth, like spices roasting. Nitin was slight but powerful, a barbed wire strand hooked with ferocity and kindness. He had inherited India and assumed America. He had his father's diligence and storytelling cadences, his mother's domestic industry and her admiration of craftsmanship. He had his mother's laugh, thick and pure as a jasmine garland's clustered bonnets.

When Nitin entered a room, I saw his mind before his body: the dark eyes' unapologetic intelligence; the arrogant, patrician chin; the long-spined, hungry pace. His skin was like a surface tension over his intent, the pate over the fine broad bones of the skull, the flexed fabric on the restless hands. When he arrived in the hospital lobby yesterday, I met him in the corridor, my fingers outstretched for his.

"Any problems on the road?" I asked. After the September attacks, brown skin was unsafe. Sikhs, Pakistanis, Yemenis, Egyptians had been beaten up, slashed. A wordless prayer for Dr. Abu flashed on the screen of my brain.

"I didn't stop," he said. He wore a souvenir National Security Agency T-shirt. "I drove straight through. Where's your sister?"

Nitin looked in Joyce's eyes as though he were studying a rare and beautiful orchid. He talked to Daddy as though the two of them were playing checkers on a front porch. He walked with Mama as though prepared to catch her in case she fell.

When the night's visiting hours ended, Nitin pulled two cups from the stacked white tower by the coffeepot. He escorted me into the elevator and through the hushed hospital, past the doors behind which doctors slept, to our spartan dormitory room. From a pocket inside his overnight bag, Nitin produced a pint bottle. He doused puddles of rum in the dark acid of warm, canned soda. We touched our cups in a silent, styrofoam toast.

"The nurse who talks to me, her name is Carol," I said. "She said something tonight. Joyce is a fighter, she said." I stared into the oily bubbles of the drink. Nitin looked at a point on the wall over my head, listening. "I mean, we all think it matters how we live our lives, you know, over the long run. But nobody knows how long their life really is. Nobody. All we get is the short run, right? So it matters she's fighting. It matters she's doing a good job. I mean, today's her life." Nitin nodded. "I don't think I've been smiling at her," I said. "I don't think I've been cheering loud enough."

She hates her own obesity. She can't accept herself. So she can't accept others who look like her. What does she think when she sees a fat person? She gauges how much the person is overweight, how fat he or she is. She feels anxiety. She thinks, Are you happy?

Do you know you could be happy? Are you trying? What are you doing to help yourself? I am so sorry for you. I don't want to have to feel sorry for you. You make me mad. Why do you have to be this way? I want to help you. I don't want to encroach on you, to assume you need help. Do you want to lose weight? Do you want to talk about your weight? And why should it upset me? Who are you to me?

You force me to confront my own responsibility and my own prejudice. I am uncomfortable. I don't know you, yet have opinions about you, and don't like this about myself. I don't like knowing that if I feel this about you, others probably feel it about me.

Mama's call to her brother Harold had in less than twenty-four hours circulated to the furthest capillaries of the far-branched Texan aunts and uncles. As if in a convulsion, Texas had responded to Joyce's distress, jettisoning a vocal, impassioned representative. "Look who's here," Daddy said. He walked beside us into the waiting room.

"W-a-a-l, hello, stranger," Aunt Mickey said, squirming out of the overstuffed sofa to clutch me in a tight hug. "I got here just as soon as I could. Harold and them couldn't get away." Aunt Mickey had aged soft and tough as chewed leather, her cigarette thinness padded now, her chop of helixed gray hair a wiry cloud. Her eyes, like Mama's, were dark and potent as day-old coffee, and like Mama, Aunt Mickey percolated East Texas in her voice. But where Mama clipped her words, Aunt Mickey drawled them long, a slow simmer of collard greens. The East Texas drawl swung in Aunt Mickey's voice like a porch rocker on a rainy day. Aunt Mickey smiled, a fresh troop on the front line; Mama, a plump knot on the sofa, looked owlish and lost. A pillow fight of emotions and sibling memory crashed on Mama's face, the complications of sisterhood a bruiseless wound.

"How long do you get to stay?" I asked. Nitin sat beside Daddy, two reluctant theatergoers in a drama of women.

"Just today," Aunt Mickey said. "I'll have to get on the road late this afternoon. I have to be back for work. 'Til then I thought I'd just stop a while here with Toppy and Norman and spend some time with Miss Joyce."

"I was just telling Mickey how Joyce was doing," Mama said.

"Joyce has been like my own daughter to me," Aunt Mickey said in her ground-pepper voice. "I hate to think about her in a place like this."

Mama's lips thinned, possessive and weary. Not your daughter: it glared in her eyes like a transformer exploding in an ice storm. She held her tongue.

"No, Aunt Mickey, it's not like that," I said. "This is the best place she could be. They're taking real good care of her."

"Like I was saying," Mama said. "She can't move her arms real well, but she can feed herself a little. The medicine makes her sleep a whole lot, but when she's awake she's real alert and I think kind of bored. We keep the TV turned to sports channels so she can watch the games. And she has a whiteboard to write on, but she doesn't like to use it. Ever since she figured out she could do sign language with Ann that's all she wants to do. All day yesterday she kept telling us to go get Ann so she could talk."

"Sign language," Aunt Mickey said, dawdling over the words. "I forgot y'all knew that sign language. I knew she used to teach it to her kids at school. She told us about that. What all kind of things does she say to you in this sign language?"

"She asks about the weather," I said. "She wants to know where everybody is all the time. And last night she started telling jokes."

"Jokes," said Aunt Mickey. "What kind of jokes?"

"Knock-knock jokes," I said. Mama oh-my'd under her breath, and Daddy stifled a laugh.

"Well, if that don't beat all," Aunt Mickey said. "Knock-knock jokes."

Knock, knock. Who's there? Mae. Mae who? Mae be I'll tell you and maybe I won't. She spelled the jokes one deliberate letter at a time, waiting for me to repeat each word. If I missed a word, she started again from the first letter. Knock, knock. Each exacting recitation ate a quarter hour, better than reading magazines or the day's sports section. Knock, knock. Who's there? Fanny. Fanny who? Fanny body calls I'm out.

"It wouldn't be so hard," Mama was saying, "only they don't have a chair in the room where I can sit down. My ankles and knees get to hurting so."

"You might ask them to put a chair?" Aunt Mickey said.

"You'll see when you go back," I said, as Mama shook her head no. "There's no room. If the nurses needed to get around fast, they couldn't have a chair in the way."

"Yes, I suppose that's their reason," Mama said.

"Well, it's about time now," Aunt Mickey said. "If they only let two at a time, then Toppy, you want to go on back there with me?"

"Y'all might ask for a cup of ice chips from the desk nurse," I said. "She's thirsty all the time."

"That's right," Mama said. "Those ice chips make her feel better."

Returning from the ICU, Aunt Mickey walked as if her hips ached. Her devilish smile had desiccated, a dead branch across the snowy face. Sorrow and shock had drained her and filled her with age. This isn't fair, I thought. You were once Joyce's daily life. You should have had more time to sift this through. I'm sorry: Joyce's heart is strong, but her fever's never gone away. Her body's fighting the infection, fighting gravity, fighting for breath, fighting internal bleeding and loss of air from her internal organs. I know you saw the sagged skin of her purpled arm. I know you saw the oxygen tubes notched into the puffed ottoman of her neck. I know you can read monitors.

Knock, knock. Who's there? Woo. Woo, who? Don't excite yourself. It's just a knock-knock joke.

She has lost weight for five weeks consecutively, then gains two pounds. She knows about normal fluctuations—water retention, increase in exercise, hormonal shifts—yet she takes aside a friend who's also on the program. She know it doesn't make sense—she knows it's irrational—but she's suddenly scared she'll die. What if she dies too, like her sister? What if it's not possible, and her body just gets fatter and she can't stop eating? This program is the last thing she knows to try. What if her last chance doesn't work?

"Oh, honey," says her friend, fond tears in her eyes. "Your feelings are real, but they're not true. You're doing great. You're going to be okay. Your feelings lie."

Daddy and I walked down the long glass angles of the breezeway. A stairwell ahead descended to dense shrubbery and statuary, a green gateway to afternoon walks in the Tulsa neighborhoods.

"I didn't get to see my girlfriend today," Daddy said. "I call her 'hugging Carol.' She hugs me just about every time she sees me."

"You know, she told me something," I said, measuring my words as sparingly as salt. "She told me they were looking at something on Joyce's X-rays called 'free air.' It's when you have air in your body that shouldn't be there. She said they're trying to find out what's causing it. Maybe that would help them know more about what's going on."

"How do they find out what causes it?" Daddy asked. Perception, inquiry at last, the roundhouse slap of an ocean wave.

"They can do a surgery, Carol said," I told him. Daddy's eyes went blank, his stride stretched and steady. "But none of the doctors has mentioned surgery yet to you or Mama, have they? So they must be trying other ways for now."

Daddy blinked. He swallowed, then sniffed. "No, the doctors haven't said anything like that," he said. The glass panes of the long breezeway flowed past us as though we were fish in an aquarium.

"Daddy, I want to tell you this. Back before Joyce went in the ICU, we were talking one day. And she told me what her favorite hymns were. So I would know them."

"That's good for somebody to know," he said. "Here's those stairs."

"Just a second, Daddy." I paused in the breezeway, unwilling to carry the conversation into the bright, green September day. "I'm worried about Mama," I said. "Does she understand what's happening? Because I can't tell."

"She knows," he said. "But, Ann—" I looked up in surprise at the old, arresting tone. In the dark of his voice spread the searchlights: pity on me, instruction, finality. He held each word in his mouth, almost to sing them. "She's not going to die," he said, settling things.

Why does she want to lose weight? That's how most people phrase the change she wants. The only reason she minds the scale is that it measures some success in her real pursuit: she wants the fat gone from her abdomen. Not because she'd be more conventionally attractive, though she would. Not because her clothes would fit better, though they would. She wants the fat gone from her belly because it feels wrong, unbalanced, an inefficiency wearing down the whole machine. It's a symptom of her habits, which are destroying her the way a parasite kills its host. She wants to lose weight; she wants to lose her round belly.

And she wants to lose weight because she feels bad about herself overweight. The struggle to stay mentally healthy and productive is harder overweight. She hates that her weight and the food she eats are topics of discussion

between her and her husband. She hates having to think about her body and
food all the time. She wants to lose weight; she wants to lose the obsession.

1988

The school year yawns itself awake, and Joyce gazes up at the closet shelf. With laborious ceremony, she selects this year's blank diary, a slim blue velveteen brick. Joyce inscribes the year, the principal's name, her kindergarten class roster. Her round, oversized print packs the paper rows like children at assembly, ready to say the pledge.

"Timothy M. was a very bright student," she writes. "Like many kids in his environment his imagination needed prodding. One day I had ditto ink on my fingers. Timothy asked me what it was. I told him that I couldn't pull my human skin on all the way that morning. He backed up all the way to his seat watching me. Pretty soon I heard whispers and kids were watching me. It worked. They started thinking of reasons I couldn't be an alien. I shot down every reason until finally someone played along with me and thought of reasons I could be an alien."

Joyce unlocks her apartment mailbox. A letter's arrived, the stamp bearing the image of a northern Italian castle. It's from Joyce's sister, who reports that she has lost another job. This time her sister's gone all the way to Italy to lose a job, on a one-way ticket no less. Joyce shrugs. Her sister has always gotten things too easy. What made her think she could be a nanny? A small child, that's not easy. Maybe this new job will go better, still babysitting, live-in. Her sister's letters are all about the scenery and how she spends her days alone while the girl is in school. The letters sound like her sister's trying to be British and from 1920, like that's impressive.

Joyce's print crowds and tilts. She speeds her day onto the diary page. "Joey D. is a pretty sharp kid. When his work started getting bad and he began to change his attitude I was concerned. I asked his mom to come for a conference. She told me that she and Joey's father had separated and were getting a divorce. Joey blamed his mom since his dad moved out. His dad was a trucker so Joey didn't get to see him very much. At least that explained why Joey had problems.

"Not too long after that, Joey asked if he could sit by my desk to do his work. I hung around my desk as much as I could so that he could talk to me when he felt like talking.

"What Joey had to say was, 'I wish you were my mother.' I was pulled two ways at once. Happy that I had a good, positive influence on at least one kid. Sad that Joey was so upset about his parent he wanted a new mother.

"Thank goodness that not long after that Joey got to spend time with his father. After that he started improving his work and his attitude got better."

An aerogram arrives. Joyce squints at the crushed scrawl on the tissue trifold. "I'm not sure when I'll come home," her sister writes. "I've gotten some work at a translator's office. I walk nearly four miles to get there. They pay me reasonably well, but I might see next summer before I've saved the money for my ticket. I already know, though—when I come back, will you meet me at the airport? I need to go home and live with Mama and Daddy. I'm afraid if I don't do it now we won't have any relationship at all in a few years. But that's pretty scary. So can I come stay with you before I go there?"

Joyce answers the same day. Her rounded print lopes along the lined fencerails. "Glad you got a job. Keep at it. Whenever you're ready, just send me your flight info," she writes. "Plan to stay as long as you want."

Waiting is not passive. It is as taxing as holding your breath. By Joyce's third day in ICU, we had begun to escape into our minds, repudiating boredom as unworthy of Joyce's chained and solitary waiting. She lay swathed in boredom. The exigencies of hospital confinement—bathing, pills, drawn blood—were executed in the hours alone with nurses. We fumbled through routines with her: Find a ball game on TV. Unstrap an arm. Describe the weather. Feed some ice chips. Babble the day's news. Wait for her jokes, her questions, her requests.

Daddy walked; he organized Aunt LaNita's household paperwork, a favor. Mama, sunken in the waiting room sofa, read a novel. She dropped her chin toward her monumental breast and peered through the glinting bifocals nudged forward on her nose. She propped and casually crossed her canvas-slippered feet on an overstuffed ottoman. Mama's hair was a fine gray fluff, and her racing mind in the round body was like a furious, epic message bobbing, bottled, in a placid sea. I scribbled occasional scarlet edits across a pile of technical drafts; I scouted solitary corners of the hospital where I could, under the pretense of writing, daydream, sometimes of Nitin's goodbye kiss, his smile before he drove away, sometimes of nothing but the clouds that raced across the windows. Driven by the Oklahoma wind, the clouds moved so fast it felt like they stood still and the hospital turned below them. The vapory events of Joyce's health sailed by the exact same way.

The strategy of information had changed. Dr. Patrick and the student residents bundled into Joyce's room between nine-thirty and ten every morning, made inconclusive noises, and bundled out again. Their conferences bent inward around the research table monitor and Joyce's thickening chart. Frayed strands of diagnoses trailed through the team's mutterings. Hematochezia. Arterial desaturization. Words and phrases spoken as if in code fell near enough my grasp; chart pages were left briefly unattended on a countertop. Each piece of machinery had a name, a manufacturer; each drug would have a description, along with the conditions that it treated, its side effects and contraindications. The fat notebook bulged with these fragments and with numbers from the rack of monitors. Nurse Carol fed me narrative, led me down the blind corridors of Joyce's progress. And on a page at the back of the notebook, a litany grew longer: Pulmonologist. Nephrologist. Endocrinologist. Cardiologist. The specialists arrived one by one to introduce themselves to Joyce. I'll be in charge of your lungs and your oxygen treatment. I'll be in charge of your kidneys. I'll be in charge of your heart.

Late on Sunday morning, Nurse Carol called me from Joyce's bedside. "Dr. Salamon, this is Ms. Vandiver's sister," Nurse Carol said. "Ann, this is Dr. Salamon. He'll be Joyce's gastroenterologist." He'd be in charge of her guts, I thought.

Dr. Salamon, five-eight and stocky, wore his thick, snowy hair parted on the side of his square head. He peered over his metal eyeglass frames, his chin lowered and his eyes impatient. His posture was straight as a wooden block, and his coal-bin voice was forceful, an East-Coast elbow through verbal traffic. "Yes," he said. "I'll be a minute. I want to look over the notes here."

I know this Dr. Salamon, Mama would say when I told her. His picture's on the social page. He was a big-time expert witness in some case last year, and he travels all over the world. I can't believe he's on Joyce's case. He's real expensive.

Dr. Salamon strode into Joyce's room, still reading her chart. He looked up. His eyes widened and he rocked backward. "My God!" he shouted, the words like bullets. He gestured, arm outstretched, hand fanned. "This—this is impossible! She's huge!"

He gaped at Joyce, at her mattress-like obesity, the buttocks rolling to the edges of the bed, the abdomen a creamy, upturned bowl. In the face that to Dr. Salamon might appear an expressionless lump, I saw that Joyce forgave him, her eyebrows pitched upward, amused as though he were a circus bear that had just loudly farted onto its trainer. Dr. Salamon struggled. "I'd been told she was obese; I hadn't pictured . . ." Loyal to Joyce's lead, I held my silence. "I'll need to rethink my recommendations," he said. He wheeled. I shrugged Joyce's own shrug at her, the clown-mouthed shrug of tolerance of unbalanced people. I followed Dr. Salamon from the ICU.

"This really presents some difficulties," he said to me in the hallway. His rational gruffness and direct gaze were his apology. "To operate on a patient of this size presents challenges."

A word can twist your arm behind your back. Operate. He thought I'd known. "Will I be able to speak with you when you know more about the surgery?"

"Of course," he said, his sandpaper voice growing more finely grained, under a lighter touch. He looked over his glasses, his white head tilted. "This must be very hard for your family," he said.

I held out my hand. His grip was firm, a hand on a tiller. "It helps to speak with her doctors," I said. Dr. Salamon nodded, his thick bangs flopping forward. I wanted to climb onto the life raft of his intelligence. But I suspected what would prove true: none of us saw Dr. Salamon again.

Back in ICU, Joyce called me near with a slight twitch of an eyebrow, a tweaked wrinkle beside her lip. Black sparks in the blue eyes bound me motionless. How am I doing? she spelled, careful and severe, staring at my face.

"You've got a rocky path ahead," I said. "Your kidneys are better, but you have to heal from whatever is causing the infection. Something besides the kidneys is making you weak and making you hurt. Now, it sounds like the doctors are narrowing down their ideas for treating you. They're figuring it out. So you have to keep fighting now. I know it must be hard. The hardest thing you ever did?"

She nodded.

"Then are you fighting?" I said.

She nodded, paused, her raised hand hesitant with a letter half-formed. My body's crying, she spelled. I cradled her hand as though it were a fallen flower. I thought about kissing her fingers. She waved me off and spelled: Fighting. My job now.

She doesn't know what she looks like.

When she looks in the mirror, she sees a beautiful woman. She sees her eyes and smile; she sees skin, its curves and hollows, shades and colors. She sees a creature with a soft, coincidental body. Except sometimes she blinks, and tries to see herself as others might see her. Then she sees an unflattering haircut, stooped posture, the receding double chin and overbite. Puffy eyes. Sloped shoulders. Flaccid arms. Fat rolls on her back, a hammock of pudding, her belly. Jiggly, loose thighs with goose skin. And she is appalled and terrified that she doesn't know which woman is real, the beautiful, unique one or the ridiculously flawed one. One disappears into the other, like two negative spaces sparring to become the foreground image.

"We know how uncomfortable she must be," Nurse Rita said. "It's gravity. She slides down in the bed and needs to be lifted back up. At first we didn't really know how to manage it. It takes at least two of us to help her. Sometimes there aren't two nurses, so she has to wait a little longer than she or we would like."

"I'm sure she knows you're not ignoring her," I said.

"The look on her face," Nurse Rita said. "That hurt look."

"I'll talk to her," I said.

"Did you know she'd gotten her period?" Nurse Rita said. I shook my head, unsure why I would need to know. "We were stunned. At her weight, no one expected her to have a period anymore. It gave us quite a fright, the bleeding, until she told us that she always still had periods."

"We weren't sure it wasn't internal bleeding," Nurse Carol explained later, in our quiet, nightly chat. "The doctors are discussing a colonoscopy to identify the cause of the free air. But in her condition, even a colonoscopy is a difficult and uncertain test. They aren't sure they could perform it."

"What would it tell them?"

"Whether her bowel had been perforated. In that case, there's a surgery called a colonostomy. Do you know what that is?" I shook my head to clear my vague and trivial knowledge. Colonostomy didn't sound too bad. "The damaged part of the colon is removed," she said. "It's a fairly standard procedure, but you realize, for her any surgery has additional risks."

"Carol," I said. "How is she?"

"She's relying on the oxygen more than we would like," Nurse Carol said. "She's still sick from the infection. Her kidneys for the moment present no problems; they're functioning. Her heart is strong and she's lucid and alert when she's awake. The one thing is, she needs to eat."

"She's not eating? Not anything?"

Nurse Carol shook her head. "We go over the menu with her every night. We'd bring her whatever might sound good, even if it's not on the list. She studies that menu so carefully. But then the trays sit untouched. I told her, 'Ms. Vandiver, you have to eat something. I know you think you need to lose weight, but you have to eat to keep up your strength.'" Nurse Carol threw a longing gaze like a fly-fisherman's cast toward Joyce's room. "She forces herself to eat a few bites now and then, but it's not enough."

"I'm not sure she's trying to lose weight," I said. "See, there's this lifelong thing with her. Nothing in the world can make her eat food she doesn't like." No force of logic, emotion, or pain would work. Could the medicine have dulled her appetite? Was food still like waste in her mouth?

"Do you know anything we could bring her? Is there anything she would just really love?"

A carousel of food whirled around the vision of Joyce's ice chip relief. She'd jut her lower lip to catch the ice, focusing on the spoon as if she were keeping an ice cream bar from dripping. "A milkshake," I said. "Strawberry. And french fries? If she can have those. Crispy. With ketchup."

Changing into her swimsuit, she faces the locker, attempts to remove her clothing strategically, to remain as least naked as possible. A taut, athletic woman walks behind her, drops a gym bag.

Fine, she thinks. Let the taut woman see her fat and naked. She disrobes completely and begins to tug her swimsuit over her cellulite. She glances at the taut woman, who's frowning. Wonder what she has to frown about. Looking like that.

Her unfairness hits her like a hammer in the ear. What does she know? Just because a woman's thin she has no problems? How does she know the woman hasn't just gotten a breast cancer diagnosis? Or divorce papers? Or a horrible work evaluation?

That taut woman has worked hard for her health and ought to be proud, not resented. She's not angry at the taut woman. She's angry because she's not more like the taut woman. She's angry because she doesn't want to face her shortcomings. It's easier to hate the taut woman than to forgive herself and begin to heal.

She closes her eyes over the wet film of chagrined, unexpected tears. I'm sorry, she apologizes silently to all the taut women she's ever seen. She slides her suit straps over her shoulders. She and the taut woman leave the locker room together, without eye contact, without a word.

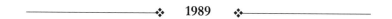

❖ 1989 ❖

"Hey. Joyce. Thanks for letting me stay here until I can get home to Mama and Daddy's," I said. "It's a nice apartment."

"You're welcome. Sorry I was late to the airport."

"Yeah, least of my troubles."

"Well. Rest up now, I guess. Look around if you want. You want something to drink?"

"Hey, is this your school diary? The one you wrote me you were keeping? Can I read it?"

"No."

(Teresita is selected to play Mrs. Santa in the Christmas PTA. She is wonderful! She has to cry out, "Santa, where are your boots?" Her mother put her in a beautiful white dress. It was covered in the play by Mrs. Santa's apron. Her hair was curled with a white bow on top of her head. That was covered by Mrs. Santa's cap. She was still the cutest kid on the stage—that's the opinion of her unprejudiced teacher. I can still see her arms flapping up and down while she asks, "Santa, where are your boots?")

"Hey, I said no! Put it down!"

"When did you get all these pictures of Grandma Roberts?"

"Grandma Hester gave me some. Daddy gave me some others. They said I could have them as long as I didn't just put them away in a box."

"Grandma was so pretty."

"She was twenty-six there."

"Your age."

"I'm glad you're back. I missed you."

"Why?"

"I had stuff to talk about. I sure wished I could call you."

"Did something happen?"

"Not really. It just—I had to get some help. I talked to my friend Skyler, at church—I talked to a counselor . . . I'll tell you about it if you want to hear," Joyce says.

"Yeah. Wait, let me sit down."

"Uh. Yeah. So. I don't know if you ever knew that I have this problem with anger. No, don't laugh. I mean a big problem. You have to remember that anger is a sin. It's just like alcohol or fornication or any other vice. You can indulge. You can use anger to feel better and hurt yourself at the same time. See, when I get angry, my stomach can stay knotted up for hours. Days. My head starts to hurt and it feels tight and I can't think right. I can't think about anything but being angry. It feels terrible."

"So how does anger make you feel better?"

"Because then I don't feel helpless. That's what I figured out. When I feel mad enough, I don't have to face the people I'm mad at or solve the problems. It's like anger is my whole response, and I'm really good at it. Apart from the anger I feel like I don't have to do anything more to fix the problem."

"That doesn't sound like fun."

"At first it feels powerful. Then it just feels sick. That's why I had to talk to somebody. And Skyler, my friend—he's great, he knew, and he'd ask how I was. He asked how I was, and listened. Skyler. I have a picture—look, he has beautiful eyes, kind of like Parker Stevenson. Anyway, I got some help. I'm better now. I'm getting better. It helps to tell you."

"You can tell me anything," I say.

"Good. Because you were the person I was mad at."

"Joyce?"

"I've been angry at you for so many years. No matter what I did, you were always right there doing it better. Wherever I went, as soon as you got there, I disappeared. I know that wasn't your fault, but I felt like I didn't have my own life. You were always there. As long as you were there, I didn't matter."

"That's not true."

"I was so angry at you."

"I didn't know."

"I know it wasn't fair. You're my sister, and I love you. Don't cry."

"All I wanted was to be like you. Joyce, you're my—look, I always felt better with you, I wasn't scared. I never meant to take anything away. I didn't think about making you feel bad. Maybe I didn't think about you. I just wanted to be with you all the time. Didn't you know that? I'm sorry."

"It's okay."

"No, no it's not—look, don't you cry too—can we be sisters again?"

"Yeah, say more soap opera things like that so I'll stop blubbering. Here, take a tissue. Take two. Blow your nose. Whoo, hey. So, listen. I need your help."

"Anything."

"When Mama and Daddy start in on me about my weight, help me change the subject."

"What about your weight?"

"Well, look at me. I've gained a bunch of weight since college and they're worried I'm going to take after Mama's side and get really big and not be able to move."

"No. They said that?"

"Those exact words. Anyway, when they start in I can't stand it. It makes me want to get away, and I get so angry. I feel like I could deal with the weight, but not the weight and the anger at the same time. It takes everything I have to deal with the anger."

"I get it. Yeah. But can I ask you, are you doing anything about your weight?"

"I watch what I eat, I really do. I eat salads and low-calorie frozen dinners, and not a lot of snacks or sugary stuff. And I go for walks, plus just keeping up with the little kids at school is plenty of exercise. You wouldn't believe how much walking back and forth there is in a day with second graders."

"Have you gone to a doctor?"

"What's a doctor going to do?"

"I don't know. Maybe help you."

"Doctors aren't going to do anything but tell me I need to lose weight. Anyhow they cost too much money and insurance won't pay for it. I've checked into all kinds of stuff. Insurance doesn't pay for any kind of weight loss treatment or stomach stapling or anything."

"You thought about stomach stapling?"

"Yeah. Insurance won't pay for it. It won't pay for special medicine or any kind of weight loss program or a visit to one of those places where they put you on a diet and exercise. I could do that in the summer but it costs way too much."

"But what about—"

"See, I don't want to talk about it. Not with Mama and Daddy and not with you. I'm going to be fine. I just have to keep eating right and walking and it'll be okay. Anyway it's not like I want to be a model. As long as I'm healthy the rest of it doesn't matter. And don't tell Mama and Daddy about the stomach stapling stuff."

"Wow. Don't worry."

"They would just get all upset, like I was worse off than I am."

"As long as you're doing something for your health, I won't let Mama and Daddy get after you."

"Thanks. You lost weight, didn't you?"

"Yeah. I walked a lot too. You wouldn't believe. Miles and miles."

"Was it beautiful over there?"

"It was."

"Tell me. Tell me what it looked like. Tell me everything."

"Right. That'll take all night."

"I'm not sleepy. I'll go get us a can of pop."

(We came back from Christmas break but Teresita came only 2 days and then was absent for several days. She returned with a long letter from her mom. Her father's birthday present to Teresita was abuse. It then came out this wasn't the first time. Dad's in jail but they are moving back home, out of state. The image of my sweet Mrs. Santa Claus is sadder now when I think of Teresita.)

"Hey! I told you not to read that!"

"Just a little."

"Give it here. I'm going to bed."

"Joyce, don't be like that. We were having a good time."

"Yeah, we were. But now I'm going to bed."

"Okay. Goodnight . . . Joyce? Goodnight?"

"I put your sheets out on the couch."

"Thanks. Goodnight?"

"Mm-hm. Look. Just go to sleep. It'll be better in the morning."

Monday, September 24. The highway's spine away from Tulsa anchored a wingspan of golden Oklahoma cropland. In my little car I soared across the wide Oklahoma sky, guided by the frail silhouettes of barbed wire, the spindly metal daisies of windmills. Then Oklahoma scrolled up behind me, closed and blank; Kansas unrolled, the sunken groove of highway edged in narrow ditches, pasture, prim country towns. The Kansas highway pitched me inexorably toward the Kansas City inter-state loop, the south-suburb malls and chain restaurant clusters, the light industry and office campuses, boulevards and convenience stores, and finally, to my own workplace, where sales associates laughed and nodded into their telephones, where software developers gem-chiseled lines of code down screens. Hardly anyone noticed my arrival. Good. I could start wrenching the world right-side out again.

But the desk, the monitor, seemed distant and transparent, as if I were dreaming them. The work around me, piles of printed sheets, zoomed close, then far away. E-mail messages, tidy bricks of query, lay stacked in the onscreen inbox. They pay me for the small tasks just like the large ones, I thought. I can complete. I can control. I can move bricks.

But my hands were already on the keyboard; what, after all, lay between me and the resumed hunt for my sister's assassins? A scarf of skin, some fragments of plastic, an ethereal network of hard fact and oversimpli-fied half-truth? Terms, tests, conditions, pharmaceuticals: prune away whatever was not written by doctors; pry apart the Latin thorns to find fruit, however small or discolored. The thorn field of medical knowledge is vast and tall; no one could know its every cubed yard of twisted stem and spike. No doctor could know it all, and I was at its mercy, lost. Yet as I ignored other work, information accumulated. Two colleagues debated database structure outside my office; a long printout hummed from a laser printer. The life in which I was supposed to participate sounded far away. I searched; I fashioned a costume of information for the invisible, leering bullies that were Joyce's ailments. Isolated terms stitched into a seam, pattern pieces of research into a shroud: dire conditions, unavailable treatments, co-morbidities, mortality statistics.

Search term: arterial desaturization.

Your blood is saturated with oxygen. Everything your body does feeds on oxygen; your body craves it. When you breathe, you bring oxygen in and push carbon dioxide out. The more deeply you breathe, the more oxygen can get to your blood. The blood in your arteries, flowing away from your heart to all your other cells, should be 95 percent saturated with oxygen's rich fuel. But when you can't breathe enough oxygen—for instance, at high altitude or in a house fire or when your lungs and heart are struggling—the amount of oxygen in your blood drops. Carbon dioxide begins to build up. If you have edema or apnea, then oxygen in blood that flows back toward your heart may be reduced as well. You can't live without enough oxygen in your blood. You can't live with too much carbon dioxide in your blood. If your body can't get enough oxygen into your blood, you will need mechanical assistance breathing. The machine that feeds you breath must monitor the oxygen, must administer it like a mother bird feeding its young.

Search term: abdominal free air.

The tubes and sacs inside your body, many of them tucked and coiled in your abdomen, contain air. Free air—visible on an X-ray or from an ultrasound—might mean you have a hernia, a ruptured cyst or ulcer. Or it might mean that one of the vital tubes and sacs of your internal organs has been punctured. Not only air but bowel wastes might be leaking into your body's cavities. Bacteria flood with the contaminants into your abdomen, soaking you in infection.

Search term: hematochezia recurrent.

Hematochezia is blood passing through the rectum. Hemorrhoids can cause it; so can inflammatory bowel disease; so can diverticulitis.

"I talked to Nurse Rita tonight," I said to Mama on the phone. "She wouldn't tell me anything, only that there's no change and Joyce was resting comfortably."

"Well, as long as that's true, there's not much else to know, is there?" Mama said. "Those nurses are busy, Ann. They don't have time to stop and fill you in."

(Kerri and our colleague Lisa had that afternoon shut my heavy office door. Kerri stretched an arm, leaned on the bookcase; Lisa, with regal, stage-manager posture, sat cross-legged on the floor. Workplace sounds ceased. The office, with its cloudy gray and beige faux-finish walls, enclosed us like a closet where we'd crept to tell secrets about boys.

"Here's the hardest thing," I said to them. "It's hard to tell the difference anymore between what I imagine, what I know, what I believe, and what I'm afraid of.")

"I was thinking," Mama said. "I noticed LaNita still has the hospital bed in her garage, the one Troy was using before he got this new one? I think, when there's a good time to talk to LaNita, I'll see if she might not sell it to us. We're going to need one when Joyce comes home. She's going to need to stay sat up with the oxygen and all. I might ask LaNita about that."

("What are you afraid of?" Lisa's dark eyes deepened, but not with challenge. She asked into my fright as though she were letting me into my own locked house. A friend, I thought—a friend walks like this with you into the dark.)

"I won't ask her today, though," Mama said. "Today would not be the right day to do so."

"Why? What happened? Isn't LaNita there?"

"No, she's at the hospital with Troy," Mama said. "He went back in the hospital last night. I need to let your daddy tell you about that. I will say this, I'm glad we were here with LaNita no matter how hard it was. I'm glad Joyce is getting such good care in that ICU we can come up here."

("I'm afraid of how I feel when I look at her. The past few years, I've only known Joyce as an unhealthy, miserable, obstinate, mean person. I still feel angry with that person. But now she's so helpless, and I'm afraid I'm giving up on her. I mean—I tend to dwell on the worst case scenario. Is that what I'm doing? Am I imagining she'll die, or am I realizing the likelihood? Is thinking she'll die the same as giving up on her?"

"You know what the doctors have been telling you. You're being realistic," Kerri said. "And you see your parents having such a hard time facing the possibilities. You don't want to put yourself through that pain if the worst happens.")

"What happened with Uncle Troy?"

"I'll let your daddy tell you that one. She just can't let him go. Ann, she needs to let him go and she just won't." But how do you let go the spark of life? It's too easy a thing to say on someone else's behalf.

("I know you're right," I said. "If she dies—oh, God, I want to say 'when,' 'if' feels like a lie—they'll go through hell. My mom and dad have hope—they believe in her getting better. I don't know how to hope. I've known for a long time her weight could kill her. I've been grieving her alive, knowing it."

"Look," Kerri said. "You're not doing anything wrong to think about what might happen. It doesn't mean you don't love your family."

"It's not your fault this happened," Lisa says, rocking in her cross-legged pose, reaching a hand to my knee. "You know that."

My breath eases, so I smile at her. Under her short shock of black hair, every centimeter of Lisa's pale-cream face smiles a miniature smile back.)

"We were all asleep," Daddy said. "It was the middle of the night. We woke up and she was yelling. We all thought Troy was going. Ann, I never heard anything like it."

("It's not wrong for them to hope," I said.

"Nobody knows what's going to happen next," Kerri said. "I think it's pretty amazing and wonderful that they've been able to stay there, by her side. How hard to see your child like that.")

Daddy sounds reverent and stunned. "It was terrible for her," he said slowly. "It was a terrible thing."

("When Mama comes in the room," I said, "Joyce's whole body relaxes. The last time that happened was maybe when Joyce was a baby. I think Joyce would hold out her arms to Mama if she could. So Mama gets to see that again. That one thing's good.")

For her thirty-fifth birthday, her husband gives her a bicycle. She hasn't ridden since she was eight years old. He buys her a helmet, shows her how to switch gears, how to slide her feet out of the toe clips, how to stand on the pedals to pump. She rides behind him on the trail, mimics his movements and poise. She stretches, one arm winged toward the shoulderblades. On a level path she drops both hands to her thighs, feeling the freedom of balance rush through her.

This isn't like the gym, she thinks. She can be good at this. They ride six, later ten, then eighteen, then twenty-five miles. A long, steep hill near their house conquers her every week as her husband sails to the other side. He rides on without her, but she attacks the hill grimly, each pedal push a curse and exhortation—do it! she yells under her breath. Come on, do it! One day, she hauls slowly to the top, panting and berating her burning calves. She crests the hill in triumph, and sees her husband waiting, off his bike, clapping and cheering for her.

Sleep shifted me back into my own world. Plans, maps of the coming day buzzed in my brain. I awoke, bathed, dressed, breakfasted, and arrived promptly at my desk, wearing the clockwork routine like a lucky talisman. Tulsa was happening to Tulsans, there were no hospitals, no sick people anywhere, and my phone would not ring.

"Ann?" The voice was light, sweet, magnolia, summer. "This is Dr. Mary Francis. I'm on your sister's primary care team?"

Things happen in the morning, I thought. "Thank you for calling me," I said.

"Your number was on the contact list," Dr. Mary said. "You need to know what's happened. Ms. Vandiver's blood oxygen level dropped critically low during the night. It's back up now, but it's tenuous." The words dropped off, silky white petals. "Frankly, we almost lost her. But now she seems all right. That is, we don't expect any immediate change."

The world was inside out again, inside a bag where black clothes lay not yet unpacked. I needed to check my tire pressure. Roads waited empty and fast. "I'm on my way there. Do my parents know?"

"They were here in the ICU this morning. They know she had a critical event."

"Doctor," I said. "Did—that is, did my parents seem upset or agitated? How'd they take it?"

A breeze, a pause, ruffled the cupped flowers and glossy leaves. "They seemed relieved and satisfied to know that she had stabilized," Dr. Mary said.

"I'm sorry to ask," I said. "Do you think they heard the same information you told them? Did they react to the fact that Joyce had almost died?"

A sigh, a scent, drifted through the phone line. "When you get here, why don't you call the ICU from the waiting room," Dr. Mary said. "Ask them to page me. I'll meet you there."

❖ 1990 ❖

I lean my head against the telephone receiver as though it were the invisible wall that separates us, as though it were a piano's wooden frame. I wait for the smooth chords of Joyce's stories to vibrate through my bones. Her stories vibrate to the marrow, to childhood.

"So Granddaddy got in a fight," she tells me.

"What? With who?" Childhood roles return with childhood comforts; stories puzzle and delight.

"With this other equally old and mobility challenged man who sleeps in the next bed. See, the man who shares Granddaddy's room steals stuff."

"What does he steal?" I know Joyce remembers childhood; her second graders' stories are like shivers under her skin. And I remember childhood because I'm afraid to forget. If I forget childhood, the wall between Joyce and me dissolves, unnecessary. She wouldn't need to wall away a stranger.

"I don't know what all. I think he stole Granddaddy's comb. Anyway, Granddaddy comes back in the room after his therapy yesterday, plunk, plunk, plunk real slow in his walker, and this other man is over in his wheelchair by Granddaddy's bed and he's trying to hide the grandbabies' pictures down in his lap blanket. It must have taken him I don't know how long to get over there in his chair because he sure couldn't get away, not even with Granddaddy poking along three inches at a time on that walker. So the nurse comes in and finds these two old men wrestling on the floor and Granddaddy yelling, 'I'm a gonna get my gun! You done it now!' Whoo-ee."

"Who won?"

"Granddaddy. He got the pictures back. And he bit the other man on the leg."

"Are they both okay?"

"Oh, the nurse gave them both a talking to and put them in bed. Granddaddy don't like any of the people at that place. He thinks they're stupid. He calls the nurses and the doctors a bunch of waterheads."

"Waterheads? What's that mean?"

"He told me, 'Them's a bunch of waterheads. Them's heads is completely flat.'"

During her summer visit to Oklahoma, neither childhood's vibrations nor amiable stories come out of Joyce's suitcase with the novel and videotapes and Bible and the new wardrobe. She unpacks denim tent dresses, elastic-waist knit skirts and flared T-shirts, wide fabric tubes that drape like tablecloths.

"So, this is all you do? I mean, when you're not teaching." She collects the old movies. She thinks Daddy might want to watch them with her. She marks passages in her Bible. Skyler has given their adult class a summer assignment. ("I can't wait to show him how much I finished.") She reads, as all the women of our family do, at idle moments, contriving idle moments for that purpose. "Don't you hang out with friends?"

"I'm happy how I live," she says. She pinches her long brown frizz back over small, pale ears. "At least I ain't trying to be somebody I'm not."

My fingers travel to my razored bob, to the dark, dyed obliteration of early gray. Her eyebrow arches, her smirk stretches. I must have flinched and am annoyed she'll think it evidence of conscience. I flinch at her grammar, which I cannot imagine in a classroom: He don't. We wasn't. Them is. At the new rasp in her voice, as though a strand of fiberglass has snaked down the puff of her throat. At her prim rejection of vanity. I flinch at the way she ignores Daddy, at the way she sneers when Mama speaks, at her punitive disgust at the food Mama cooks and her haughty disinterest in cleaning the dishes she's helped dirty. I flinch at each dainty snip she makes with teeth and lips, one oily french fry after another, and lower my glance resentfully to the fries on my own plate. I want to jam them in one handful against my teeth.

We're cramped in our old bedroom like two pieces of a malfunctioning kitchen appliance that won't fit back into its packaging. Our friends have disappeared into their own lives, Lorena and Susie into marriages and back to the Baptist church, in another town. Joyce and I cannot simulate their companionship. My irreligiosity angers Joyce, and her narrow code frustrates me. We avoid and blame each other. We are like houses with the windows boarded shut and deadly petals of broken glass embedded in the weeds.

"I don't know what gets into the two of you," Mama says. "Y'all were always such happy kids. Thank goodness we had one child that wasn't moody." Hunter, home between shifts of his two summer jobs, is six-five now, with deltoids like Volkswagen fenders. He's able to lift me as he would a sleeping toddler, heavy as I am, chest-high in his arms. At Mama's praise, he plasters on a showy grin. I knock him on the bicep with a loose fist; Joyce squeezes a tight frown down her raw-biscuit cheeks.

"Whatever," I say, my voice flat. "Daddy, you headed out to burn the trash? You want me to carry anything?"

"If you want to stand around and watch trash burn, I guess I won't stop you." He adjusts his ball cap visor, a tidy up-and-down jiggle. Across the pasture, in the excavated pond, Daddy sets a lit match to a newspaper wad. Bags of trash slop over the pyre, and white smoke sweeps off the burning debris. We stand at the hot lip of the ragged dirt shell. Shallow lines rivulet down Daddy's face; the blond fringe over his ears is freckled with gray. His pale blue eyes are still honest as a boy's. They reflect the orange flames. The fire's shadows stripe his nose and chin.

"How much more you going to dig on this pond?" I ask.

"Huh. To tell the truth, I started filling it back in about a month ago."

"You're not giving up?"

"No, I just don't need all that big a pond. I'll use it to burn trash for now. Maybe one of these days I'll find some way to make a little goldfish pond up here. You remember that concrete goldfish pond my Grandma Roberts had in her back yard? You were probably too little."

"Orange and red goldfish," I say, "and a turtle."

Daddy shoves his hands deep in his jeans pockets. The buttons on his cotton shirt glow in the firelight. "You can come back home whenever you want," he says. "I don't ever want Joyce to move back in."

He takes it for granted that I understand. He wants to love her. Otherwise, it wouldn't matter where she lived.

"Granddaddy don't really have a gun. But speaking of guns. I want to tell you a story, but you can't tell Mama and Daddy."

"Yeah."

"Last year I had a gun pointed at me at work."

"What?"

"No, no. It's okay. Here's what happened. This girl in my class had been acting out all day, and I told her if she didn't stop she was going to have to stay after school. So when the last bell rang her grandmother came to get her and I told her that Latisha was staying a few minutes after for punishment. And the grandmother starts yelling at me, 'You let her out of that chair right now!' And I wouldn't. So her grandmother was gone for a few minutes—they just live a half-block away from the school, and when she came back I was standing with my friend Ms. Lopez, and the crazy woman pulls out this gun and points it right at me and starts yelling, 'You let my kid out or I'm going to shoot you!'"

"What did you do?"

"What else could I do? I told her, 'You can shoot me if you want to but Latisha's staying at least five more minutes.' I thought Ms. Lopez was going to faint when I said that."

"She didn't shoot?"

"No, she just wanted to bully us. She wasn't fixing to shoot anybody. She put the gun back in her purse and wandered off, a-mumbling and grumbling. What does it tell that kid if I back down to a threat? If I say you stay fifteen minutes, you stay fifteen minutes."

"Huh. That's showing them."

"You better believe it. In my classroom, I say what goes."

"We're not able to diagnose her properly," Dr. Mary said in her magnolia voice. Her eyes were round and dark, like dolls' filled teacups. Short and slight, she wore her long white coat the way a gymnast wears chalk, ready for hard work. "She just can't fit into the MRI scanner or the CAT scan. The X-rays suggest free air, but it's very hard to see because of the large, hard masses of tissue in her abdomen. What we can see is all shadows, hints. We wait and watch, hoping the diagnosis will become evident."

The hospital felt flimsy and transparent around us, its gray and pink walls a bubble. Dr. Mary's exploratory concern, her lonely reprise of Dr. Abu's old, haunting aria, echoed as if inside a misty, ammoniated dream.

"While we wait, she's weakening," Dr. Mary said. "We don't know which available treatment could prove fatal. If we treat the kidneys, we worsen the infection. Treat the infection, and we clog the kidneys. How much food to give her, if the problem is in her digestive organs? How much oxygen is safe?" Impulsive, she squeezed my shoulder, slid her hand to my elbow. "You should be prepared," she said. "We're reaching a critical point. We can't wait. We'll have to decide what to do to try to save her life."

When she loses ten pounds, she thinks, this feels clean. She feels clean and empty. Her clothes don't feel tight. She doesn't cry zipping them up.

She doesn't sneak food. She eats what she wants, wanting more to stay within the guidelines she's accepted. She doesn't care who approves or disapproves of what she put in her mouth. They're not in charge.

She never wanted to keep a food record before. It seemed punitive, one more tool to beat guilt and doubt into her conscience. What good is a list of everything she ate today? Making the list won't stop her from eating. And at the end of the day, incapable of analyzing her choices, the invoice of food illogically reinforces her idea that she's either escaped or confirmed that day her laziness, lack of control, and idiocy toward food.

But now she's keeping a food record that reveals, for every choice, its place in a pattern of nutrition—calories, fat, fiber. It isn't a bludgeon, but an education. She sees the nutritional merits of her choices, how quantities and composition of food are related. It dazzles her, stuns her—she sees in black and white the point at which her satisfaction and pleasure perfectly balance with nutritional health. She holds her breath as though she were holding the truth in her throat:

success is not a weight, a number—success is keeping the balance. She can, for the first time, see a goal.

The beige cotton wrist restraints held Joyce down like a billowing tent. She was losing weight and looked loose in her skin, partially deflated. She seemed to be spreading like a melting brie platter, the needles like fondue forks in her arm. Her blue eyes blinked, placid, in the hopeful globe of her face. I wanted to run away, to write, to tourniquet with a notebook page and shoot up with words.

"Hey. Has your doctor been in today? Sorry—yeah, you have what, like a hundred doctors now. The cute one. Blond. The pulmonologist. Dr. Schroeder. Has he been in today?"

Joyce's struggle to remember was like a game of freeze tag on her face. Recognition was tapped, unfrozen, and ran away. She flapped her hand in its cotton restraint, dragging my attention to her plump fingers. There was a man, she spelled.

"A man? What man? Another doctor?"

There was a man, she spelled again. He was sixty. He met a sixty-year-old woman. They got married. One day a fairy came to the man. The fairy said, I'll grant you one wish. The man said, Make my wife twenty years younger than me. Poof! The man was eighty.

Toppy and Norman, she spelled. Her eyes drooped, sly with achievement, and in the electrostatic silence of ICU, my laughter clattered like a dropped metal pot, an escaped aluminum lid. Nurse Rita, moving past with her slim and angular propulsion, shot us an investigative glance. Joyce waved the nurse buzzer button at her, then looped slow, meticulous lettering across her whiteboard like icing script across a sheet cake. There was a man, she wrote. He was sixty.

"Ms. Vandiver, you told me that one already," Nurse Rita said. "She got us last night. We thought she was trying to explain what had happened before she was hospitalized. It didn't make sense. Then we got she was writing a joke."

Joyce pretended to watch the muted television. Her faint, subversive smile betrayed a sliver of daylight under the pulled shade of her blank face. "When she buzzes us in," Nurse Rita said, "we can't take the chance. She might need any kind of help. She might really be trying to tell us something. But she starts again on this same joke."

"It's a long joke," I said.

"It takes forever," Nurse Rita said. "But she gets upset if the nurse tries to leave when she's writing it." I followed her out of the room with Joyce's empty ice chip cup.

"She seems disoriented," I said. "Sometimes she's forgetting how to spell things. She knows when she gets it wrong. It confuses her to get things wrong."

"That's the medicine," Nurse Rita said, spiking the full paper cup with a plastic spoon. "In the mornings she should be more alert. Afternoons and evenings, it depends."

Back in the dim room, I tilted ice chips into the slow, pleasured movements of Joyce's tongue and lips. Her encyclopedic eyes flickered over me, dark, dilated, patient. Why does the butcher, she spelled. She halted, then tried again. Why does the butcher put so much meat on the sandwich?

"Why does the butcher put so much meat on the sandwich. I don't know," I said. "Why does he? What? Joyce? Was that a joke?"

No, she spelled slowly. Not a joke.

"Oh," I said. "Oh. God. Then the answer is still I don't know." I wanted to run away, to write, to drink the ink and spit it up onto the page and drink the words again. I smoothed silky strands of hair from her sweaty temple. "Are you fighting?"

She nodded, a pout blossoming under the dark creases of her closed eyes.

"Then it's fine," I said.

Giving up food is a negative habit. It's harder to stop doing something than to start doing something. Positive habits, not diet, have changed her health. When she doesn't run, walk, lift, or swim, her leg muscles ache and itch. She fidgets and grumbles. When she doesn't feel air moving past her face, she sighs and grouses.

When she doesn't drink water, her breath is shallow, her sleep, fitful. She feels mordant and cynical and weeps easily. Water's become like a drug. With it, her mood swings disappear. She thinks of walks, of books, of friends, work, and accomplishment, not the dulling of pain. The want flattens and folds itself away.

She clasps the positive habits, floating splinters of wood in a stormy sea. She will float on them to shore, she thinks, to a life where she doesn't remember hating herself.

The dormitory phone rang against the concrete block walls and into the stale loaf of sleep. "Your sister wants you to come down," Nurse Rita said. I want Nurse Carol, I thought, waking into uncharitableness and misplaced priority. And Joyce? My sister Joyce? Joyce doesn't ask for me; Joyce wants me to go away. "She's fine," Nurse Rita continued, "but she's asking for you. You can come down for a while and stay with her. It's all right."

I pulled my sweater over my T-shirt and listened to the elevator's old moan in the absence of hushed human voices. Night dimmed the waiting rooms, where a man and woman with graying hair and slack, exhausted faces slept leaning together on the sofa, their hands warmed in their armpits. I brushed past the ICU No Admittance sign. Nurse Rita smiled a thin, efficient smile and waved at me from the desk. How do ICU nurses smile? They did it all the time, but how? "Don't stay too long," she told me.

Joyce strained to tease her bulk upward in the bed. Hungry, she spelled. Thirsty.

"Do you want ice chips?"

She scraped her unused voice from her throat's floor. "Cherry limeade," she said, a parched, imperious croak. "From Sonic."

"Okay," I said. "Wow."

"No," she said, hearing laziness in my easy agreement. Adamant words cost her breath. Her voice imploded. "From Sonic."

I knew the drink she craved, its fresh-squeezed, curvy lime wedges, a gulp of sweet cherry juice, slushy ice. She would sluice cherry limeade through the long straw, summer in a cup, the freedom of her car, her arm out the window pushing the drive-in speaker button.

"You know it'll be flat by the time I get it here."

She shrugged a shrug at the edge of peevishness.

"Anyway, Sonic's going to be closed now. It's almost midnight. They open in the morning. Can you wait until lunchtime?"

She pivoted her head from side to side. She fumbled for the whiteboard. NO. The word blackened the entire, small rectangle.

"Morning? Can you wait until morning?"

"If I have to," she wheezed.

"Don't try to talk. I promise, in the morning," I said. "First thing." Simultaneous urges swamped me—to hug her, to stay the night; to run away so that the morning would come sooner. I planted my palms on the nurses' desk and bounced on the balls of my feet. "Rita," I said, "she wants a cherry limeade. Can she have that? Can I bring it in the morning?"

"She asked for food?" Nurse Rita said. Her brown curls fell behind her shoulders as she looked up sharply. The second nurse, an energetic and matronly woman with hair the color of pumpkin shell, swiveled in her chair, her lips buckling with a quick intake of breath.

"She says she's hungry. Maybe she'll eat now. But I promised her the cherry limeade if it's okay."

"She can have whatever she wants," Nurse Rita said. "That's the first thing she's wanted, isn't it?"

"Since she got here," I said. "Can I go tell her?"

"Then you'll need to go and let her get some rest," Nurse Rita said, with an offhand pointedness that made me suspect I, not Joyce, looked worn and dizzied.

But I felt like a third grader winning a relay race. The sun shines and teacher cheers. I sheltered my hand under Joyce's on the bed. She patted my hand, a gentle four-beat rhythm. "I love you," I said. "I'll see you in the morning." Dutiful, triumphant, Joyce closed her eyes.

1991

The phone rings. It's Saturday evening, late summer, and college students return to Norman, Oklahoma. Like water rising in irrigation trenches, they fill the apartments, bars, and restaurants. In a few weeks, the quiet, ten-minute walk to campus will rattle with students, and the feathery fragrance of beer, books, stale pizza cheese, and deodorant will hover on the walkways. I pick up the phone.

"It's nothing," Joyce says. "I just feel like talking."

"Okay." I swing into her lie. "What do you want to talk about?"

"I don't know. Whatever you want to talk about." Today her voice is clammy like shower mold. Her eyes will be blue butterflies struggling under a dropped net.

"Huh. Okay then. Did you know I'm going back to school?"

"Mama told me."

"Classes start in two weeks. I'll quit my job at the hotel but I'll still clean houses."

"Hm." She drops the syllable down her throat like a tongue depressor. Tension coils on her sigh. When she used to cry, she'd wipe her tears as though they blistered her.

"Okay," I say. "Okay, now. What's wrong?"

"Skyler's getting married," she says, and her voice cracks. "Skyler. He's leaving."

"Wow. Are you okay?" There's a trick to feeling out for pain, feeling into its acid-eaten shape. It's like looking at a stereogram until the two images snap into a picture. You look at the objects around you, but without interest, as though they aren't real. You can't touch them. You let your world lose meaning and suddenly, snap, only the other person's voice is reality, and you can feel every pinhole, every crumb on its surface. I stare at the proof of my life: the high wall of pine and cinder-block bookshelves, the secondhand volumes, the ceramic plates piled in the sink, the empty, greasy pizza boxes, the thrift-shop blouses on wire hangers in the closet. Things lose their names and then their shapes, then disappear. And when she speaks, I feel it: pain at two depths, a rug burn over a broken rib.

"No, I'm not okay. I feel so stupid." She sniffles. "It's not like there was anything. He's had this girlfriend a long time, and she's really nice. That makes it worse. He said he wanted the two of us to be good friends. I don't want to be her friend. I don't want him to move away." She sets her silence between us like a picnic basket, then unpacks it.

"He wrote me a card last year. I was having a lot of problems then. He wrote that he loved me and felt close to me. Now I think he just said that stuff because he was going to be a minister and he cared that way. Not how I wanted him to care."

"What did you want to happen?" She's twenty-nine. She's never known a man's naked body on hers, the unpredictability of hands, lips, legs. What does she do with sex? Is she Christ's and pure, the ache worthwhile, or is she afraid? Until twenty-five, I'd kept myself aloof in fear, the armor of resolute sexlessness intact. Sex is like a drink of water in a hot belly; I can no longer accept thirst. Which is worse, the intensifying dehydration of virginity, or the protracting drought that follows? Does she recognize her ache as sex? Does she call it love, or depression? "What did you want from him?"

"I don't know," Joyce says. "I wanted him to—I don't know. I just didn't want things to change. Good grief," she says. "It's stupid. Let's don't talk about Skyler. Tell me what classes you're taking. Mama said something about architecture or economics or something and she didn't sound like she knew. I don't need to talk about it. It's hard to say his name right now."

"Joyce, if he cares about you, he'll still be your friend." The words slouch and fold under my own self-image of misshapen lumpiness, my own distrust of attraction. "If he cares, he'll still be in your life."

"But not the way I wanted. It's the same every time I like a guy. I'm a friend, and that's all, and they get married. It hurts so bad. Why do I do this every time?"

Sexlessness, a mummification, a smothering, sorrowful hope. You're handsome, so witty, so good. Take my dignity, never kiss me. My body doesn't matter. Only don't send me away. Only let me love you.

I bubble shallow breaths through the long silence. The silence will eventually curl on itself, break, and splash into sentences.

Wednesday, September 26. "I'm not supposed to do this," the hospital coffee shop girl said, slipping a shot of cherry syrup and a lime into the soft drink. "But I can ring it up as a coffee."

"I appreciate it," I said, "thanks." Not lazy, I told myself, assessing the beverage's non-Sonic shortcomings. Not lazy. Practical. She'll be mad but she'll drink it.

Nitin, who'd left our Kansas house at four in the morning, stirred a second packet of sugar into his coffee. The hospital pulsated with morning activity. The lobby and hallways, deserted through the night, filled with the flat stroll of nurses in white shoes and varicolored scrubs, with lost tribes of fatigued, disoriented families. Nitin raised his steaming coffee cup in a parting toast as he veered into the smaller waiting room. "I'll watch for your mom and dad," he said. I carried the soda. Its sugary perfume drizzled toward the ICU, over the bland antiseptic cake of bandage-and-ointment odors.

"No," called Nurse Rita, her brown eyes thawed at her long shift's end. "Wait. She can't have that. Her chart's been changed. Nothing by mouth. She can't have any food or drink this morning."

Nothing by mouth. I know what it means. (Anything can happen. Your foot can get stuck. The train can come faster than you think. You won't believe it's happening and you'll freeze on the tracks.) "Not even a soda?"

"No. Nothing by mouth."

"Oh," I said.

"Are your parents here?" Nurse Rita ducks her head, forces me to look her in the eye. "The doctors are waiting for your parents."

(The train is just around a bend. The whistle swells the bones.) "They said they'd be here this morning. I can try to find them."

"Good. Dr. Schroeder'll be here soon. He wants to talk to all of you."

Beyond her open doorway, Joyce lay patient in her floppy heap of flesh. The incisive blue eyes, the tweaked pink smile, the delicately precise hands didn't belong to that mountain of fat, didn't belong to the surgery that awaited it. I wanted to pull her from her body. I wanted to run away with her.

She's lost twenty pounds. She's going to need new clothes soon. This will be easy from here on out, she thinks. She knows what she's doing now. Yet the mirror shocks her. She can't see the new leanness that the scale and her loose jeans indicate. Just like when she was gaining weight, she can't see the changes in her body. The fat is going from her belly, but she can't see the difference with her eyes. She feels a shock of fear. If she were to slide and start eating insanely again, the new fat on her belly would be invisible to her. It would be the same as before; she could damage herself blithely, be too far gone before she knows she's going.

Mama and I paraded behind Daddy into the ICU, conspicuous in our colorful blouses against the tunnel of white coats. Mama posted herself near Joyce's monitors. Daddy sidestepped toward Mama to make room for me. The three of us planted ourselves, a windrow, alongside the elevated angle of Joyce's bed. Dr. Schroeder, the slim, intense young pulmonologist, chased his blond hair back with a chiseled hand. Joyce relaxed near him, calm as he studied her face. She waited limp with trusting curiosity. Her wrists unstrapped, she folded her hands atop her belly.

"Ms. Vandiver," Dr. Schroeder said in prep-school tenor, soothing and grainy. "Here's what's happening. There's some free air and bleeding in your abdomen that we can't explain. The other teams of doctors haven't able to isolate its cause. But based on what we're seeing, we think we may need in the next few days to perform a colonostomy or some other type of surgery.

"Now," Dr. Schroeder said, "if we need to do a surgery like that, you're going to need more oxygen than you can get from the respirator. We'd like to do a surgery now so that your lungs can get the oxygen you need. In the surgery, tubes will be placed down your throat, to connect you to a machine that can regulate your breathing. We believe you need these breathing tubes to survive any later surgery.

"If we need to perform the second surgery we would have to place those tubes in a big hurry. We'd rather put the tubes in now, so we can take our time. We think that if we wait, we won't have time to do both the intubation and the other surgery you need. Do you understand?"

He searched subtle details in Joyce's serene face. Yes, she nodded.

Dr. Schroeder bounced quick glances at the family. Mama's face pinched inward, her lips tight. Daddy shifted his weight from one black sneaker to another, slid involuntarily jolting hands into jeans pockets.

"You have to give us permission to do the intubation," Dr. Schroeder said. He raquetballed a hard look off Mama, Daddy, me. "So before we go further, do you have any questions?"

Joyce motioned for her whiteboard. She checked Dr. Schroeder's face for clues of haste or boredom, then curved the marker tip slowly across the slate: What is the other surgery, the colonostomy?

Dr. Schroeder read the board and popped his head up in surprise. He struggled to hold propriety, a briefcase lid, on an escaping, looseleaf laugh. "I'm sorry," he said. "I'm not making light of it. It's just—well, ICU patients don't print this neatly. They simply can't. I've never seen it." Joyce fringed her eyelashes downward and with effort, boosted her right shoulder up, the shrug of dignified pride.

"My daughter's an elementary school teacher," said Mama, laughing too in the relief of participation. "You can take the girl out of the classroom . . ." Joyce raised her eyes to Dr. Schroeder and smiled: You understand my mother's nervous. And I'm still waiting.

"We're not sure yet that a colonostomy is what we'd need to do," Dr. Schroeder said, his returned smile shrinking. "In that type of operation, the surgeons will look at your colon and small intestine and remove any parts that might be damaged. We might do an exploratory, to see what's causing your symptoms." He handed the board to Joyce. "But we're not sure yet what we'll need to do."

Joyce nodded.

Dr. Schroeder leaned forward on the bed rail again, the blond hair blown back from the forehead, his eyes serious as Bunsen burner flame. "Now, there are a couple of things we have to talk about," he continued.

Joyce nodded again.

"First, before you agree, you need to understand. Once we put the tubes in, it may be very difficult to take them out again. You will have to be much stronger and able to breathe on your own. The longer we leave them in, the more difficult it may be to take them out. Do you understand?"

Joyce nodded. Mama nodded. Daddy nodded. I stared at Dr. Schroeder, feeling suddenly hypothermic. It's not just until after the surgery, I wanted to say. Her lungs can't do it on their own. Artificial respiration, months and months of it, right? Right?

Joyce wedged an additional word on the whiteboard. When?

"We need you to decide as quickly as possible," he said, "right now. As soon as you tell us, we'll start getting you ready. Now, I can tell you're lucid. You can make your own decisions. But you need to tell me, do you understand the decision you're making?"

"Yes." Her thirst squeaked and cracked.

"Ms. Vandiver, do you give us your permission to do the intubation today?"

"Yes."

A sigh rippled through the interns. "All right," said Dr. Schroeder. "The second thing. Now, these are standard questions. Any time we do this type of surgery we need to know whether you want Code Blue procedures. Do you know what those are?"

Daddy's narrow jaw trembled. Under his bald, freckled head, his forehead wrinkles deepened. Mama's lips thinned to pink toothpicks. Her black eyes darted from side to side.

"Code Blue procedures are the extreme, life-saving techniques we will use if you would otherwise die in the surgery. Like paddles," he said. Joyce nodded. She sent a glance, a tentative bounce as with a playground ball, toward Daddy, and then swiveled her attention back to Dr. Schroeder's silver-screen diction.

"It means that if your heart were to stop, we would use any means necessary to keep you alive. Now, before you make your decision, you need to know that these kinds of measures are risky to a person in a weakened state, and they can cause you to suffer effects that lead to death. This is a very personal decision," Dr. Schroeder continued. "We want to make sure your wishes are followed. Do you understand?"

She hesitated. I understand, she wrote.

"Ms. Vandiver, do you authorize the use of Code Blue procedures?"

She bounced the playground ball at her own feet, considered a pass, wondered if she'd get the ball back. "Do you want a few minutes to talk it over with your family?" Dr. Schroeder asked. Joyce nodded, relieved. "That's fine," he said, "we'll leave the room. But don't take long. We need to know soon." Dr. Schroeder turned the welder's flame of his eyes on me, on Daddy and Mama. "A few minutes only," he said.

"Well?" Joyce dropped her whisper down the swirl of Daddy's gaze.

"You have to tell them what you want, Joyce," he explained. "You know what I think. But it's not up to me. You have to say what you should do. Your mother and I can't say." He chided her willful silence. "Joyce, they need to know."

Mama slid her hand along the bed rail. Daddy placed his hand over hers without looking at her. Mama drew her shoulders back, looked up at Daddy, grateful, strengthened. What private admissions of possibility, emotions secret from daughters had passed between them? He thinks Code Blue is death in life, I thought. He pictures Joyce plugged in, her brain evaporated. Daddy looked in Joyce's eyes. "It's okay, Joyce," he said at last, his voice thick. "Whatever you say to do is all right with us."

Outside the glass bowl of Joyce's room, interns and Dr. Schroeder paced, strapping the message of hurry to flaming-arrow glances. Joyce's eyes cleared, like a girl who has finished and folded her Christmas list. Her face unclasped its doubt. "Do you know what you want?" Daddy asked.

Joyce nodded. She drew a deep breath, summoning a command she meant to hammer into us like nails. She separated the words, the pauses like the hammer rising. She nearly shouted it. "Keep—me—GOING," she said, and glared at our stunned aftershock.

"Good for you," I said, shaking off the trance. Mama and Daddy clung to the bed rail like magnets. "I'll go tell them."

She decides she'll learn to run. She finds an online training schedule that builds toward a 5K run. She only has to be able to run thirty seconds at a time to start. She can run thirty seconds.

She runs so slowly that people walking briskly pass her. She turns red, wheezes and puffs. Just keep going, she tells herself. You can. You can.

The day she runs a mile, she wants to jump and laugh. No one can take this away from her: One day, she ran a mile.

"She wants Code Blue." Dr. Schroeder hopped forward from the nurse's station, dropped his jaw to call the team together. "Wait—" I said, "please, talk to my father."

Irritation like the shadow of a hawk darkened Dr. Schroeder's face: Be quick, his somber eyes said—I want to be patient with you.

"My dad thinks Code Blue means Joyce might be left a vegetable." Dr. Schroeder's sudden focus was like a hot match head pressed to my face. I dared not flinch. "My uncle is in the last stages of ALS up in Bartlesville. My parents go there every day, shuttling between the two hospitals. My dad's afraid. He thinks he'll have to watch Joyce die slowly, on artificial life support, like he's watching my uncle."

Dr. Schroeder's face absorbed the pain, my parents' daily pilgrimage. The young, aristocratic face sagged. "I'm so sorry," he said. He nodded through the window toward Daddy, who strode, startled and obedient, toward a waved summons.

"I was telling your daughter," Dr. Schroeder said, "Code Blue is different from life support. If we use Code Blue," he said, "it's to keep Ms. Vandiver's heart beating throughout the operation. If she were to go into a coma or a similar state and needed to be kept alive artificially, it would be another situation. In that case, you would make a whole other set of decisions."

Daddy's courteous smile swung, a kite tail, on his pent exhalation. "I see," he said, with the faint quaver of prayer. He put out his hand for Dr. Schroeder to shake. "Thank you for letting us know."

"Thank you," I repeated, but Dr. Schroeder was already moving. His team's flurry barely admitted a brush back into the room to tell Joyce, whose own eyes stared in meditative, stubborn preparation, that we loved her. I left my parents there, in their goodbye, and hurried to Nitin, who stood, his lean angles unfolding into rapid lines. He ran a profit-and-loss calculation on my face. "They're intubating," I said. My voice clotted. The watery cherry limeade waited on the table. I sat the cup in the bottom of the trash can.

Nitin wound past me to my parents. "Norman, how are you?" he said. Daddy slowly shook his head, his blue eyes drooping in their hollows, toward the pronounced cheekbones. Mama touched the back of Daddy's arm. Her grimness was replaced by stiff-spined resolve, a forming, secret list of actions.

"Toppy?" asked Nitin.

"Well, they're going to do a surgery to put breathing tubes down in her," Mama said. "The nurses just told me it's a short surgery and not a very big deal. Joyce should be back in her room inside an hour, and we can come see her this afternoon."

"Do you want to go get some rest? Ann and I can stay here."

"No," said Daddy. "There's no need for everybody to stay. They'll call us when she's out of the surgery."

"Norman, I want to stay here," said Mama. "Why don't the three of you take a walk? I'll stay here and wait. Anyway, I'll need to call Hunter and them. You all go on now. Go on."

1992

"February. Jeremy C.'s dad died. He had a terminal disease which name was never told to me. He goes to counseling and therapy every day. James M. lost his dad a year ago in a robbery. I put the two of them together and they talk about their dads.

"... Sonia W. came up to me after school one day and said she brought me a present but I probably wouldn't want it. I told her to let me see it. She opened her hand and there was a yellow golf ball. I said, 'How did you know! I live across the street from a golf course and I couldn't play because I didn't have a ball!' The smile on her face was worth it. I still have that golf ball to remember that smile.

"... We were discussing the news and were on the story of the whale who died at SeaWorld. We were talking about how scientists would study samples from the whale to determine why he died. Jonathon S. said, 'You know why he died, don't you, Ms. Vandiver?' Reminder—kids still believe in adults and their knowledge. The All-Knowing Teacher is alive and well in someone's imagination."

My mother calls. Her East Texas twang swallows vowels like loose change among sofa cushions. Cancer, she says—cancer riddles Granddaddy's kidneys and liver. "They're not going to try and do anything for him," Mama says. "They're just going to try and make him comfortable. The doctors say it's a matter of days and weeks. I talked to Mother," she says, "and she's just Mother, she's just says it'll be a relief to her, you know, she's been expecting and waiting for a long time now."

A week later, on her birthday, Mama's voice is even softer. It's the voice of a woman floating in salt water, almost dreaming. "The phone rang this morning and I picked it up," she says. "It was Mother, and she just said, 'Well—happy birthday.'" Granddaddy's mind was clear to the last. He wasn't long in pain. "Mother said the funeral's Saturday. Have you talked to your brother? Mother says all the grandsons are going to be the pallbearers. I don't know if I told him that this morning. They're going to get the family spray, eight red roses and one white, for all the kids. Mother said if she died first they'd have them eight yellow and one white. If Daddy died first they'd be the red."

"Mama?" I want to hold her hand. I want her to hold mine. "Who's the white rose for?"

"That's for Jerry Don," my mother says. "Hadn't you ever heard us talk about Jerry Don? That's the baby Mother had that died, the last, when he was eighteen months old. He's buried there in Sardis Cemetery."

Responses clog the pocket at the back of my throat, and images fog thickly—Granny, alone, her dark eyes like muddy topsoil, her easy smile bitten inward. Granddaddy, his grin like a camp lantern, stretching his wrinkled hug from the VA hospital bed.

"Sardis Cemetery," Mama says. The car tires crunch down narrow lanes. Clouds gather. Pines sway in the November wind. "Ann, I've been coming here all my life. It just gets smaller and smaller." In Sunday shoes, we totter over gravel paths. The pallbearers lift the casket from the hearse.

Driving into Linden, Mama had pointed out the cramped frame house where she was born, the cropped lot where Granddaddy's soda shop once stood. She waved at a yellow-brick house. "Ann, I used to think that was the biggest house in the whole world," she'd said. She'd remembered the way to the funeral home, where Uncle Harold waited for us. Thin weeds of gray fought through his barbered brown hair. He led Mama and Daddy into an adjacent room. Stacks of pamphlets—"Ouch! It hurts to say goodbye"—reclined in tabletop display sleeves. Harold and Daddy returned to the foyer and spoke quietly. I wandered into the adjacent room. The casket there gaped open like a mouth full of candy.

Granddaddy's body had lain airless and strange in a blue suit and striped tie. Mama, pinched and wordless, ran her fingertips over opulent, crimson petals, eight red roses escorting a single white in a gown of ferns.

Now, at Sardis Cemetery, Mama leans her blocky curves on Daddy's angular frame. Hunter looms among the cousins carrying the casket toward the grave. On the basketball court and in the classroom, Hunter has always moved slowly, quietly, his aggressionless face an ice-caked deep freeze. But when Grandpa Ralph had died, Hunter had cried his way into seclusion; for months he'd spoken to no one. Steady and serious now, he lowers his corner of the silvered box.

Joyce guards Granny's graveside chair. During the service, while Granny sat shrunken and troubled and the aunts and uncles dabbed their eyes, Joyce had gripped my sweating hand. She'd passed the casket without stopping. Her conical body swayed in wads of denim dress. On the side-walk, she'd sobbed once, tears beading her eyelashes. We'd clasped our arms around each other's shoulders.

The pallbearers detach white carnations from their suit lapels and drop the flowers onto the casket. Hunter, last in line, bends and places his blossom carefully to one side. Duty complete, he links his arm in mine to keep away the cold. While Mama begins to cry in her own older sister's arms, Hunter and I walk for a while, reading the names on the stones.

We return to the ambient brightness of the Dallas metropolitan night. The aunts and uncles and cousins unlock their darkened houses, unfold rollaway beds, and show out-of-towners the spare towels and the travel alarm clock. Age has massaged itself into the aunts and uncles. In Uncle Shorty's sun-mapped face, lines radiate like desert cracks. Aunt Mickey's black hair is drizzled with wiry gray. Aunt Mary Elma's face looks like Granny's, apple-cheeked, soft lips drawn slightly inward, narrow-lidded eyes quick and shining.

Their photographs sneak among the frames that crowd Joyce's mantle. Unguarded school-photo smiles speckle the layered mural of sepia stares, family portraits. Joyce lifts a photograph from the mantle, toys with its wooden frame. Her frizzy hair falls in a fan of split ends past her straining bra hooks. Coarse black hairs arc around a flat mole on her second chin. The same faintly stale odor that clings to her bathroom wafts from the tented dome of her dress.

"Ann?" she says. "Tell me something." She speaks as if each word were a footstep further into a lake, her skirt weighted with rocks. "How did I get like this? How did I get so big?"

I stare at her, stupified. "To me," she says, "in my mind, I look like I did when I was twelve. Then I see myself in a mirror, and I just want to cry. How did this happen?"

"I don't know," I say. I avert my eyes from her distended, tallow bulk. I grope for judgment. I look to the crate of videotapes by the TV, to the kitchen housing frozen dinners and leftover Chinese takeout. "I mean, I don't know how you live."

"I try to eat right, and I don't eat all that much. Not more than other people."

Searching for a right response is like searching with toes for houseshoes in the dark. After a while you give up and walk barefoot on the cold floor. Briefly, I feel around for words: I love you. You're okay with me. You're a good person. I love being with you. "Do you exercise?" I ask. "I mean, not just walking at work. Do you go to a gym?"

"I don't like to feel sweaty. Sweat makes me feel hot. I can't stand it."

"Sweat cools your body."

"No, it don't."

"Yeah, really, that's how it works."

"Not for me." She pouts, defiant. "I get overheated when I sweat."

"Do you ever think about cutting your hair?" I ask.

"What's that got to do with anything?"

"It would look better."

Joyce catches her breath, signals the rigidity of anger. But her eyes soften. A thin smile forms, a dent in metal. She pats me on the arm, a goodnight, a dismissal. She turns away. "It's okay," she says. "I knew you wouldn't understand."

No one mentions her weight loss until she loses twenty-five pounds. Do others find it indelicate to mention weight loss? Maybe it's a safeguard. What if they say, "Wow, you've lost weight," and she says, "No, you remember me as larger than I am." Besides, everyone has seen a diet fail. If they congratulate her now, do they risk witnessing her failure as the fat returns? Or maybe nobody notices—maybe this change, central to her life and thought, doesn't register at all.

It's strange to her that people who meet her won't be meeting the same person she herself knew six months ago. They won't perceive obesity as others did just six months back. It scares her a little that she'll still know herself obese and might not see herself as others do. She still sees herself as a person struggling for health and balance. But that's no longer obvious. That image lives now only in her mind.

In the hospital, Daddy walked as though trying to stay inside the lines of a path only he could see. He walked as though in a glass anatomy, where any casual bump or sidestep might break a heart or brain. His shoulders succumbed to their accountant's slope. His hands hung like empty work gloves.

But outside, in the endless stadium of thick grass blades and Oklahoma sky, Daddy's adventurous gait returned, each joint easy and precise in its ball-and-socket range. He held his arms loose, his hands in jacket pockets, his long torso square over the trim hips. His long, graceful steps were like wide gear teeth, rolling backward the sidewalk's wheel. From under his ball cap brim, he noted the passing trees, buildings, clouds. When I walked with Daddy, I always felt we meant to find something worth seeing.

Nitin kept pace with Daddy. I walked behind them, two men in their ball caps and fall jackets, one graying but loose as a giraffe, the other sinewy, ready to spring, to hit something with a racket.

"I want to show you something I found," Daddy said.

We walked north of Utica Square, its long, green-gloved, asphalt fingers holding glass storefronts like loose gems. Spanish and Georgian houses at discreet but neighborly distances sank their backs into sloped yards. High and sparkling windows crowned velvet lawns, yew hedges, spiraled topiary. "I was just walking and I found it," Daddy said.

At the park's entrance, a berm of azaleas encircled a sandstone tower. Atop the tower, a full-sized bronze swan landed atop bronze water. We single-filed past the statue's stretched wings into the park. Black chain link hugged the pathway, separating us from a sunken lake. Hollow brown stems and pale green grasses with white seedhead tufts buffered the lake's algae'd edge. A goose in a sleek, black-striped cap sailed past a red-eyed male wood duck in its emerald helmet. Brown-marbled females tightroped up a low branch above the pure white backs of black-capped fowl. An upturned rowboat rested on a bank. Along the path, benches on iron feet sat under spongy puffs of trimmed green pin oaks. Caladiums nodded their palmy heads. Daddy and Nitin and I walked slowly, silently around the lake's long finger. And then we stopped. Trumpeter swans slept where water crept toward a willow. One swan wound its pearly neck and tucked its head against its vast, snowy back. The other kinked its neck, eyes closed, and dipped its black bill forward to its breast. Birds in the trees, birds floating, called across the water.

The surgery doesn't scare us, I thought. It feels like progress.

Daddy stood still and easy, hands in pockets, not shifting weight. A golden duck trailed a raised pincer of water. A breeze spanked a gingko branch; a turtle splashed into the lake. "I want to bring your mother here," Daddy said.

She has new habits. She wants to exercise, to eat so that her body feels clean, light. She doesn't want her gut to be constantly full of digested overfeeding. She has more energy, more self-respect. She knows there are some differences in how thin people are perceived and treated and she knows she will benefit from them. But thinness itself won't change her life. The self-respect will change her life.

Sometimes, when she sees lean women in the gym, a reflexive jealousy shoots through her but just as quickly dissipates. She knows that when she reaches her goals, no one will know she used to be obese. She too might then look like she couldn't possibly understand the challenge and pain of being fat. And that won't be true. So why should she assume these women couldn't understand? They're humans, hence will suffer or have suffered. Maybe they don't know fatness—but would she want them to? Would she really want others to feel that horrible, just so they could understand it? There's plenty of pain without that, she thinks. And maybe—God, she hopes—there could be plenty of understanding, too.

Search term: intubation.

The breathing tube slides in through the mouth. You lie sedated, under anesthesia, while your tongue is moved aside and the tube is inserted down your airway. When you wake up and feel the tube, you may begin to gag. You won't be able to speak or eat. The tube is painful in your throat, and your already exhausted body is racked with irritated coughs. But sedative drugs will dull the pain, and you will be able to breathe. While your nasogastric tube is attached to a bag that drips your food, your breathing tube is attached to the box that feeds you oxygen, that feeds you life.

Mama and I trundled down the hallway to ICU. I inherited Mama's short stride, a gait that lends itself to dawdling, to lollygagging. We don't move quickly enough to go anywhere by accident. Our legs are sturdy, the reliable props in the changing scenery of our weight. When Mama walks, she doesn't sway or waddle, but balances the heft of breasts and torso and moves with deliberate economy.

When her children were young and her hips curved out from a short waist under winter-squash breasts, Mama glided with purpose toward whatever she intended to do next. She stood, knelt, or sat: peeling a carrot, scrubbing a shower floor, hemming the sleeves of a dress. Then she moved purposefully toward the next thing. Mama never looked down, but always forward, blind with thought, ready to be distracted, ready to notice small things. She had a walk meant for a cruise ship, meant for companionable conversation, meant for small children to walk independently alongside.

Now, she rolled slightly to the outside of her feet, testing her heel or arch for some patch that did not ache. When her knees hurt, she walked slowly, as though pushing a vacuum. She edged into the ICU ward ahead of me, both of us scanning for silken blond hair, for the honest and realistic smile.

"She came through just fine." Nurse Carol pauses in her swift pass toward another patient's room. "No problems."

Joyce's freshly swollen face lay lax, dozing in the grog of pain medication. Thick, yellowish tubing depressed her lip's central pouch. White tape encircled her neck, raced up her cheeks. The tube draped toward the ventilator and monitor. Mama sidled through the room, contemplating the objects that enmeshed her daughter.

"I would stay in here so much more," Mama said, "but I just can't stand up that long. My knees get to hurting so I want to cry. Norman brings me ice packs, and it helps a little until I have to walk a ways again." She tapped the plastic sac of liquid nutrition. "This bagged food," said Mama. "I was talking to a woman from church whose husband had bagged food. I don't even want to tell you how much this costs per bag. Do you know how expensive this is? I don't even want to tell you." Her tired voice dangled from the words like an abandoned playground swing in the wind. "How many bags of this do you suppose she goes through every day? However many it is, it'll be more now, I guess. She won't be able to eat now."

Mama sighed. She tipped her salt-and-pepper crown backward on the hinge of her neck, and waited at the monitor as though it were a New Year's countdown. "Before, when we were in here. Did you see her pulse?"

"Yeah," I said, "after I saw you watching it."

"It didn't go up, not once that whole time. They explained about the surgery and the tubes and she stayed calm as anything." Mama touched Joyce's shoulder, tentative of hidden, taped tubes under the spread napkin of the gown. "I just couldn't believe it."

Thoughts tumbled like dice in a cup. "You know what we haven't done?" I said. "We haven't let any of Joyce's friends know she's in the hospital."

"I don't know who there is to tell," Mama said. "There was that one teacher, that Ms. Lopez, that was her friend in Dallas, but Joyce said they hadn't written in a long time. And Joyce never saw Lorena or Susie anymore. Joyce said they would be too busy with their own goings-on to get together with her."

"So there's nobody?" Desire throttled me. I wanted to see Joyce walk, how she balanced the enormous weight of belly and buttock over short, strong thighs and moved with deliberate economy. I wanted to hear the voice, whether the low, watery melody or whispered wheeze or the fiery anvil-slam.

"Well, I wouldn't say nobody," Mama said. "Mickey came right up. Joyce was always closer to family than anybody else. At least as far as she ever said."

Where would we look for clues to Joyce's life? For the past year, she'd lived behind the closed door of Hunter's old room. The small bedroom groaned with her: the flattened, full-size bed, the stereo equipment and TV, spilled piles of videotapes, cassette tapes, notebooks, craft supplies, genealogical research, scrapbooks. Joyce's smell, the smell of dried urine and discarded bloody cloth, the smell of rotting flesh, permeated the carpet and seeped under the closed door. What would confront my parents there?

"Mama? Say, I just thought this. If you're going to try to bring the hospital bed from LaNita's, what would you think if Nitin and I went and cleaned Joyce's room for you and took down her bed? Then you'd have room. And I know Joyce's room needs to be cleaned, if it looks like the last time I saw it."

Mama's relief was soft and pliable. "Well, now. That's a good idea," she said. "Would you do that? That would be a real big help." Mama grazed Joyce's shoulder with the backs of her fingernails. Her dark eyes glowed, fresh coffee for nighttime travel. "You've been a real big help," she said. "You've been a real big help to me and Norman through all this."

Both of us looked down at Joyce, at the tubes rubbing into her face, the needles buried in her arm, the beige thongs fastened tight around her wrists. I felt my way into her waking, discomfort, shock.

"Ann. We need to tell the nurse not to take off those straps any-more," Mama said. "If Joyce gets it in her head to do, she'll try to pull those tubes right out."

◆ **1993** ◆

"I'm in trouble." Joyce's voice is salty like blood. "You can't tell Mama and Daddy. I'll tell you but you have to promise not to tell them."

The hair prickles on my arms. "If you're in trouble, I might have to tell them."

"No," she says, firm as a padlock. "Mickey knows. Mama and Daddy can't find out."

"Okay," I say.

"It started two years ago. Me and Mickey went to one of those time share shows? Where you get a free radio for going to look at the place?

Ann, it was such a nice place. They had a lake and trails and it was so quiet in the morning. And only a little ways from Dallas. They had little apartments where you could stay. There was a program where you could order your food to fit a special diet."

"Oh, you didn't."

"Well, I had the money. Anyway, they said how a lot of people joined up to lose weight. It was supposed to be a good place for me to go and get healthy. I was so excited about it. I got to thinking how I could get away from all the stress."

"What happened?"

"When I wanted to use the place it was always booked, and I could never go. But I figured oh, well, and I paid them off. It took me a long time. And now they're saying I never paid them and I owe them six thousand dollars. They say they don't have any records that I paid them. They're going to sue me."

"Joyce? What are you going to do? Can't you work it out with them?"

"What is there to work out? I say I paid and they say I didn't. And they sent a whole bunch of notices and even though I called and called they won't talk to me and now they're going to take me to court. I don't have six thousand dollars."

"What's Mickey doing?"

"She got me her attorney. I think it'll be okay—I mean, it has to be—I paid them everything I owed and I never even got to use the place—but I just feel sick. Nothing turned out like it was supposed to. I wanted so bad—I had to tell somebody. It's a relief to tell somebody."

"Are you okay?"

"I guess so. What choice do I have? Mickey says the attorney is a good one and everything'll be okay as soon as he straightens it out."

"Do you have enough money to pay for the attorney?"

"Mickey's helping. I'll pay her back."

❖   ❖   ❖

She wishes for a world where fat people are not ridiculed when they attempt health. She wishes for a world where no one rolls their eyes when a fat person eats a salad. She wishes for a world where people spontaneously, sincerely applaud the fat man in the gym who manages his first full lap around the track. She wishes for a world where a fat woman never feels like she doesn't deserve to wear a pretty dress. Where the person who says, "What's the point, most people just gain it all back," is shunned by polite company.

Thursday, September 27. Fall began in northeastern Oklahoma with lazy sunlight, a golden noon after white-hot August. Sparse rainy days were chased by sweaty stretches, the clouds drifting low. Green deepened in tree and roadside weed. Sweet gum burrs turned brown, dangling yet on branches, and the river's summer shine sank into its long blue vein.

Nitin and I drove in shirt sleeves, our jackets spooning in the back seat of his car. Toll road, state highway, county road, and old river road funneled us toward the mission: we planned to leave her room not only clean, but empty, to box the scrap and froth of her collected life and burn the rest.

I pictured the cramped bedroom as I'd seen it last, dirty clothes in piles, dirty dishes stacked on the bureau. Joyce lived behind the closed door. She'd plod out to fill a plate, then rock under her furry cape of brown hair back to her sanctuary, to her own TV channel, to solitude. Cautious as an armadillo, she'd wait until Mama and Daddy's car wheels spat the last of the driveway gravel backward. Then she'd creep out, safe, to slide a record album onto the turntable spike; to balance her lower back across a chair and click a chain of links on the desktop computer screen; to breathe, unwatched, unscrutinized.

"Daddy wants us to look for her papers," I said. "Bank records, checkbook, insurance, anything like that. I think they told him at the bank he can arrange to draw on her account."

"How hard will it be to find that in her stuff?"

We turned up the driveway's gravel slope. "She doesn't throw anything away," I said. "None of us do. Oh, and Mama said to go ahead and burn the mattress and box spring. They're old and hard and flat, she said."

The little brick house sat modest in the trim green lawn. Daddy's pear orchard towered, tall green flames, over the pasture. Toward the pond, locust and oak trees clustered, hilltop guardians. My house key admitted us into the silent laundry room, the darkened kitchen. Closed drapes divorced the living room from the day outside. Hunter and his family were out, but were still in temporary residence. Their folded laundry and open suitcases strung across the living room floors. Sticky breakfast plates sat like dealt cards near the kitchen sink.

We carried rolls of trash bags, cans of carpet freshener, packets of yellow rubber gloves. The sweet, faint smell of rot floated under the closed door of Joyce's bedroom. I hauled air into my lungs and turned the knob. Sunshine through the open curtain blinded us. The acrid smell, an engulfing wall of fetid odor, rushed from the room. Nitin dropped supplies, tourniqueted his upper arm around his nose. We edged into the stench and the debris.

Nitin's watering eyes darkened with pained amazement. "First," he said, coughing, "everything off the floor. Let's clean the carpet."

"We'll need those rubber gloves," I said. I waded through fast food wrappers, between towers of paperbacks. I unlatched the window and hammered the frame upward with the heel of my hand.

Air freshener dissipated, useless. Joyce's body odor seemed to saturate not just the carpet, but the paint. The smell hung in the closet with her clothes and wafted from the squashed bed. Hands in rubber gauntlets, we stripped the sheets and stuffed them with the pillows in a plastic trash bag to be burned. The mattress was a canvas of layered oval browns and yellows, a history of incontinence. Nitin heaved it upright. I followed him bumping toward Daddy's trash pit, which the family with intractable loyalty still called "the pond." The tossed mattress sledded down the unburnt brush pile. The box spring sailed into the pond after it, a platform for the dozen bags to follow, stuffed with litter that had been her life. Wadded paper, graying flags of soiled underwear; plates and bowls caked with dried milk and ketchup; bread crusts and fried pie wrappers; dresses, skirts, bath towels balled up and stiff with dried urine; we threw them all away. Into the trash bags went her hairbrush and comb, half-used body fragrance sprays. Nitin began to sort and stack: five large cartons of videotapes. Five more of books. Four of music, compact discs and cassettes. He shoved the boxes against the wall.

"Do you know how much money this represents?" he said. "How did she spend that much money on these useless things and claim she had no money for her health?" He bent and tossed a spiral notebook toward the half-filled trash bag.

"No, not that," I said.

"Look at it. It's just a bunch of sports scores she wrote down from TV, the ballplayer rosters. Here's another one, a list of random people with the movies they were in." He flapped an open notebook at me. Joyce's round print paraded across the top line: Research on My Favorite Actors.

"It's in her handwriting," I said. "It goes here, there's an empty dresser drawer. All her journals go here. Jewelry, her keepsakes, any photographs you find. I guess we could put the cameras there, too. How many are we up to now?"

"Nine," Nitin said. He handed me a snapshot camera. "And four tape recorders. Why did she need so many cameras?" He shook his head, his shoulders tense as an archer's, his eyes and lips severe. "I don't understand. I don't see how she could live this way. I don't understand how your parents let it go."

"What would they do?" I said. It is what it is, I thought, no answers.

"It's their house, their property she was destroying. They could threaten her. Give her a month. Get help, get counseling, or get out."

Loyalties snapped at me, sets of pincers. Sister: Let me fight my battles alone. Husband: There's a time to say "should," a time to impose, to act. Parents: Where will she go outside our acceptance, when she can't even clean herself? You cannot, I thought, put yourself in someone else's shoes insisting the shoes be repaired first. "It's evident she was sick," I said. "I can't imagine how hard it's been for them to face."

We rested, disagreeing in silence. Then, while Nitin vacuumed powdery coats of carpet freshener, I spread Joyce's papers on Mama and Daddy's trimly quilted bed. Insurance records, pay stubs, bank statements, pension correspondence, all in separate piles. I slipped a letter from its envelope. "Ms. Vandiver," it said. "We're frankly shocked you've asked for your deposit back. You left your apartment in a state of filth, with broken furniture and a foul odor that required repeated fumigations. Your deposit did not cover the costs of cleaning. We have enclosed a bill for damages." My head felt heavy as if with sleep, as if I'd breathed exhaust fumes, the doctors' voices, mortality statistics.

"I'm glad we did this today," Nitin said, reading the letter. "This would have been terrible for your parents."

I felt like letting go, like drowning in Joyce's paper past. "She's really not coming home again, is she," I said.

"It's hard to hear your parents talk about it." A quick spasm of painful compassion tugged Nitin's face, dragged iron filings of sympathy through his voice. "It's hard to hear your mother looking forward to Joyce coming home. Throw it away," he said, handing the letter back. "We'll burn it."

1994

"Hardest story of the year.

"One day about 12:30 Rachel's mom comes and signals me to meet her in the hall. She has been crying. She tells me that her year-old daughter had been living with a foster family. That morning there had been a shooting close to the family's house. A bullet had found its way to the baby. It hit her in the head, killing her instantly. Rachel was being taken home so she could be told.

"The day before Rachel came back to school I had a talk with the class. It was rough. They had so many questions that were unanswerable. The counselor arranged to come in for a session with the whole class.

"By this time 2 weeks had passed. Rachel was going to counseling with her mother. We were all concerned about Rachel because she hadn't cried yet.

"The counselor came and read the class a story about someone whose grandpa had died. It worked. When the story was finished the counselor asked for questions. Rachel's hand went up first. She told about seeing her sister in a coffin. Next person asked a question. All of a sudden, Rachel began crying uncontrollably. A couple of kids hug her. The counselor helps Rachel up and turns her around and Rachel sees me. She ran and buried herself in me. After she calmed down the counselor took her to her office.

"Rachel would talk to me often about her feelings. She would be angry that someone would hurt her sister. She would miss her and pretend to play with her. She would be scared someone was going to shoot her.

"It was a long process but after 4 months Rachel finished her therapy. She laughed more and her bad dreams were almost gone."

We are incontrovertibly adult, twenty-seven and thirty-two. We see the stories of each other's lives like lightning on the other side of mountains. An event flashes, a hot hand in a windowpane, and we count toward the thunderclap, the next installment of the story. One one thousand. Two one thousand. And the days drizzle by in our own lives until we are together at Christmas, attempting to recollect our old life under the shared umbrella. We peer at one another. Can we still divine the girls we were, the girls we knew? In the wood-paneled, shag-carpeted formidability of my converted-ranch duplex, we sit politely as unacquainted dinner party guests.

Talking, I press my adult life flat like an origami swan. I tell Joyce I have a job, but not how I dread it; tell her the weight gain but not the depression; tell her Nitin is a friend. I don't tell how I have fallen in love with his voice, hard as peanut shell and hiding a sweetness, sustenance—a voice infused with Bombay exhaust and coastal salt, with left-behind hard-liquored college nights, a voice like an architect's rendering, dark lines and soft, hand-swept color.

"We see each other most weekends," I tell her as we pull on our coats. "In the summer we went hiking a lot. And when I was really sick last winter he took care of me."

She nods, courteous. I expect we will tour silently through the electric market of color, the Oklahoma college-town yuletide. But in the car, weaving slowly through suburban decks and tents of light, Joyce opens like a chest of drawers. She flings over me, like quilts over a mattress, stories of teaching and stories of children.

"I'll tell you what really gripes me," she says. "I mean this really gets my goat. People complain and complain about the system but nobody wants to read to their own kids. Parents want to drop their kids at school to learn math and reading and basic thinking and to use their imaginations and right from wrong and all the social skills. They want the kid to come back home all fixed and then they ignore him! I can't tell you. Getting parents to go over the kid's homework, or even care what the kid is doing in school—it just kills me. There you have some bright kid, and his mom won't even come to one parent-teacher conference. What does that tell the kid?"

"Mom doesn't care."

"It's more than that! It tells the kid they don't have to care, that school and reading is all just a big waste of time. And who's the kid supposed to believe, me or Mom?" She shakes her head. I suddenly notice she's combed her long hair sleek, a painstaking effort. "And then, like this one kid, the counselors wouldn't test his learning disabilities because his mother wasn't emotionally stable. I felt really sorry for that kid. He wouldn't take any help from anybody. He's the only kid I ever gave up on helping."

"Really? The school can decide not to test a kid if the mom's not stable?"

"Well, what good would it do if it sends her over the edge with the kid every time the school implies he's not cutting it? The bureaucracy can make me a little crazy. I had this one kid, Marco, who got bumped up to second grade. But due to, I don't know, some crazy law, he had to stay on the first grade roll. They say they want kids to achieve but then they punish them when they do. These kids," she says, "a lot of them come from tough home situations."

"Poverty?"

"Violence. Last month one little girl who is always there on time didn't show up. The security guard came around to say her aunt had been killed in the house by an intruder. Sara saw the whole thing happen. She never came back to school."

"But is that typical?"

"Ann, it's all the time. Sometimes it's—not funny, but I don't know the word for it. There was this one boy, Henry. I was trying to explain about broken bones and casts and I didn't have any kind of props. I remembered Henry's mom had her arm in a cast. Henry sat me straight though. His mom didn't break her arm. She was shot! I asked him how that happened and he said she was breaking into her boyfriend's house and he shot her. Then other times . . ."

"What?"

"Well, last year one of the dads had beat up the mom and had threatened to kill the kid. That was when I was teaching in the portable, you know, basically a trailer? Anyway he was seen stalking the portable. He said he was going to kill me and his kid. We had to have security walk us back and forth everywhere for a month until he got caught. Don't tell Mama and Daddy that one."

"Uh. Yeah."

We turn a corner. Three large houses blaze white in the cul-de-sac, the rooftops thickly frosted with red, blue, green. Buckets of live poinsettia, scarlet in the incandescent drip, skirt entryway pillars.

"Oo-wee," Joyce says. "Look at that."

"Hey, you want to look at Christmas lights when we get to Muskogee?"

"Sure," she says.

"I haven't been back in a while. I don't know where houses like those are, do you? Do you know where the nice houses are?"

Even in the gray interior light of the car I can see her face tighten in reproof, her eyes widen with pity, with the inability to give up on me. "Nice houses are where nice people live," she says.

She loses thirty pounds in seven months. She can, looking backward, say it in one sentence, as though it were quick, easy, encapsulable. To sum it up denies the rigor of daily confidence, with no proof that her goal lies ahead in the fog of her future.

In the past ten years, she's lost and regained fifty pounds twice. What makes her think she'll keep the weight off now? She shoves the thought aside. She's lost thirty pounds. She has to stay the course and hope to find out, eventually, why this time is different.

Mama stripped the papery garlic peel of her question. "There's one thing, I don't know what will happen. If Joyce doesn't get well enough to sign those papers she won't qualify for state medical benefits. You know how many specialists come see her now? And I don't want to think about the medicine." Her square hands spidered over a fanned stack of waiting-room magazines. "Norman and I were meaning to ask you. Do you think you and Nitin could find out from the hospital about the bills? What happens to the bills?"

I promised to find out. Nitin and I wound through the glass tunnel connecting the hospital's buildings. We presented ourselves in the business office like siblings at Santa's lap. The office's lunchtime hush was symphonic with glass door hiss and elevator hum. The administrative assistant's large eyeglasses glinted under the fluorescent panels. We traded a series of declarations with her, capped with a single question.

"My sister is a patient, uninsured and indigent. My parents are concerned about the bills."

"Your sister is an adult, and the bills are in her name. She is responsible for her own bills."

"Good. What happens if she dies?"

"Have the doctors told you that?" The woman raised long fingers to her lips. "Is that really likely?"

And what do I believe? Is it likely Joyce will die? Am I betting on her death? Where is the line between likelihood and belief, between belief and knowing? Nitin rested his brown hands on the desk as though he were closing a lid. His rich voice compelled the woman away from her question and back toward ours. "The doctors say she could die," he said. "It's something the family needs to be ready for."

"Well." She trips, barely regretful, on office habit. "You can't get blood out of a turnip."

"Oh. Yeah. So what happens to the bills, if they don't transfer to my parents?"

"Even if we can't collect," she said, "your parents aren't responsible."

Search term: morbid obesity.

The medical profession has set a range of ideal body weights for each of us. These are the weights at which our bodies are the least likely to develop health problems due to excess fat around our bones and organs. There are words for people whose weights are lower than the ideal, or higher than the ideal. For a certain range above the ideal, that word is "overweight." For the next range higher, the word is "obese." If you are one hundred pounds over your ideal weight, or 50 to 100 percent more than your ideal weight, a hospital will note that you are "morbidly obese." Statistically, you are at much greater risk of the killers—diabetes, high blood pressure, strokes and heart attacks, arthritis, and complications unraveling from your lowered blood oxygen levels.

Joyce lay awake in the cramped glass cubby of ICU, a living, breathing prize in the metal and plastic claw arms of bed and machinery. "Hello, turnip," I said. Joyce abridged her eyes into a half-blink, impatient with blithe nonsense. Chips, she spelled.

"Right here," I said. "Only I'm not sure how to do this now." The plastic tubing had immobilized her mouth. She couldn't lift or turn her head on the flimsy pillow. "You sure you can still have them?"

Ripples of impatience flexed the light brown eyebrows. Chips, she spelled.

"Here, let me show you." Nurse Carol breezed into the room, her chin pointed under a white smile. As though I had been embraced from behind, my shoulderblades saluted one another and my breastbone lifted. Cool, sterile, ICU air doused my lower lungs. I'd been standing hunched; Nurse Carol made the room safe to breathe. "Like this," Nurse Carol said. "You try."

My sweater sleeve brushed Joyce's gowned breast. A single ice chip swished in the miniature spoon's white bowl. I steadied the spoon's edge on the heavy tube and depressed the corner of Joyce's lower lip. With my fingers I pushed the ice chip onto her tongue. Joyce's lips felt like overripe apricots. The ice chip melted against my finger as it passed into her fevered mouth. "That's it," Nurse Carol said. She poured her warm smile like a sink bath over Joyce, over me. "She'll be thirsty all the time now. She can have lots of those ice chips; they're good for her."

I pressed another ice chip into Joyce's mouth. "She looks so young," Nurse Carol said. "Ms. Vandiver, it's hard to believe you're thirty-eight.

You don't have even a strand of gray hair." Joyce's eyes shift, briefly buffered with crinkling lines, toward the compliment. Thank you, she spells. Joyce's hair, the brown of a halved pecan, was like an Amish woman's, untouched by spray or gel or electric heat. Her skin, unadorned, unclogged by makeup, was smooth and dewy, the creamy color of mock orange blossoms. Her eyes, light blue coronas around dark pupils, fixed on her visitors with calm acceptance, patient curiosity. She waved her strapped right hand in loose circles to recapture my attention. Dark purple and black bruises bloomed in her white tulip arm.

"More chips?" I asked. Joyce's nod was like a slowly pressed piano key. Tallmet, she spelled, then winced and waved her hand to erase the garbled words.

"You're tired," I said. She nodded, lifting her eyes and gathering her concentration. Talk to me, she spelled.

I chased an ice chip out of the spoon into her mouth. "Don't try to move your head if it makes you too tired," I said. "I remember the signs for yes"—she made a loose, knocking fist—"and no"—she finger-cymbaled her straightened index and middle fingers to her thumbtip—"yeah, so just do that, okay? Now let's see. What have I got to talk about . . ." Her chest rose with an artificial breath and fell, sinking flat. She watched me, a child waiting for a bedtime story.

"The nurses and doctors say you came through your surgery just fine," I told her, pushing another ice chip. "But I guess you know that already. There's no more talk, at least today, of any other surgery. They'll be taking a lot more X-rays to see if they can figure out the problem."

Xrays every night, she spelled. Not new.

"Oh. Well, here's something. Did Mama tell you that I cleaned your room?" The finger cymbals clicked together: No. The blue eyes narrowed, wary. "We wanted to go ahead and get it ready for when you come home. And Daddy had me collect up all your bank records and stuff in case of paperwork."

Papers, she spelled.

"We organized everything into a big accordion envelope. We put all your videotapes in those big clear plastic boxes. Don't worry, I didn't take any of your books or music or anything. It's all there waiting for you."

Papers, she spelled again. In garage.

"Oh," I said. "We didn't go out to the garage."

You, she spelled, grappling for a simple verb. You sort papers. Not Mama, Daddy.

"You want me to go through your papers before Mama and Daddy do." The loose fist knocked: Yes. "Is there stuff you don't want Mama and Daddy to find?" The fist knocked. Her stare gripped me.

"Okay," I said. "I'll make sure. I'll tell Daddy that's what you want. Hey, Joyce? You know that Nitin and I have to go back home this afternoon?" Her fingers rest on the sheet. The lower lip works against the tube. "I know, I want to stay here too. But I have to show up at work sometime, right? Carol says nothing's going to happen for a few days, that you'll just rest and recover from the breathing tubes." Joyce's chest rose and fell. "Look, I know you're fighting, Joyce," I said, "but I want to see you say it."

Go home, she spelled. I love you.

"Then tell me you're fighting," I said. "Tell me."

1995

"The whole class looked forward every morning to Ms. Vega coming to the room. She would say, 'Good morning, Ms. Vandiver. Good morning, class.' The class replied, 'Good morning, Ms. Vega. If it's to be, it's up to me. Se tiene que ser, depende di me.'"

Owning a camera is like owning the world. Whatever you see, whatever touches you, can be both captured and set free. Captured: the children in their caps and gowns, forever six and smiling. Set free: children liberated, if briefly, from the fight to believe that they matter.

The moment of prying a new camera from its packaging is sacred as a nun entering her prayer. It is the world, waiting in an untouched box. It is the world, waiting behind Joyce's eyes. Joyce has forgotten how many cameras she owns. She buys them, coveting the black mirror of each new lens. She chooses snapshot cameras as premiums with purchases or with credit card applications. She cancels the cards and keeps the cameras.

A snapshot camera nests in her shoulderbag. Another rides in her glove compartment, a third in the back seat floorboard. A camera sits ready on her fireplace mantel. A camera lies with the yellow wooden ruler and attendance chart in her school desk drawer. Other cameras in storage and at the bottom of dresser drawers wait like the dead in graves before the resurrection.

On a Saturday morning, golden in oblique autumn light and quiet in the remnant peace after Friday night high school football games, Joyce picks a compass direction and drives out of Dallas. Her car seat molds to the broad speed bumps of her lower back and thighs. She rewinds a cassette tape—standards from the forties, corn-syrup melodies and brassy ditties—and she sings along, her raised voice loopy, cracking. She stops wherever she wants and snaps historical markers, scenic outlooks, the colors of tree and sky, cattle nudging close to barbed wire. She drives to east Texas, to spend the day with Aunt Mary Elma and to hear stories of faraway childhoods and our grandparents' youth. She drives to the zoo, where she carefully presses coppery film into the camera's chambered teeth. She can't walk far without tiring, hurting. She sits on a stone bench, waits to center the viewfinder on the wild flesh of a great, furred animal, a gorilla, a polar bear. While she waits, she trains the lens on a thick-waisted clump of black-eyed Susans by the path. She shoots the clouds, searching out the shapes of dragons and of angels.

She memorializes her classroom. She staggers down to a single knee, to child's-eye-view near a tabletop scattered with construction paper triangles, pillared with glue bottles. She corrals the children in the frame as if in her arms. She clicks, captures a small girl, tongue between teeth, puzzling out a new flash card word. She embraces the children by pressing the camera button. The shutter opens and closes like her heart valves.

She takes pictures as a form of love. It is a way of taking and of giving, of worshipping her world. She goes out alone, independent, like a prophet fasting for God's visions in the desert. When she takes a picture, she acknowledges beauty and states her faith that she too has a place in that world. A picture is a prayer. A picture is pure thankfulness, pure joy.

She fills the film with images, and stress falls away like flaking paint from an old house. Expectations slough like flecks of skin in the bath. Defiance and bitterness crumble away from her smooth, expectant face. She is restored. Brimming with images that she chooses, she frees herself of all the images that have been projected onto her. She soars from the spine-smashing weights of perfection and imperfection. Camera in hand, Joyce makes herself visible. It is the way she looks to herself, the self she believes those who might love her would see. Picture by picture, she builds her own portrait. Frame by frame, she sets herself free.

The therapist says, "You talk like you believe you weigh three hundred pounds." The therapist means to point out that she doesn't see herself correctly. But she thinks, Three hundred—that's the magic number? It would be okay to despise myself if I weighed three hundred pounds? I'd be right to feel ugly at that weight?

It dawns on her: there is no magic number. The emotions of overweight and body image are the same for everyone. It doesn't make any difference how her actual body looks to herself and others. The feelings have nothing to do with measurable weights. A woman twenty pounds overweight can feel as miserable and ugly as another at a hundred and twenty pounds overweight. One person may be saddened looking at an obese woman—another may be equally dismayed looking at a spouse who's let five pounds creep on. She herself finds women silly who think that five to ten "extra" pounds doom them to unattrac-

tiveness and unhappiness—yet she believes in her own doom at thirty pounds more than a numerical goal.

No matter what weight she is, she thinks slowly, one person might think she weighs too much while somebody else thinks she's healthy and attractive. So she can't base her self-approval on how she thinks others see her. She can't base her love for herself on how she views her body. But she's done that for so long . . . if having a body isn't about the approval of others, or her own self-judgment . . . then it can only be about health. It's about keeping herself alive and able to move and do the things that bring her joy. Her body isn't about her weight. She wants to shout, exultant. It's about her life.

Autumn and October slid over eastern Kansas with a lighthearted gaudiness: trees burst from their green cocoons, orange and red and gold against a turquoise sky. A day passed, then two, then three, and routine returned. Calls to the hospital, reports of Joyce's stability bracketed the day. She's the same, the nurses said. She's doing fine, said Mama.

I worked from early morning, when the offices were still dark, until late, when my colleagues had gone home. Technical documentation projects had piled up, like a fortress I could hide in. Documentation made sense. Nothing left ambiguous, nothing a guess. Step through a task, one, two, each paragraph an accomplished goal, the reader gaining confidence, the writer building a legacy, expertise. I littered my workspace with documents in progress. I collected the junior writer's projects for winnowing, for editing. In her early twenties, bright, willowy, and eager, thoughtful, she listened as I explained how to prepare the reader for difficult procedures, how to see into the reader's doubt, how to differentiate between simple accuracy and the truth. She lay an arm across her draft and stopped me.

"How's your sister?" she said.

"She's not well."

"She'll get better."

"Chances are she won't."

"No, you can't say that," she said, startled and dismayed. "You have to stay positive, hope for the best. Right?"

"This—it makes me feel good—that you want to cheer me up. But look. Sometimes people don't get well. The chances are very, very high that my sister might die. That's not defeatism. That's the truth. See, we don't have to talk about it." I edited my stern face, looped a small, closed smile over my chin. She nodded in sad compliance, laying her concern aside like a book she'd read when I wasn't watching. She courteously refocused on the red ink. "See, it's a thing that's happening," I said.

Nitin, at home, cooked rice and spicy yellow lentils, antithesis to the hospital warming trays and vending machines. At the stove, Nitin stirred, sniffed, tasted for salt. His hands sure on knife and vegetables, he sliced fine flakes of onion, tender tomato cubes. As he cooked, he sang to the cats and practiced his golf grip, the lean torso torqued to swish an invisible three-iron through invisible fairway. "Mmwah," he said, kissing me hello. "Dinner's almost ready."

"I have to call my parents first. They're at the hospital. I think they're pretty tired."

Nitin deftly blotted the scowl that sketched itself on his cheekbones. He stared impassively into the soup pot. "Where's your brother been?" he said.

Loyalties clashed; I groped for an explanation that wouldn't sound like an excuse. Where's Hunter been, indeed. Where's he been since boyhood, since we knew without saying it that he saw things differently, or didn't see them; where's he been since childhood anxieties first pulled his words back into his sinuses, only to emerge as a blurred string of sounds; where's he been in the years he fought toward fearlessness, a marriage, professional promotions, the ability to counsel, to lecture, to teach. Where's he been since he first learned to fling his smokescreen, I know! I know! at family unpleasantries. "I don't think he knows," I said. "Start without me."

Preambles drifted away while the phone was ringing. I didn't care how thickly I plastered my reputation for high-handed superiority and bossy, imperious foolishness. "Hunter," I said. "You need to go see Joyce."

"I know," he said, curt, fending off the cudgel.

"No, you don't know. Look. I'm not trying to harass you here. Hunter, she's really sick. I bet Mama and Daddy haven't even told you how sick she is."

"Not really," he admits, gruff.

Hysteria, like steam from dry ice, drifts into my voice. "Hunter, you need to go see her. She asks for you all the time. She's really, really sick. You need to go see her now."

Once, Hunter had caused a car accident. Daddy had driven across three counties to bring him home from an emergency clinic. Alone with Hunter late that night, with his smile and his leafing through the refrigerator, my panic and furious impotence had burst out; I'd yelled at him, hit his chest with my fists. Don't ever do something that stupid again! Don't ever do something like that! And Hunter had grabbed my wrists, pulled me close, a bear hug against his tall, heavy frame. Sh, sh, he'd said. I'm all right. I'm all right. It's over now, it's okay.

"Ann," he said, soft now as a pencil rubbing of a gravestone. "I'll be there this week."

1996

"Will your sister get some help about her weight?" Muskogee pin-wheels past the car windows, drab and wintry. Nitin drives to the hotel. Five days have passed since a handful of friends witnessed our courthouse wedding, then gathered around our kitchen table with wine and tortellini and crimson-sugar roses sashed on white sheet cake. It's Christmas now; my family has gathered along with the new son-in-law, whose question startles and hushes me. We saw her in the summer, in Dallas. She'd wedged herself into a top-tier ballpark seat to sit unmoving through nine innings, sweating, frustrated. Her head poked like a tiny, grumpy mask from the sloping beanbag of vast knit skirt and flowered T-shirt. Her stomach squished over the armrests; her urn-shaped calves buckled inward from waterlogged ankles. It's no surprise he'd ask about Joyce's weight. But I hadn't expected that he, remote, pragmatic, would care for her, would extend himself. I'm used to no one daring to ask. I'm used to us ignoring what must be pain.

"I've asked her. I've asked her about doctors, about diets, about programs. She says it's too expensive, or that it won't work."

"Well, if she doesn't do something soon she's going to get sick and that's going to be more expensive." A muscle twitches at the back of his jawline.

"What do you mean, sick?"

"A person can't be that overweight and not have health consequences."

A dream recurs. Granny is alive and Joyce is sturdy, healthy. In summer dresses, they wait for me in a park. Granny laughs; she wants to walk down the flower garden paths. Joyce's eyes glow and she holds out an expressive arm, motioning me closer. She wants me to move faster. She wants things to move forward. After this dream, I wake blissful and sober as the dream cools: I can't hug my Granny, and my sister wrestles her own body to make it walk or stand.

"Well, sure," I say. "Eventually there could be consequences. But I don't know what else she should do. She says she's trying to eat healthy. All that's in her refrigerator are frozen diet dinners."

"And how many diet meals does she eat at one time?"

It's justice, someone besides me disapproving. She disapproves of me, too, after all, of references to irreverent movies, of eye makeup, of godless friends and churchless Sundays. She disapproves how I've forgotten childhood games, jokes we once shared. But her disapproval means she hasn't given up on me. Her disapproval makes me loyal. "I don't know. I do know the only kind of snacks she eats are diet snacks. Sugar-free, fat-free stuff."

"Diet snacks? Those are still just empty calories! What about fresh vegetables? Does she get any exercise?" A photograph slides into memory, Joyce leaping in mid-layup near the back yard goal.

"I think she walks. She stopped exercising, really, after she left college. She used to walk all the time. She doesn't like to sweat. She says it makes her feel hot and miserable. Yeah. Can I tell you? I get scared every time I think of her. She's been gaining weight for years and she always says she eats healthy. It's to the point I can't think about her without feeling sick and scared, and mad that she would let herself get this way."

Yesterday, Daddy and I had walked to the pond. He lit a newspaper torch and shoved it into the pit of wood and trash. Hands in windbreaker pockets, Daddy had watched the smoke rise. "I'm real worried about Joyce's weight," he'd said.

"Mm," I'd said.

"Your mama's awful worried. But she thinks there's not much that can be done. Do you know? Do you know anything we could do?"

"Daddy, I don't know." God help me. I'm the child. Don't ask advice from me. "She needs to go see a doctor."

Daddy's voice had creaked like wet wood in the fire. "Where did we go wrong?" he'd asked. I'd taken his large, rough hand in mine, mute in protective sadness.

White hairs had crept, like mice from the cold, into his blond tonsure. He was shorter now than before. Of course there were indictments. He suspected them: perhaps the past is not the way he remembers it. Perhaps the past is not what he believed. It would be evil to lay childhood's wounds on my father, to crush his heart, gentle as a cricket. I'd stood with him by the open fire and squeezed his hand: You're no longer held to account. You're not in charge of my harm and healing. And I'm still here with you.

"If you love her," Nitin says, pulling into the hotel lot, "you're going to have to talk to her. And now I have to talk to you." He turns off the ignition. He drops his hands to his lap, and turns to me. "I love you," he says slowly. "I don't want to lose you to a heart attack at forty. Please do something. Please exercise. Please lose weight."

*T*hen, her weight loss stops, fifteen pounds higher than the medical guidelines for acceptable weight, fifteen pounds from the goal range set by the weight loss program. Some people would tell her to reject the guidelines. But she sees the fat on her abdomen, and she wants to bend without feeling its compression. She wants to run without feeling it bounce.

She also knows that to reject the guidelines would be, for her, an excuse to discard the plan she's following. Then what would she do? Her behavior isn't safe. She can't trust herself to eat sensibly. It's her dark secret and her growing fear. The want has returned.

Migrating monarch butterflies, erratic orange stitches, scalloped the highway's center line. I sped southward with them. I felt close to the outdoors, close to the road noise, the sun in the fields, the grime of small towns. I curved past landmark hilltops, grain silos, creek bridges; finally, Tulsa popped, an art deco bicep, off the long arm of the plains. The tattoos of glass office buildings, gardens, bungalows, and chain restaurants melded cheery and unassuming into the city's concrete skin. St. John rested in the intersected crook of boulevard and residential side street. I traipsed up the long, glass breezeway, my ribcage lifted high, breath deep and relaxed. The concrete dorm room smelled like fabric softener, mothballs, antibacterial tile cleaner. I tossed the half-empty leather-trimmed bag on the bed, locked the door, and sashayed through hallways as if through a summer resort. I rode in a full elevator. It paused at the nursery floor, released families like celebratory balloons. A ringing waiting-room phone snagged me; with courtesy learned from other families whom we had begun to recognize and greet, I called a name into the larger waiting room, inventoried visitors' silent headshakes, then wrote a message on the small room's whiteboard.

I walked with a bounce into ICU, where the sheet, turned back, clung tight and flat to Joyce's bed. Her mattress was an empty slab, forlorn, adrift in a machineless room. The cold, white countertop was wiped clean. Nurse Carol rushed, caught me as I wheeled, adrenaline spiking, gag reflex convulsing, Joyce a blur in the next room, like a paperweight rose, embedded in glass behind glass. "It's all right," Nurse Carol says. "She's right in there. See? She's been moved into isolation. Oh, that must have been a scare. It's all right, you're okay." Nurse Carol touched my cheek, inspected receding panic as though checking a fallen child's abrasions. Her smile was a warm compress, a sheltered lap. "Now," she said, brisk again, "you can still go in to her. You'll need to wear a gown and gloves, and afterward, wash up carefully. I'll show you."

My feet, my tongue felt like flat tires, sluggish. "Why's she in there?"

Nurse Carol nodded, decisive, a pushpin stab. "Her doctor wanted to talk with you about that. I'll page her." Her? That would be Dr. Mary, with dark, percolating eyes and explanations mild and smooth as cocoa.

"But what can you tell me. Carol."

Nurse Carol measured out a dosage of words. "It's an infection. Her body is resisting the antibiotics. The kind of infection she has can spread very rapidly to other patients. That's why she's in isolation."

"It can spread? Can it spread inside her as well?"

"I know you have questions," Nurse Carol said. "The doctor will be here in just a minute. In the meantime, let's get you gowned. I'll show you about the washing. Then you can show your parents when they come."

Search terms: Vancomycin-resistant enterococci. VRE.

The word in print curls like a snail, and spoken sounds like a blister under the eyelid. Enterococci. En-terr-oh-cock-eye: bacteria that live in human feces. Every one of us harbors enterococci in the caverns of our intestines and genital thoroughfares. These bacteria don't harm us as long as they stay under house arrest. However, if they break out into the body, they will infect the urinary tract, or the lining of the spinal cord or brain, or, opportunists as bacteria are, the vulnerable tissues of a wound. Resilient, the enterococci have mutated into strains resistant to the strongest of antibiotics. These vancomycin-resistant enterococci—VRE—lie harmless in your body like other enterococci, unless given the opportunity to infect and kill.

VRE transmit themselves from person to person on the hands; they can jump easily from infected surface to uninfected surface. The bed linens, the bed rails, the gauzes and tubes and the skin of a patient with a VRE infection are crawling with the VRE bacteria, swarming with its high mortality rate and its easy contagion. Such a patient must be isolated. Her visitors must be gowned and gloved. The risk of the infection's lightning spread across the hospital is far too great to risk a kiss, warm fingertips on a forehead, a bare hand laid against a fevered cheek.

The long-sleeved gown, a pale blue square from the clean-laundry cart, clung to my sweater arms. Tapes looped in a rough bow at the nape of my neck. Sterile gloves smacked tight against my palms. I closed the sliding glass door behind me as instructed. The empty room, the glass antechamber, was perfectly silent. The nurses buzzed by outside, silent. I stationed my purse by the stainless steel sink. In the mirror, the rectangle of my face was grim, dark half-moons puffing under my eyes. I folded my eyeglasses and hooked them on my purse strap. I didn't trust myself not to jab them up the bridge of my nose with a bacteria-laden finger. Anything we took in, Dr. Mary and Nurse Carol told me, stayed in. Magazines, newspapers. We could take ice chips. Be sure, they said, to throw them away inside the room.

Joyce lay beyond the second sliding glass door. I closed it behind me, and then the room seemed like any other hospital room. The bank of monitors towered over the bed, and festoons of tubing emerged from her dry lips, from the trunks of her arms. Joyce slept. Her face was childlike in its mask of tape and tubes. Her breast and belly rose and fell with the hiss of the machine. I wanted her to wake; I wanted to see her eyes; I wanted her to sleep; I wanted her expression always this peaceful and protected. The clock hands crept, a quarter-hour, a half-hour. She slept.

Reluctant, I retraced my steps. Opened and shut her sliding glass door. Peeled off the sweat-lined gloves, dropped them in the trash. Wadded and dumped the gown in the dirty-laundry cart. Coated my hands and forearms with antibacterial soap. Watched my own serious eyes as I massaged and rinsed my fingers in hot water. Looked back to see her breast and belly rise and fall. Opened the door to the ICU noise, the ringing phone, the click and shuffle of chair, pill packet, keyboard.

"So, are you okay?" Nurse Carol met me in the quiet zone by the central pillar. We stood, bound by words we felt rising between us.

"She's sleeping," I said.

"I'd like to ask you something." Nurse Carol drew back her chin, as if cushioning refusal. "All the nurses here have been wondering, trying to figure it out. How did she come to be so overweight?"

"What do you mean?" Calories in, calories out. Isn't that the line? You tell me. Can't medicine tell me how she gained weight?

"Patients as overweight as your sister are usually very depressed people," Nurse Carol explained. "But she's so young, and she was able to hold a job that she enjoyed, and she's surrounded by family who love her, and you can tell—you can just tell she's such a sweet person. What happened?"

I itched with words. Where do I start to tell you? I thought. I wanted to scratch deep, to get rid of the words, even if it bled. What would I write? (The planet is not round today. Its gravity and all words are warped, and I wish for quick deaths for us all. Let her go easy. Don't let her be scared. Give the doctors some sign. Let them know what to do. But wait for her, God. Let her tell you she's ready.)

"I don't know how it happened, exactly. I've tried to piece it together for the doctors when they've asked." Words sank into my pause like shoes into mud. Keep moving, I thought. (My sister, my sister.) "She started gaining weight in college. After a while, it was like not only she couldn't lose weight, but that her body just gave up. It got harder for her to lose weight, but easier and easier for her to gain weight." Like she was tumbling downhill in snow, I thought, until she was a giant snowball at the bottom of this hill. "I wish I knew how much she weighed," I said.

"What do you mean?" Nurse Carol frowned.

(My sister, my sister.) "They told me when she came in that she couldn't be weighed. That there wasn't a scale that could weigh her."

Nurse Carol drew a sharp, indignant breath. "That's—no—that's just not right," she said. She pulled a champagne ribbon of hair behind her ear. "Of course she was weighed when she came in. Every patient is. Joyce weighed five hundred and fifty pounds when she came in. I'm so sorry. I don't know why someone would have told you that."

(My sister, my sister, my other body—)

The number swelled, a wave in my shipwrecked ocean. I clung to the number, a splintered raft, and floated on the black and freezing sea. Five hundred and fifty. How had she stood? How had she walked? How had she lifted five hundred and fifty pounds upright, the short spine straight, the shoulders back? How had she carried five hundred and fifty pounds? What horrible strength had returned to her bones with every morning's waking? (I don't want to leave you. I want to love you. I'll sing to you. I'll show up at visiting hour.)

I wound my way back to the dormitory, legs heavy and ready to stumble. The idea of dinner waved at me repeatedly like a child on a carousel. I hated every need of my body, the need to eat, to sleep. The craving to write throbbed. I wanted to mummify my head, to plaster pages on the pounding clusters of words. (I promise you I will teach someone to read. I promise you something you tried will live.)

The fat notebook was like a weapon in my traitor's hand. I could find words, find relief—my god, I could find dinner. I sprawled on the knotted twin bed. Whatever would happen in words must happen quickly. I could visit her again that night, and I would need to smile. The planet is not round today, I scrawled, aimless and wild, feeling selfish and rotten with words. (Oh God.) Its gravity and all words are warped.

(Give us quick, give us all quick deaths.)

PART FIVE: ISOLATION

1997

"So are you coming home for Christmas this year?" A stale crust of petulance smothers Joyce's thickened, alto croak.

"You know I'm not. Joyce. You know I can't." Cross-legged on our bed in the small apartment, I look out at the first flakes of a Michigan snow. The white kitten pounces at my toes, assaults my loosened sock. Nitin's away at the business school library, and the apartment's quiet.

"I'm sorry," I say. It's true, I'm sorry she's peevish and lonely. It's her choice. Joyce drives from Dallas every year to sit in the conversation-less glow of Christmas television, to link herself back to the house where her secrets were formed and to the parents, who were necessary. Secrets cannot be sacred without someone to hide them from.

"It's not your fault," she says, her croak fluid and strong. "I know it's not your fault, but I still get so frustrated and mad. It's every Christmas. The three of us open presents and then it's all over and we sit and look at each other. It's lonesome."

"What can I do?"

"I don't know," she says. "That's up to you."

"Well," I say. "Merry Christmas." White dumplings of snow fall now past the window. The white kitten sleeps on my foot. Love for my sister resonates like a bass drum through the pause where she doesn't say good-bye. "Joyce?" I say. "Did you get that letter I sent you?"

Dear Joyce, this is the hardest letter I've ever written. I've got to say some hard things to you and I'm afraid I'm going to say them all wrong. But I have to try, because I love you and I am afraid I'm going to lose you. I'm afraid you're going to die because of your weight.

I know you said you don't know how you can be gaining weight, since you eat healthy and don't eat much. That's why I'm worried. Something could be really wrong with your health. It's not normal for a person to eat healthily and still gain weight. Please, go see a doctor. Please. I know the doctors will only say you need to lose weight and stop at that because that's all they ever did with me too. But you can ask for tests to make sure you don't have a serious problem. What if you had diabetes and didn't know it, or heart disease, or something the doctors could help you with? And if there's nothing wrong, then at least you'll know, right?

Joyce, why? Why are you killing yourself? Because that's what you're doing, even if it's not on purpose. If you need help and don't get it you are killing yourself, and I don't know why. I love you so much. You're my only sister and I am so scared for you.

Please get some help. I know there are counseling services that don't cost much and there are people you can talk to. Is there some way through your work you could talk to somebody, or is there somebody at church? Please, if you need to talk to somebody, just do it. Please figure out why you are letting yourself get sick. If there's something medical that's gone wrong in your body you can find out what it is. Or if there is something you can do to lose weight you can go to a program or start an exercise plan. Or if you need to talk to a counselor it's all there for you. Please take care of yourself.

If you ever want to talk to me about this just call. I don't have all the answers but I love you and want to know what you are doing to be healthy and get well. I just love you so much. I know you might be mad at me after you read this letter but I know you understand, too. You can talk to me anytime. I love you. Ann.

"Yes," she says. It is a yes that sounds like love. It is a yes that says, don't pay attention, of course Santa Claus is real. "Yes," she says, "I read it."

"I love you." Can I wrap my voice in colored paper and tape and ribbon? Can you open it and find everything you ever wanted, everything you need?

"Maybe you'll come home next year. I love you too." She sighs. "Merry Christmas," she says.

She begins to binge again. She restrains herself enough not to gain weight, but she doesn't know how long that restraint will last or her body cooperate. What can she do? She was already on a level path, already following a plan that could help her. She has all the tools, yet she's failing. She doesn't know what more to learn, what more to try. If she can't stay with the best plan available, what hope is there?

All day, she presses back anxiety to face the world and her commitments in it. At home, alone, she won't face anxiety; she wants to numb it, stifle it. Food helps her do this. Her want for food intensifies. Her drive to satisfy the want slips out of her control. She leans back into the lifelong panic, and hides her eating. Dread, panic—they no longer register as abnormal states, only as suppressed ones.

What is she thinking? She isn't thinking, any more than a weak swimmer, throat full of chlorine, thinks about proper stroke mechanics. The want drowns her. She flails, she reaches for the nearest floating object—chips, cereal, bread,

lunch meat, ice cream—but flailing with food in hand she only gulps more
want.

In the steps and turns of our hospital minuet, Mama and Daddy and I met in waiting room or cafeteria line or elevator. We smiled condensed smiles and sat together silently. With words like half-learned dance steps, we signaled when we meant to go to her, to gown and glove.

"Norman, you want to go back?" Mama slid her half-worked crossword puzzle into a tote bag.

"No, I'll go later," he said. A troubled thought raced across his expression. It was as clear as if a thin film had been peeled from his face imprinted with the image of him in the blue gown, swaying on his sturdy black sneakers, claustrophobic in his crowd of feelings as he looked down at his supine, silent daughter.

"Well, Ann, we can tie each other's gowns on," Mama said with busy impetus, as though I, the ICU ward, and Joyce were ingredients she were setting out to mix and bake. Daddy settled in the armchair. Chin in hand, he looked out the window at the empty movie screen of sky.

Mama crossed glass thresholds while I collected the day's trivia. BUN, creatinine edged upward. Temperature still elevated. Oxygen the same. "Oh, and," Nurse Carol said, "her skin is weeping."

"Weeping? What's that?" I'd left the fat notebook with Daddy.

"Her body's releasing excess fluid through the skin. You'll notice it. I don't want you to be shocked."

Joyce's skin was thick and moist, like chicken noodle. Her skin seeped milky sap. Joyce's eyes, blueberry magnets, flattened and glared. Embarrassed, I straightened and smiled. "Hi," I said. "How are you feeling today?" She shrugged: a grasp and release of the right hand, a lift of the left eyebrow, a twitch of the tube-bound lips.

"I guess she don't have the whiteboard anymore," Mama said. "Joyce, do you want anything? We brought some ice chips. You want those?"

Joyce's nod was a careful and focused dip, her chin into her neck's cape. Mama, jaw firm and eyes steady, administered flecks of ice. Joyce lifted her eyes like wildflower Mother's Day bouquets, to follow Mama's face.

"You want the TV, Joyce?" I asked. Joyce tried to transmit a mild grimace through a shake of her head, her right ear shifting by millimeters toward the pillow. She pinched her forefinger and middle finger to her thumb. No. "Okay," I said.

"You don't need to try to watch TV," Mama said. "You need to get plenty of rest. I'm going to go on out now and see if your daddy's ready to come tell you good morning. Ann, you ready to go?"

"In a minute. I want to stay just a little longer."

"Don't stay too long. Your daddy likes to come back here by himself. I think he just doesn't like me around when he gets his hugs from Carol."

Joyce trained the thickened slits of her eyes on me, intent, as if she were poking me with a stick. Mama, outside, dried her hands on paper towels. "You want to ask about the weather," I said. Joyce nodded, her right ear shifting by millimeters forward.

"Okay. It's supposed to rain tomorrow. The sky's gray. It's cold. The leaves are falling. They say after it rains it's supposed to be warm again. But I don't think it will be, not really warm. There are pumpkins in bins out in front of all the supermarkets." Joyce's eyes relaxed. "Now my turn. You know what I want," I said. "But here. I know your answer. I just want you to know for sure that I believe you."

The right ear shifted forward. A breath puffed the eroded peaks of breasts. Joyce's fingers, dry at the tip of her weeping arm, engineered slow and malformed letters. F. I. G. H. T. I . . . her hand, restrained, sagged to the bed.

"You know I think you're doing something remarkable," I said quietly. "You're doing great. It doesn't matter, you know, anything that happened before. It's just—awesome—to watch the way you're fighting now. I love you so much."

Okay, she spelled. Tell Daddy. Not worry.

I laced my rubber-gloved fingers through her fevered ones. "He's fine," I told her. I hiccupped as though teasing, laughing.

She'd thought the want was gone forever. Yet here it is, driving her. She thinks of food and her own weight—ways to eat and ways not to eat, from the time she wakes and in every idle moment. She's horrified that she's letting the want take over. But she can't think how to stop.

She tries to remember how she first lost weight. What helped at first? When did she know she had found balance? Remember when the habits that saved her life were novelties? She drank water. She started to exercise. She kept fanatic records, writing down everything she ate, planning ahead.

The switch from harm to health was not like putting on the brakes. It wasn't like a hairpin turn. It wasn't like choosing a different path. It was like waking up from a long sleep. She's the same person she was asleep, but waking would never choose the things she dreamed.

How does she wake up again from want's insane dream? How does she wake into health? She thinks, I don't know how. But I have got to do it. Wake up! she screams at herself in the mirror, out loud, alone at home. Wake up! Wake up!

Gray cloaked the drive home from Tulsa. Low gray clouds hung on graying trees and fields; the long gray highway stretched like an arrow's shaft from the car's chest. Pewter rainstorms bunched on the Kansas horizon. On my car antenna flapped a dead orange flag, a snagged monarch butterfly pinned to the wire by the wind. A gray workweek lay ahead, into which I'd slip like a Chinese checker marble, unremarked. News like volcanic ash weighed on my colleagues: anthrax had poisoned Florida, bombs pounded Afghanistan, and smoke streamed upward from hot New York rubble. Then, days passed. The rain crossed Kansas City and a cool October sun emerged. Lisa leaned into my office. "Let's picnic tomorrow. I need to get out of here a while," she said, her dark eyes and posture strong and open, like a Soviet sculpture. Her voice sung like low clarinet notes. "I expect you do, too."

The park was a ten-minute drive from our office. Picnic tables dotted a hillside over a small, bucolic lake. On a concrete shoreline trail, women pushed babies in strollers and small children ran from plump, insistent geese. Lisa uncapped a plastic container of salad; I unwrapped tuna sandwiches. We anchored napkins with soda and water bottles. "So tell me," Lisa said, lowering her pointed chin. She prodded the wooden table with a taut finger. "Spill it."

I swallowed moist bites of sandwich. "So she has this new infection. I've been reading about it. It's called VRE. The mortality rates—you know, if you have VRE together with this or that condition—Joyce has more than one condition that has a mortality rate above 80 percent, when VRE's present."

"Wow," Lisa said, her black eyebrows arching. "No wonder you've been a little distant. It's just one thing after the next, isn't it?"

Joyce's sicknesses emerged like runway models. "Infections, kidneys, lungs, fever. You know, my dad made a joke. 'Well, at least she's not pregnant,' he said." A gust skimmed the picnic table, tossed a stray napkin to the grass. By the lake, three white geese waddled. "My mom told me something sad. She said the ICU nurse—you know, the one who's been so good to my family—she told Mama that the nurses were amazed to see us there so much. It didn't make any sense, because why wouldn't we be there? Then I counted up all the patients who are just there, alone. There are a lot more full beds in ICU than there are people in the waiting rooms."

"It's good for Joyce she doesn't have to go through this alone."

"I mean, all these people right at the edge of life and death. You know, they think they see all this devotion between us and Joyce. But we've had such a frustrating relationship. She's a difficult person."

"Because of her health problems?"

"No—well, yes, that makes it worse—but she's always been kind of hard to live with. Stubborn. A little vengeful."

"Maybe the nurses see better than you do."

"Maybe. At first I felt so guilty, because I wanted to say, see, I told you this would happen."

"How do you feel now?"

"Yeah. She can't change how she got where she is. I look at her, how she's living her life right this minute. She's not giving up. She hasn't complained once or asked anybody to feel sorry for her. I just—if I'm ever in her place, I'd hope to do a tenth as well. I'd hope to be that brave."

Search term: diverticulitis.

The jelly-slick tubes of the intestines are like a relay-race team carrying the baton of food. Each intestinal section runs its leg, processing the food with enzymes, releasing nutrients into our bloodstream, and passing the baton of leftover material toward the next kink in the tubes. We hardly know the contractions and expulsions as the long coil pushes its parcel onward. Naïve and ignorant, we trust the pink stack of ribbon compressed in our bellies.

The intestinal walls aren't invincible. Weak spots can pouch out in the walls of the large intestine's five-foot canal. These little pouches are called diverticula. The same weak spots can form in the twenty-foot, snaked length of the small intestine. If your intestines carry the thinned bulges of these little diverticula pouches, you have diverticulosis. Most people as they age have some. But diverticulitis is when the weak pouches have become small, stagnating pools for fecal matter, bacteria, and infection. With diverticulitis, your lower abdomen will cramp severely, and you'll run a fever as you would with any infection. You might find blood in the toilet; you might be constipated; you might feel like throwing up. Doctors use a CT scan or X-rays to diagnose diverticulitis.

If you don't get treatment, the infected pouches bulging from your intestinal walls may fill with pus. If you still don't get treatment, the diverticular pouches can tear, and through the perforations, the pus will leak into your abdomen. If the infection leaks out and contaminates the sac that holds your abdominal organs, you have peritonitis, and you will need emergency surgery to clean the abdomen and take out the damaged parts of the intestines. Peritonitis can be fatal.

Medical experts believe that the common cause of diverticulitis is a diet low in fiber, which increases pressure in the colon. Other things that can weaken the intestine's walls are not drinking enough water, not getting enough exercise, and holding in bowel urges.

Search term: peritonitis.

Our guts lie pouched in a membrane, a sterile sac, the peritoneum. Whenever an intestine is perforated, its contents spill out in a hard splash of infection, contaminating this tender sac and everything in it. A perforation like this infects the abdomen and requires emergency surgery. Doctors rely on CT scans or X-rays to see where free air, along with toxic leakage, is escaping into your belly. Or the doctors might need to perform immediate exploratory surgery to find the damage and decide how to repair it.

Untreated, the peritoneal infection can spread into your blood; fluid can leak from the bloodstream into the abdominal cavity. The lungs or the kidneys or the liver can fail. The surgery needed in critical cases to save your life carries its own risks—the surgical wound can become infected easily, lying near the body's wastes. Or, the surgical wound, amidst an onslaught of organ malfunctions and the body's disrupted nutrition, can fail to heal.

"I'm sorry," I told Lisa as we trudged up the long grass hill to our cars. "I haven't asked how you're doing. What's going on with you."

"Oh, give me a break," she said. "Don't put that guilt on yourself, and don't put it off on me. You're in pain right now. You'll be there for me some other time."

"Yeah?"

"That's how she goes, chickie." Lisa climbed with shoulders back, lunch pack swinging, short black hair shining in the noon sun.

"I feel like I'm leaning awfully hard on you. And on Kerri, too. She's been listening to all this since way before Joyce went in the hospital." My breath felt like a sack of gravel in my chest. The hillside grass slid underfoot.

Lisa stopped on the hilltop, at the lip of the parking lot. She dropped her lunch pack. She held her arms open wide. The stubborn gravel sack resisted across the floor of my chest until I let go, into the steady, warm crescent of my friend's embrace. "That's it. Go ahead," Lisa whispered as I crossed my arms against her back. "Lean on the people who let you."

 **1998**

Adulthood: roots grow too deep to be transplanted again. Our values and opinions anchor us in the dark, humid soil of adult fears, regrets, plans, and loyalties. Roots spread, powerful as rumors. They creep and push into foundations, under fences, under walls. Long, fibrous fingers, our roots tickle toward relationships, validation, reward. Sometimes, two plants grow so close together that their root systems weave inside the earth. If the plants are of the same species, the roots can graft together, forming a single plant.

Joyce and I share the nutrients and poisons of an old conversation. We are past the first discovery of our singular and mutual dismay at our own fat bodies, at each other's.

"I don't know what to do to lose weight. I try to eat right and nothing works," Joyce says.

"Have you gone to a doctor?"

"Doctors cost money."

"Being sick costs more money. Will you go to a doctor?"

"Ann, doctors cost too much money and anyway they don't know anything. They just say to lose weight and they look at you."

"What do you mean, they look at you?"

"They look at you like you don't deserve to even be in their office."

"What doctor did that to you?"

"It was a long time ago. It doesn't matter."

"I think it does. But anyway. What about a group, like a program, a support group?"

"I don't want to go in with a bunch of people. And anyway, all of that costs money. The special food costs money. And I went with Mama to her meetings and it didn't do any good I could see. Don't you remember how upset Mama got when she couldn't lose weight even though she tried to do everything the program said? I don't want to be like that."

"Okay, then what about this low-carbohydrate diet. A friend of mine told me about it and I've been trying it the last couple of weeks, and I've lost five pounds. I didn't want to say anything about it to you until I knew it would work and that it was something, you know, you can live with."

"Do you have to buy a lot of special food?"

"No, and as long as you can eat salads and fish and chicken and eggs and cheese you can do this diet. And every day you can eat some carbohydrates, so it's not like you totally have to give them up. You might try that."

"I'll get the book. I'll do that."

"And will you go to a doctor?"

"If things start going wrong or I feel bad I'll go to a doctor. There's just not any reason to go when they don't want to help me and all they do is say to lose weight. I know I need to lose weight. I don't need to pay a doctor to tell me that."

Search term: ileostomy.

Our delicate intestines don't heal like skin when they are ruptured or torn. Surgical repair for extensive damage is both harsh and elegant, a reconfiguration of our plumbing. In one type of this surgery, an ileostomy, the surgeon removes the large intestine and prunes the small intestine, removing the septic portion from the twenty-foot coil. Then, the surgeon cuts a hole in the abdomen, and hooks the healthy remainder of the intestine to this opening. After that, the body's wastes exit through the abdomen and collect as liquid in an odor-proof bag that surrounds the opening and is attached with adhesive against the stomach's skin.

Friday, October 12. Nurse Rita's voice chiseled a jagged path through my morning's bland schedule. "The doctors decided this morning they needed to perform an emergency surgery, an ileostomy," she said. "Your sister's being prepped." Nurse Rita anticipated the melting-wax drip of my reflex question, shoved an answer under it. "Your parents are here," she said. "They know."

I stared at my monitor, at unflickering lines of text that five minutes before had proven my importance in a workplace and in a world. I felt foolish and duped. The fat notebook exposed work as bloated, hollow. A folded scrap of paper fell from the notebook's heart. The pressed digits felt like sorted pills under my fingertips.

"I'm on my way to the hospital now," Harry said, his honest voice reassuring as the swish and thump of a gilt-edged King James. "I'll be there with your parents soon. Less than an hour."

She decides that it's okay that it's hard to name and face her pain. It's okay to be afraid her pain is stupid, or trivial, or freakish. But, she decides, it's not okay to let her pain dictate her actions blindly. It's not okay to be the puppet of her pain.

Surgery occurred underground, in the subconscious of the hospital. A labyrinth of narrow, undecorated hallways piped around the surgeries. Down and beyond glass doors, the waiting room splayed like an airport lobby. Armchair fortresses dotted the room's expanse, circling ceiling-mounted television screens. Mama and Daddy had laid claim to a secluded corner, a gauntlet of couches under recessed lighting. Mama looked up, her eyes sharp as a whittled stick. Daddy stood, his blue windbreaker hanging loose.

"How was your drive?" Mama's eyes softened, cream stirred into coffee.

"Not bad. Have you all been down here the whole time?"

"Your daddy got up and walked around a while. They told us we shouldn't expect any news for a few hours. Did you get yourself some dinner?"

"I stopped and got a sandwich."

"It's kind of early for dinner though, wasn't it."

"Well, I didn't want to leave once I got here. What about you all? Are you hungry?"

"Hunter and Maggie went out to get something. They're supposed to be bringing something back for Norman." Mama looked down at the magazine in her lap. "I don't think I can eat anything right now."

Two other families, quiet as deer herds nestled in woods, sat across the waiting room. "Where's Harry?" I asked.

"He said you called. He had to go visit a woman in another hospital. Though I don't know what he's doing out, with his bad back. We told him we didn't need him to stay, but he said he'd come and wait with us. Oh, you should see, he's in a lot of pain with his back now."

"Huh. Can't they do anything for it?"

"Oh, they can, but he's having just a terrible time with the insurance. So he just has to wait until they decide to cover what he needs, and you can see the effort. You just know he's hurting."

"That's a shame," I said.

"Diverticulitis," said Daddy. He offered the word, a pocketed candy he'd forgotten and now wanted to share. "I was trying to think of it, what they said she had that made them do the surgery. She has real bad diverticulitis."

"Lots and lots of people have diverticulitis," Mama said. "That's a real common thing. At least they think they finally found it, what's causing all her other problems, they said. They'll know what to do for it." She slid her glasses down her nose and raised the magazine like a mirror.

Daddy twisted on the couch. "Look," he said. "See that red phone?" He pointed to a red handset by the door. "They'll call us on that phone when she comes out of surgery. Then the doctor's supposed to come down and talk to us."

"Is that so," I said.

Daddy folded his hands in his lap, his eyes alert as if the coach might call him off the bench. "They didn't know how long it'd be," he said.

What would I lose by trying it? she thinks. When I eat, I'll think about what I want, not just what I'm allowed. She's shocked by the result. Thinking about the day's boundaries between herself and food, the want to eat swells in her like a storm. Thinking about what she wants, she's forced to consider she wants not only food, but health. By freeing herself to think of what she wants, she frees herself to think of her desire not to eat.

An hour expanded around us like an air pocket in a rising loaf of bread. Nothing, not Nitin's comforting voice on the phone, not the smell of fast food in paper bags, not fitful conversation, reached the quiet center of waiting. Mama folded her attention into another magazine as though she herself were a bookmark. Hunter and his wife, Maggie, watched the ceiling-mounted sitcom and sucked cola-flavored remnants from giant cups, through long straws. Maggie, whose cordial laugh rasped across the grain of her apprehensive eyes, lost herself in the TV's vivid, shallow tableau. Hunter sighed and gazed, but his eyes didn't dart with the television's action. Daddy glanced at the TV, at his fingernails, at me. He wore his patience and stillness like muddy work gloves.

"Hey, Norman," I said. "I don't think I ever asked you how your garden did this summer."

Daddy blinked. His eyes widened and he cupped his hand behind an ear. "What's that?"

"Your garden." I pictured the lush, crop-ribbed rectangle nestled among the pine and apple and pear.

"His tomatoes made all right," Mama said without looking up from the glossy columns, "but we didn't get as much corn as we thought we would."

"I don't think I'll grow corn again," Daddy said. "Too much trouble for not enough results."

"You know," Mama said, "there's a woman at church who has one of these colostomy bags like they're putting on Joyce. You'd never know it. She comes to church and drives around and does just whatever. The way they can attach these bags now, they say it's no big deal. You'd just never know, even looking at her clothes, that this woman had this thing."

"Hunter, get up and change the channel," Maggie said. "I don't like this show. I don't like that show," she said, with a convivial, apologetic smile.

"My big project for next summer is I have to cut down a bunch of apple trees."

"No! Apple trees? Why?"

"Oh, they want thinning. The apples don't come out as good. Besides, we can't use them all. They just fall on the ground for the birds." Daddy looked back at the television. Mama sat her magazine aside and interlaced her fingers at her navel. Hunter sighed. And time sealed us in, even as it edged its yeasty prison outward.

She reads weight loss success stories. Some start at 165 pounds, with the writer remembering how bad it felt to weigh so much. That's her current weight, midway to her goal, and she feels fit and strong, pleased with her progress. She gets it: there's no absolute fat. But for each of us there is a perceived absolute thin, the image of the finish line, perfection. She thinks, If there's no absolute fat, then the absolute thin is a lie, too. There is no finish line.

There is no final success in losing weight. There's only how you live your life every day. There is no "lose it and you're done." There's only managing your habits, your body's predispositions, tending and caretaking your body every day. She's used to thinking that problems have solutions. But problems with weight don't have solutions. They have countermeasures. That's the good news, she thinks. They have countermeasures.

If the tendency to obesity is with her always, then she's not curing her obesity but managing it. If there is no winner's tape, no day when she can say she's done, then she never has to worry about winning again. For if there is no finish line in weight loss, there also is no such thing as failure to cross it. If there is no permanent triumph, but only the task, the everyday challenge—then she doesn't have to win to be proud of herself. She only has to keep going, keep tending, keep caretaking her body every day.

If she doesn't have to be perfect . . . she snags on the thought—it's too good to think it fast—if she doesn't have to reach perfection, then she doesn't have to be afraid of failing anymore.

In the fourth hour of surgery, the hot cells of claustrophobic imagination began to multiply. Is it a good sign, that it takes so long? Is something wrong, to take this long? Is four hours long? They haven't given up. What would it be like, to cut into a body? How many surgeons suctioned, clamped, tunnelled through the flesh to vulnerable organs? Sometime today, I thought, gruff Dr. Salamon had shouldered the burden of decision, the recommendation for surgery. I wouldn't do it, I thought. It's like Harry's work, it's one of the honorable things I'd never have prepared to do.

Harry'd arrived, walking slowly but without a bend or jerk in his podium-ready posture. He'd hugged me and Mama, shaken Daddy's hand. We'd prayed, then Harry chatted with Mama and Daddy, his narrow eyes shining behind the thick lenses. Thirty minutes crept, forty-five. I wandered the room, rifling the ragged stacks of outdated news. Harry watched me. He nodded and smiled at Mama, then shifted and stood. His hand on my shoulder was strong, the fingers sensitive, easy. Silver hairs punctuated the dark, dry sweep off the even hairline. The square face wore its honest, humble bravery like a soldier's insignia—experience, not sophistication; interest, not ambition. He looks, I thought with surprise, like my uncles.

"How are you feeling?" I asked him. "Mama said you'd had some back trouble."

"Oh, it comes and goes," he said. "Don't worry on that count." He moved a half-step closer, waited to see my eyes. "Your mom and dad told me how it's been going. I'm so thankful you've been able to be here with them. I'm just so sorry," he said, "so sorry I wasn't here sooner. If I'd known . . . I had no idea, Ann, how bad off she was."

"Nobody's known," I said. "I'd thought they'd called you. I think they thought it wasn't serious enough, that way, to tell anybody."

"I would have been here," Harry said.

"You're here now." I didn't work to convey my trust; he'd see it, as he'd seen a thousand faces, sick and sad people, people swollen with painful love for the sick and sad. "Hey, Harry—how do my mom and dad seem to you?"

"What do you mean?" He watched me closely, the scholar squinting at marginalia.

"Do they seem like they're able to process it? I can't tell if they grasp what's happening. I can't tell what they feel. I'm awfully concerned for them, for what a big blow this might be."

"No, no, I can see that. Surely they know on some level how much danger she's in, but I agree, it doesn't seem like they've been hit yet with the full impact of it. Yet I can't imagine what it must be like, to grieve the death of one baby and then have another child in such peril." Harry looked over at Mama, sitting quietly as a snow globe, at Daddy studying his calloused hands. Mama still held an invisible baby she had never mentioned to me. Daddy still held Mama, mother of his boy. "Parents just can never be ready to lose a child," Harry said. "How hard it must have been yesterday I can't imagine, passing the anniversary of your brother's death here in the hospital with Joyce in that bed." I nodded, stricken, learning.

At her family reunion, she plays cards with an obese cousin, a cousin who belittles himself as a means of jesting but who rarely smiles. She wants to reach across the table and grab his shoulders. She wants to say, Listen to me. This is important. Someone wonderful can love you.

In the seventh hour of waiting, night and the weariness of fear had befogged us. We had stopped speaking, as though the words might thicken the white shroud and separate us further. Mama slept, head back on the couch, mouth open. Harry rested his face toward his chest, his eyes closed. Daddy propped his elbows on his knees, his chin in his cupped palms. Maggie watched TV, the sound low now. Hunter paced, slumping slightly, as though he were too tall for his own bones. His long head, in its military buzz, hung forward. His thick-lidded eyes, blank with thought, followed the toes of his shoes. But when the red phone rang, Hunter flashed the plank of his arm as though snagging a long line drive. His pale blue eyes filled, a child's pages with crayon swirls, and he nodded toward our sudden, stiff alertness.

We bunched together like cattle under a dark green storm sky. The surgeon, who after seven hours in blood and bowel had changed into clean scrubs, was tall, lean and taut as clothesline cord, his sharp cheekbones and jawline like concrete bridge trusses. His deep voice step-laddered up and down the words. "Joyce came through the surgery all right," he said. "She's going back to ICU. You can see her tomorrow. Now—I'll be frank. There were a couple of times we didn't think we were going to make it. But we didn't want to give up if she didn't." He floated his next words atop Mama's exhaled pride, relief. "Joyce has a strong heart. As long as her heart kept beating, we kept working," he said.

"The diverticulitis was widespread," the surgeon continued. "We had to remove all but this much of her small intestine." He held his hands about sixteen inches apart and surveyed Hunter's dropped chin, Mama and Daddy's expectant faces, my wide, horrified eyes, and Harry's distorting struggle not to exclaim. The surgeon pointed his comments as though he were knighting me and Harry with a sword. "Her bowel is now attached to an opening in her stomach. There's a stoma bag around the opening." The surgeon's voice trailed into a microscopic collapse of posture, as though the discs in his spine had compressed, fatigued beyond design. "You can see her tomorrow," he said, "but don't expect her to respond. She'll be resting most of the day."

"Thank you, doctor," Daddy said, and extended his handshake as though he might steady the surgeon's elbow instead.

The surgeon snapped his posture upright and reached for Daddy's hand. "I can answer any questions you might have," he said, taking a flat, elliptical census of our faces. We shook our heads.

"Will you pray with us?" Mama asked. The surgeon hesitated, weaving on seven hours of foot-strain. He drizzled a gaze into Mama's trusting face, into her gratitude and panic.

"Of course," he said. "Of course."

Then, in the wake of Harry's brief and graceful benediction, the surgeon strode away. We gathered purses and jackets. Hunter and Maggie stayed behind with Mama and Daddy, while Harry suggested I escort him through the maze of hallways. We walked in silence until we were sure we were alone. "I'm so sorry," Harry said, and paused. His storyteller's voice was low and soft in the echoing hallway. "You know," he said.

"I know," I said.

"Ann . . . I've seen a lot of patients in a lot of hospitals. This isn't good," he said. "This just doesn't look good."

"It's okay, Harry. I know. The doctors have been telling me."

"I just don't hold much hope for your sister." He bit his lip as though he wished the words less utterable, less able to do harm.

"No—no, oh, Harry, thanks for saying it out loud. That helps," I said. "I don't think my parents know."

"No," Harry said, "they don't seem to." Kindness broadened the lines in his face. He collected me into a strong hug, then stepped back. "They'll understand it in their own time. Just be here for them."

———————————— ❖ **1999** ❖ ————————————

Some days, adulthood feels like being lost in a department store. You can't remember how you happened to slip from your mother's side. You wind up wandering a shiny jungle of home appliances—the path forward is not the one you had imagined, and you're not sure where you're supposed to meet the people who love you.

I unpack books in the new, suburban Kansas study. The white cat dozes atop heavy cardboard crates, and the calico kitten bats a crumpled ball of looseleaf paper. The phone rings. Joyce greets me in her rusty alto. If I'm lucky she'll have a new story about Aunt Mickey. If I'm unlucky she'll want to tell me what she's eaten today and how she shouldn't have eaten it.

"I've got some news," she says.

"Yeah. What's up?"

"I'm moving back home with Mama and Daddy. Hey. You there?"

"Yeah. Just—huh. Wow. Are you okay?"

"I feel better than I've felt in a long time," Joyce says. "This is a good decision."

"What about your job? What happened?"

She clears her throat. "It was by mutual agreement. We had a conversation at the end of the school year, and the principal and superintendent and I agreed that I would take a year away and make some changes and then I could come back. I need to make some improvements with my health."

"Oh, Joyce."

"No, no, it's a good thing. I can really make some changes now. I'm going to focus on losing weight and getting my health together. That's what the school and I agreed to. They said—well, I don't want to say too much about it. I have to make some improvements. It's not just my weight and health. There's another—there are other problems. One. But it's too embarrassing. I don't want to tell you."

Intuition crawls on my skin. I can almost smell what she's talking about. "But I know what it is."

"How could you?"

We straddle a long silence, a see-saw. "Because I had the same problem, and people had to tell me, and it was awful."

Joyce bounces lightly on her end of the see-saw. "Well. Well. I don't want to talk about it. I'm taking steps. I'm taking steps now."

"What do Mama and Daddy say about all this?"

"Well, I called and asked them if I could come home. I told them what the school and I agreed to, that I would take a year and get my health improved and then come back to work. And they said it's okay."

I remember wood smoke. It spirals up blue and white, and Daddy says never, never. "Uh, I'm not sure how to ask this. You think you can stand living with Mama and Daddy? They won't make you crazy?"

"Oh, it'll be fine. I have my car and they're out of the house in the day times mostly. And anyway they need help with Grandma and I can go in and stay with her some." It's true, Grandma sees things as if through a telescope, now through the wrong end, now through the right end. She must be fed and bathed. Joyce, companionable to the elderly and young, could relieve Mama through the hours of Grandma's repetitive chatter and terrified laments. "I think it'll be fine. It's not like when I was in high school. And I need to stay with somebody and save my money. I thought of calling you. But you just moved into your house and all." Where will they put everything, her TV and stereo, her hundreds of videotapes and CDs, her books and her teaching materials and the amassed memorabilia of her life? Our bedroom's gone, a sewing room now; will she fit her adult life into Hunter's old bedroom, that freight elevator of a room?

"If things don't work out with Mama and Daddy, you can call."

"I hoped you'd say that."

"You can't come live here but you could come stay for a little while until you find a place or things cool off and you can go back home."

"Oh."

"So here's the big question, Joyce. What's wrong with your health that you have to leave your job? Anything I need to know?"

"No, it's all stuff you already know."

"Did you see a doctor?"

"I did see a doctor. That was part of the school requirement. I'm glad I went."

"And what did the doctor say?"

"That my health is fine now but I'm borderline for all kinds of things and that I need to lose a bunch of weight."

"Borderline for what?" I picture her body, the prize-winning, mutant pear. I picture her antic, crooked smile.

"Just borderline for different things. You know. Nothing's wrong with me right now. I just need to watch it is all."

"When do you go home?"

"Tomorrow. All my stuff is packed. Call me at home, okay?"

"Shoot. You call me. Call me when you start to go crazy, because I think you will."

"This is a good thing, Ann. I'm going back on the low-carbohydrate diet and I can concentrate on it now. This is going to be a positive step, and I'm going to get better."

"Okay. You know I'm here though."

"I know. I'm glad. Listen, I'll e-mail you."

I put down the phone. I listen to my house, to the way the television seeps through floors, to the far-away rustling and pacing of my husband as he sorts the mail. In this house, the news won't rifle through the drywall and air ducts. News must be relayed.

"Does she have it in writing?" Nitin says. "Because they just fired her."

"No. She says it's by mutual agreement, more of a sabbatical."

"Did she get it in writing?"

"She didn't say. It sounded like more of a conversation."

"Then they fired her. She might believe they'll hire her back, but unless she loses more than a hundred pounds it's not going to happen. She can hardly move around. How would she get to a sick or hurt child in her classroom?"

"Mm." A child fetal, unconscious, scissors lying open and stained, Joyce rocking slowly through the tiny desks, unable to bend without kneeling. The words are like glue in my mouth. "She thinks she'll go back. She thinks it's all fine."

"She can do it," Nitin says, "if she starts exercising. All she has to do is walk every day. Just walk a little, and build up over time. She could lose a hundred pounds."

"Do you really think she could?"

"It's not a question of what I think. It's a question of what she does next."

She jogs around the gym's track, past the aerobics class floor. A formation of lean, leotard-clad women stretches in the advanced routine, hops, bends, kicks. They lower themselves to their step boards and begin slow tricep dips.

Ow, she thinks—that's really hard. She watches the toned, focused women from the corner of her eye as she huffs slowly past. Suddenly, she wants to cheer. She wants to cheer for herself and for all those women on the floor.

Oh, good for you! She wants to yell. That's really hard! Way to go!

She smiles and keeps running, shuffling toward the next full mile.

Saturday morning, October 13. Joyce slept, her lips soft around the pacifying respirator tube. Her dark eyelashes feathered on the wheat-flour cheeks. The unwrinkled white sheet divulged a squarish bulge over her right abdomen. The isolation room felt soft and predictable as cotton balls—the antiseptic smell, the tick and puff and beep of mechanical breath and monitors. I held her hand. Mama and Daddy waited outside with Nitin, who, when he finally saw me coming, bounced his car keys in his fingers.

State highway 75 between Tulsa and Bartlesville was wide and empty. The road glared under low morning sun. Nitin set the cruise control and nodded to classic rock, the volume low. Mama tapped me on the shoulder from the back seat.

"Ann, have you been up to see Troy since he came out of the hospital?"

"No. The last time I saw him was when they were living in Wichita, in the hospital there."

"He's gone downhill some since then. Don't be surprised when you see him."

"Okay."

"Nitin, it's a shame you didn't get to know Troy before he got sick."

"Mm."

"I think you all would really have enjoyed talking to each other, smart as both of y'all are. Don't you think so, Ann?"

"Mm-hm."

"And don't be surprised if you hear LaNita talk about him getting well. She keeps saying he looks better. Ann, I just don't know what to say to her when she talks like that. She just can't accept that she's going to lose him. She just doesn't know how to face it. What do you say to somebody in that situation?"

"I don't know," I said.

"Neither do I," said Mama, her drawl faint, her voice brisk and deft. "And I don't know if while we're up here today would be a good time to talk to LaNita about her hospital bed. Norman? Do you think I ought to go ahead and ask her?"

Daddy shrugged. He looked out the back seat driver's side window, watched the grassy median, the pasture land slip by.

"Well, if it seems like the right time, I'll see if I can't talk to her about it. They got that newer hospital bed for Troy and the one out in the garage won't be used again. Joyce is going to need something like that. But maybe I'll wait until she comes home."

Nitin's jaw muscle jumped, a tight brown pouch near his chin. His knuckles spoked up from his grip on the wheel.

"Yes. When Joyce comes home, we'll see about getting Troy's hospital bed for her. It'll be kind of big to get in that room but it'll be easier if she has to have the respirator. You know, I had a thought—we never did bring her up any music. She really would've liked that, if we'd brought her tape player and her music. Do you think we can bring it now?"

"We could," I said. "Once we take it in that room we can't bring it out again. I'd hate her to lose her tapes and CDs. But a radio, what could that cost? Surely it'd be worth it. Mama, what a good idea."

"Well, I'll ask the nurses," Mama said. "If they let us take it in I'll bring one next time we go home."

She's walking the dog; the spring morning smells like damp earth and new flowers. She feels like singing, and it hits her: She has to do something other than eat when she wants to feel good. It's so simple. She has to find the things she loves more than eating, things that make her feel—not numb, but happy. She can cling to these things. They might save her.

"Come say hello to Troy." Aunt LaNita led me, her soft-bosomed welcome embrace flowing into a hand-held tour through the impeccably vacuumed and cushioned elegance of her house, to the converted guest room, clinical now with wide, tilting bed, portable respirator, trays of medicine, monitors. "He likes visitors."

Uncle Troy lay brittle and papery, his long limbs thin and wasted. A clawlike tension crooked his fingers, and his mouth hung slackened. His eyes rolled like flowers when the stems are too long for the vase. They rested on me with the cleared glass gleam of recognition. He had been an engineer, a patent holder, a professor with a sly, wry sense of humor. Now, behind the dwindling musculature and vanished speech, his intelligence sparked and faded, recognition full, communication impossible.

"Troy, look who it is. It's Ann. Norman and Toppy are here, too, and Ann's husband. They'll all come say hello in a while." LaNita bent her pear-shaped body over the bed, touched his cheek with the back of her hand, slid her fingers under his and squeezed. Her gapped smile flashed. The childlike blue eyes sparkled at him under her ginger-brown fluff of bangs, but her voice was plain, unadorned, everyday. She'd learned to suction his mouth, removing fluids he couldn't swallow, to regulate the dozens of medications, traditional and experimental, and change the catheter, yet had not forgotten her respect for him. She spoke to him as though he guided and protected her still. Loving her, wanting to defend her from the charge of denial, I felt strange suddenly, as though I were detaching from something—a sea anemone trying to loosen from a rock.

"Ann," she asked me quietly, glancing toward the door, "did your brother come up to visit? Your parents said he hadn't been."

I remembered Hunter, silent as if numb through the seven-hour surgery. I'd followed his paced track into a corner of the waiting room, tried, when he paused, to touch him like powdery moth wings. "Hunter? What do you remember from when we were little? What do you remember about playing with me and Joyce?"

"Not a lot," he'd said.

"Oh, come on, you remember something."

"I don't remember a whole lot. You and Joyce were always together in your own room. I wasn't in on that stuff." And he'd looked at the red phone, the pain raw in his face.

Loving him, wanting to defend him, I was humbled in my ignorance of his entire life, his private kaleidoscope of memory. I felt the pull again, deep in my ribs, as though I were struggling to uproot, to release myself from an anchor. "He came earlier in the week," I told Aunt LaNita. "Then he was there with Mama and Daddy through the whole surgery. He stayed pretty close to Daddy the whole time."

"That's good," Aunt LaNita said. "That's really good. You know I told Lanette about the surgery and she was just shocked by how bad off Joyce would have to be to have that done."

"We're glad they found the problem," I said. "It's been so hard to diagnose."

"Lanette said it sounds pretty bad."

"It is pretty bad," I said. "She just has too much to fight now."

"I'm worried about your mom and dad," Aunt LaNita whispered. "They don't seem like they can accept what's happening with Joyce."

I listened to my parents bustling in the kitchen. Undemonstrative and private, Mama and Daddy dovetailed into one another, merged immutably like the broken nutrients in rich garden soil. I couldn't remember a lie that either of them had ever told. Blessed are the meek: I wasn't competent to explain them. Loving them, defense became irrelevant.

"They'll be fine," I said.

"Are you sure?" Aunt LaNita's face sobered.

I felt it then—detachment—as though I were floating, disconnected, cauterized from time, as though the room and the people around me were no longer real, as though my body and mind were illusions, life a closed and forgotten book. I don't want to explain love, or right or wrong; I can't figure anything out, I thought. I can't even feel it now.

"They're leaning on each other," I said quietly. "They really do know how sick she is. They're doing whatever they need, to keep being there with her. It's all right. They'll be all right."

"Now, if you're sure," said Aunt LaNita, "then I won't worry. But tell me how you are."

"I'm okay," I said. I'm floating, I thought. Don't try to touch me.

"You really ought to call Lanette," Aunt LaNita said. "She said to tell you. She said you ought to come have dinner with her. She'd be a real good person for you to talk to."

I imagined Lanette's deep, warm voice, her throaty laugh, her eyes, sharp with the appetite of ideas, impatient curiosity. Lean on the people who let you, I thought. "I will," I said.

◆ **2000** ◆

Joyce's claret-colored sedan hisses and shudders in our driveway. Oaks and maples click and sway up and down the suburban street. Pale leaf buds tint the brown branches; spring's coming. Tulip leaf blades salute like scimitars; winter-dappled lawns nudge a green rag edge toward the sidewalks; purple petunias gush from juniper fountainheads. Behind Joyce's windshield, her scowl flattens into sulky stoicism. She flings her car door open, her pyramidal bulk teetering on truncated feet. She wraps her water-balloon grip around the porch's metal railing. The threads of our last conversation pop in memory at once, like two flashbulbs.

Joyce had said, "Do you think you could find out if there's a shoe store somewhere close to you that stocks special shoes?" ("How can I stay on this diet when there's never any food in the house? Mama and Daddy don't keep healthy food in the house. They don't like the food I want to eat, so I don't get to eat it. I can't wait to be away for a few days.")

I'd said, "What kind of special shoes?" ("Why don't you go buy your own groceries?")

"Extra-wide sizes. My shoes are all busted out at the sides. One pair doesn't fit on my feet anymore. I can't go to church because I don't have any shoes that look good. ("If I buy my own groceries they just get used for other things.") I can't even go for walks. I can't find shoes in Muskogee and Tulsa. I was hoping there'd be a specialty shop in Kansas City." ("Most days I just end up running to get a hamburger. It's all that sounds good.")

"What shoes do you wear?" ("If the diet's not working, maybe you should try something else. What about a support group? Or see a counselor? You have to find something that works for you.")

"The tennis shoes, the pair that doesn't fit. I kind of fold down the back and wear them like sandals." ("All of that stuff costs money. And it don't work. I've thought about it. None of it's going to work for me.")

("But—")

("Look, it aggravates me talking. I just need to stick to it, keep positive. That's all I want to say. Now. What did you think we'd do while I'm up there?")

After dinner at our house, Joyce props her empty plate on her stacked-beanbag belly. With a finger's thick taper, she gathers gobs of barbecue sauce to poke between her lips. Finally, I take her plate and rinse it in the sink. "You want dessert?" I ask.

She shrugs, a shrug in a foreign tongue. Her eyes are dull like dying plants.

"What do you want to do tomorrow?" I ask. She shrugs again. I know the game. She'll make me guess, turn spiteful when the guesses are wrong, then finally stew in silent irritation as I try to placate and please her.

Days pass. The upholstered chair snugs on her like a crust, like her analgesic silence. She dawdles through the vanilla folds of a monolithic novel, absently stroking the white cat that nestles on the chair arm. At intervals she wiggles and heaves her hips forward, then lists upstairs to the bathroom. Her back is straight as a iron bunk frame from which swing the bulked hammocks of her belly. Our chair's padding, now flattened, concave, has absorbed the tang of her skin's odor and her cloying, floral body spray.

Are you okay? I ask. Are you bored? Are you hungry? Are you mad? She tightens her lips and refuses to answer. She's not behind the wall. She is the wall, encased in it, intractable.

"I know," I say. "Let's go to that shoe store."

"Oh!" she says. Her eyes blink up like thank-you notes on blue rice paper. "I was starting to think you forgot all about it. Just point me the way." Cheer rises like baking cookie dough as she drives. She musters a cocky panache turning the wheel. I crack the window; her acrid odor floods the car. French fry crumbs coat the carpets and the gear shift skirting. Wadded hamburger wrappers and crumpled soft drink cups mulch the back floorboards.

"The people I worked with at school said they worried about me, for my feet," she says, with a quiver of remembered surprise. "They said

my feet were hard to look at. It made them hurt to see my feet like this."
She shrugs, forgiving. "I wish it didn't bother them, but oh well. I told
them they don't hurt. It never crossed my mind to think it's all that bad. It's
just my feet."

The shoes, on jutting display platforms, are crafted for the arthritic,
the diabetic, those halted by malformed toes. Joyce savors the shoes,
strokes the suede uppers. A french-cuffed salesman deposits Joyce against
the backrest of an ample chair as though she were a diamond chip in tweezers. "I'm going to ask some questions about your feet," he says. "We can
select shoes to make you comfortable and provide adequate support."
Joyce extends a leg. She hikes the voluminous denim tunnel of her skirt up
the tight casing of knee-high stocking. "Are you diabetic?" he asks.

Joyce shakes her head. The salesman props her heel on a padded
footrest. Beyond the skirt hem, a pallid knee flashes large as a basketball.
Her ankle, an overripe cantaloupe, bulges over the shoe collar. The salesman eases her cracked, ripped sneakers, tight as foot binding, from her heel
and instep, which have constricted like putty inside the shoe form. "About
how long have your feet been swollen to this size?" he asks.

"About two years," Joyce says, eager, honest, helpful. She swishes as
if in a prom dress, testing chunky tennis shoes and blue suede sandals. "I
can wear these to church." She grins. The shoes cost over three hundred
dollars. I sidle close in the cashier's line.

"Do you have the money for this? I can help."

She hesitates. "Don't tell Mama and Daddy," she says. "I have a lot
of money in the bank." The black line item in the checkbook shouts, its
trio of zeroes like round, open mouths. "So really. Don't be worrying about
me."

I try to force a word out, any word. Anger and fright freeze in my
teeth. "But you can afford to go to a doctor," I say. She shrugs, shedding
accusations with the drop of her shoulders. She wears the new sandals
home. The salesman throws her tennis shoes away.

"Come on, try those new shoes out," I say. "Come for a walk with
me and Nitin."

"No." Embedded in the upholstered chair, she shakes her head. The skein of her thinning hair trails around her neck, and happiness recedes from her eyes like airplane lights vanishing toward the horizon. "Y'all go on," she says.

Nitin and I walk up the long neighborhood arterial, past the elementary school and into short, oak-sheltered streets. The pink-pearl glow of street light and sunset softens the white and brick ranch homes and the wide stripes of concrete driveways. A gust rattles sticks of budded forsythia. I hop and stretch to keep pace with Nitin's loose and rapid stride.

"If we won the lottery," I say, "I'd send her to a spa, to a health center, to get therapy."

"It's no good unless she chooses it herself." So Joyce is on his mind, too. The crisp edge of his voice grasps the words.

"I don't know how to talk to her about it. She shuts down."

"The kindest thing to hope, if she doesn't get help soon—and it may be too late—" he says, "is that when she dies, she dies quickly. Because there is no question, this is going to kill her. A person can't put this amount of stress on her internal organs. Pray," he says, "that when she gets really sick it isn't with diabetes, in a wheelchair, with extremely expensive medicine. That will ruin your parents financially and it will drain their health. If she refuses help, then pray that when she goes it happens quickly."

He's from a world where death is visible, like a street vendor or a stray dog. He can look at the living and see death and remain untroubled. I resent his death pronouncements but accept his absolutism, the two reactions colliding silently like hot and cold water.

"She's chosen this," Nitin says. "She won't get help. She makes no effort. She's been off from work what, almost a year? All she had to do was walk. If she's trying to eat healthily, as she says, all she had to do was walk. A block a day. Then two blocks. Then a half mile. All she had to do was get up and move. She's been in our house almost a week and has hardly moved from the chair except to go up and down the stairs to bed. If she's making no effort then she'll never get better, and she will be much worse. You can't live that heavy."

Reactions ferment in my stomach. I don't want him to be right. Yet he's right. My sister's dying. Amidst the quickened breaths of walking at his pace down the even sidewalk squares, I breathe a silent apology to him for my resistance. Perhaps he hears my silence as agreement, or acquiescence. Perhaps he hears it as stubborn rebuttal forming. I hold my silence out like a hand. A street light flickers above us.

"She's lying about eating healthily," I say. "She's lying about not being able to afford a doctor."

Nitin has a special frown for the regret of waste. It skates briefly across his face's lean brown curves. In me, a seed of nausea splits, and a pale sprout of fear worms from the cracked seed casing. "I don't think she knows the difference," I say. "I don't think she knows she's lying."

"How old is your sister?" he asks.

"She'll be thirty-eight this December." Claws stretch in my voice. "She's ruined our chair. It sags now."

"It's only furniture," he says gently.

"It's hard to face," I say. I concentrate on the rubbery rhythm of shoe soles over concrete.

He nods, a heavy beat, his ripe-fig eyes solemn and untroubled. "Then you need to prepare yourself," he says.

On Sunday mornings, fewer hospital visitors barnacled the elevator walls; fewer doctors lurked and darted in coral-branch hallways. Near the cafeteria, a glimpse of receding white coat tails hooked and reeled me. Black hair, broad shoulders, panthered step, a sidelong whisk of profile— trim beard, a flake-obsidian eye. I rushed my flat, lethargic step. He clapped a hand across the closing elevator door. Fighting breathlessness, I stepped inside. My smile wavered with doubt; I might be an encumbrance, an intruder.

"Hello," Dr. Abu said. He smiled down gently, scarves of dark clouds chased from the moon by a warming wind. "How are you?"

"All right," I said, opening my face as though turning pockets inside out, begging him to look for hidden fear, contraband pain. "We've missed you."

Dr. Abu checked my eyes as though they were the darkened corners of a nursery, as though he were listening for breathing. "I've been following your sister's case, as I can," he said. "I heard about the surgery. They've told me it went as well as anyone might have hoped."

"You know about the VRE then," I said.

He nodded again, a soft scoop of the bearded chin. "How does your sister seem to you?"

(Joyce, motionless now, as if she has sunk to the depth of her bathysphere body. Joyce, with the barest blinks and winces, conveys attention, irritation. Her arms, pale loaves, lie at her sides. Her fingertips twitch. Ice chips melt inside the worn clutch purse of lip and gum.)

"There are some good things," I said. "She knows us when we come in. And she's had more visitors."

(Daddy'd said, "Do you remember Charles Cole? Elder Cole, from church?"

"Sure I do," I'd said. "He's the one who taught us sign language, when we were little."

"Why, he sure was," Daddy'd said. "I'd forgotten that. He came to visit Joyce today. I guess Harry told them all at church that Joyce was up here."

"Really? Well, that's good of Mr. Cole to come. I'm sorry I missed him."

"He cried after he saw her," Daddy'd said, perplexed, sobered.)

"She may not be able to show it," I told Dr. Abu, "but I think it would make her happy that people came for her."

"And how are your parents?" Dr. Abu asked, the infusion of concern spreading, palpable.

(Mama's said, "I think it's starting to wear on your daddy, that is, not getting any exercise and eating hospital food. He's starting to feel awful run down."

Daddy's said, "It's not good for your mother's back. Sleeping in that bed, standing up so much in Joyce's room. She's starting to hurt.")

The elevator bell dinged. "They're hanging in there," I said. "They're tired. Look," I said, "this isn't my floor. I just wanted to say hello to you."

Dr. Abu held his palm against the pocketed door and leaned on the elevator frame. I could not name the feelings that lit his eyes, a controlled bonfire on a starless night. "I wish I had something to share with you," he said. "If I knew anything more, you know."

"Yeah," I said. I piled up a small smile, an altar of thanksgiving. "I know."

How will she control her anxiety toward an overweight person? How will she acknowledge all that is part of fatness without making it her only index of that person's character? How can she offer an overweight person help with a weight problem? She can't, she decides. She won't try.

Nobody can forcibly help anybody else lose weight.

But she can give an overweight person help with the pain problem. She can assume it's there, not because of the weight, but because we all have pain problems. She can listen for the pain, and try to point toward silliness, if not joy, and be interested. She can do this for anyone. She can be a friend.

She knows well enough that the smallest bit of acceptance might be the foothold that steadies a person; the smallest bit of love might persuade a person of their worth. The smallest bit of kindness might seed an addiction stronger even than the want for food: the need to care for oneself, the need to feel good, not numb.

I slouched on a padded pink bench in the breezeway, pretending to write a letter, daydreaming in the Oklahoma sunset, its apricot scraps and lavender suffusing the hydrangea sky. A trim, brisk figure emerged from the hospital doors and glided up the glass breezeway, swinging a rectangular duffel from one hand. She dropped it by my shoes. I capped my pen. Nurse Carol held her freckled arms wide for a hug.

"I'm glad I found you here," she said. She hooked a blonde strand over her ear. Her smile was a fragile seashell. "I want to talk to you about your sister. There are things not so easy to say, back there." She motioned her head toward the hospital. She spoke as though I were a child getting ready to cross the street alone for the first time. "You know the odds aren't good, don't you?"

"I know," I said. "But I don't know the details."

"Okay. Let's talk." Carol sat with me on the bench, scrub pant knees trimly together. She paused, smiled at me, sighed. "First—because of her weight, she'll have a very difficult time healing from the surgery."

I suspended her sentence in my mind. She meant to tell me the truth now. All I had to do was chew and swallow each new, bitter bite, and she'd feed me. "I hadn't heard that before," I said. "I don't understand."

"It's gravity. Its just—gravity. The surgical wound in her abdomen might not heal. Gravity is pulling the wound apart." She watched my battle for composure as I repeated this sentence silently also. "Then, the VRE is there and may infect the surgical wound. Her medication is continuing to weaken her kidneys. And she's still on the respirator. We're having to give her more and more PEEP—that's sort of a forced breath, and high levels of it are dangerous. Sweetie—I don't think she'll be able to come off the respirator. You understand what I'm saying, don't you?"

I swallowed the acid bite. This was it, the rare, ripe morsel: the prediction, the certainty. I nodded again.

"I'm just so sorry, so sorry for your family." Her touch was feathery, as if she'd massage my hand with just her fingerprints.

"Carol? How will it happen?"

"Her lungs will fail. That's what's really killing her. She won't be able to breathe. Her respiratory system is getting weaker and weaker. All the things she's fighting—her lungs can't bear it." Nurse Carol tipped her head back; she stared at the ceiling a moment and then looked directly at me. Her wide-set, inexhaustible eyes reflected weeks of aggressive observation, even more aggressive compassion. "Your parents still don't seem to know what's going to happen."

My voice was lethargic, overfed. "No one's telling them."

"We're trying," Carol said. "They don't seem to hear it, or want to hear it." She stood. She shook her head. "The surgeons went to heroic lengths to save her. She's so young, and her heart is so strong. But here, how are you holding up?"

"Carol," I said, standing with her arms' reach. "I want to know what's happening to her. Am I right, thinking the other statistics don't matter now. The ones I call and ask for."

Carol nodded, a slight pinch of sympathy at the corners of her calm eyes.

"It's all about the oxygen, isn't it?"

"Yes," she said. "That's it. And what you'll hear over the next few days is her dependency going up. You'll hear us talk about that. Her kidney function will decrease, but mostly you'll want to watch the oxygen."

"I know it doesn't help her for me to know what's going on in—in her body."

"But it helps you. That's reason enough, you know."

"It's just—it's not right, that she could die without anybody paying attention. Without anybody knowing what she's going through. I don't know how to say it." I want to feel it with her, I thought. I want to take the sickness away from her by knowing it. I want to know what's coming, and be with her there, before it. "I feel like I'm leaving her all alone."

Carol's mouth formed a tiny "oh." Her smile was not dismissal, and she squeezed her arms around me. She patted my back. She stepped away and plucked the duffel from the floor. "It's okay," she said. "We'll tell you what we know. We understand."

Search terms: Mechanics of breathing. Respiratory assessment. Mechanical ventilation.

The lungs aren't oxygen's final destination. The lungs are a collection point, a transfer station for oxygen on its travel through the blood and toward the tissues of our bodies. The true test of sufficient breathing is not how much oxygen flows into the lungs, but how much oxygen has entered the blood. Machines that help you breathe also monitor a host of "mechanics," numbers that show exactly how much oxygen the machine is giving to your lungs and blood, and how well your body is using it.

Even the basic words were tricky surrounding these mechanics of assisted breathing. For instance, I thought of the "ventilator" as a machine to help Joyce breathe, but "ventilation" actually meant something else. You suck in oxygen with air—you vent carbon dioxide back into the atmosphere. So "oxygenation" is when you breathe in, getting oxygen into your blood—ventilation is when you breathe out, expelling the acid of carbon dioxide. Entirely separate sets of monitored numbers show whether the blood contains enough oxygen or too much carbon dioxide.

Joyce's daily charts had filled with these new numbers and words. Blips, numerals, and jagged lines freckled the tidy rectangular monitor screens for lungs and heart. PO2. FiO2. O2 saturation. Tidal volume. PEEP.

Tidal volume is the easiest to understand. This is the amount of air you move in and out of your lungs. During your regular, quiet breathing, you inhale and exhale about a half liter of air.

One of the mysterious numbers is "PO2." When Joyce's PO2 was low, the nurses' faces became somber and respectful. PO2 shows how much pressure your lungs would feel if you were only breathing the part of air that's oxygen. So if you're breathing a lot of oxygen, because you're on a ventilator, but your PO2 is low anyway, it means that the extra oxygen isn't helping the little sacs in your lungs fill up. The oxygen isn't getting into your blood.

"FiO2" stands for "fraction of inspired oxygen." This shows what percentage of the air you're breathing is oxygen. The normal air we breathe is about 21 percent oxygen. If the oxygen in the blood is low, then the ventilator includes more oxygen in the mix. But high FiO2 is dangerous. Pure oxygen is toxic.

"O2 saturation" is measured by a small probe clipped over your fingertip. The probe pulses a light. If your blood is rich with oxygen, it will absorb less light. Your blood should be 96 to 99 percent full of oxygen. When the saturation level drops low, the nurse monitoring your spiderweb of machines knows that your organs may be soon damaged, that you could suffer brain damage, that you could die.

And then there's PEEP.

Search term: PEEP.

Pure oxygen is a poison. It burns and scars the lungs. If you need high levels of oxygen from your ventilator, the nurses and doctors can use PEEP to try to give you less pure oxygen. PEEP stands for positive end-expiratory pressure. When a nurse gives you PEEP, the machine adds a little extra push when you inhale. This forces more air into the little lung spaces where oxygen moves into the blood. PEEP keeps your lungs a little more full, so that you feel like you can't breathe everything out. It eases your breathing, but has its risks. One risk of using a high level of PEEP is pneumonia. Another lies in the pathways to the lung's air spaces. They can rupture.

The Monday after surgery, while I slept next to my packed bag, Joyce's blood oxygen level dropped. "It was so low, they thought they were going to lose her," Mama said the next morning. "It came back up but they said it was tenuous, was the word they used." She chased a last lump of scrambled eggs across her plate. Daddy wedged his fork into a waffle square, watched the syrup spill slowly onto the plate. "So we didn't get a whole lot of sleep," Mama continued. "And Carol said this morning one of her doctors would come talk to us, out in the waiting room."

"Talk about what?" I felt sick, as though sleep had been poison, as though the food I had just eaten had been mercury.

"I don't know, Ann," Mama said, clipping her words, wiping her mouth with a paper napkin. "Just to bring us up to date, I suppose. Maybe they can tell us whether to expect middle-of-the-night calls. If that's so, Norman, we'll need to stay in the hospital, not sleep away at LaNita's."

"I don't know about that," Daddy said. "They can call us there just as well as here." He sighed, looking up at the TV, regretting his admission. "I don't know how many more nights I can do of that hard, lumpy bed. My joints have got to hurting."

We rode together to the eighth floor. In the small waiting room, Mama picked up the handset and dialed the ICU desk number. "We're up here in the room," she said. She and Daddy sat at the round table in the corner. I shifted from foot to foot, unsure whether I belonged with them or whether I should defer, a bystander. "Doctor?" Mama said, twisting, looking past me.

"Yes," the woman said, her straight teeth a bouquet of white roses against the satiny bitter-cocoa skin. Tall, she wore floral silk under her starched white coat. In delicate, colonial accent, she said her name, a string of syllables like a flower necklace. Her smile bloomed and disappeared, bloomed again for Mama and Daddy. Daddy removed his cap, and the beautiful doctor shook his hand. She touched Mama's shoulder, sat down at the table, then touched Mama's hand. I lowered myself into the armchair near the table. The beautiful doctor sorted her words as though they were tiny and easily breakable shells.

"The things we need to talk about," she said, "they may be very difficult for you to hear. If you need at any point to stop me and take a few minutes for yourselves, simply say so." Mama and Daddy exchanged wordless surprise and agreement.

"It's all right, Doctor," Mama said, her drawl comforting and dignified. "We know there are things that aren't easy for you to tell us."

"The prognosis for your daughter is not good. I am so sorry." The beautiful doctor gulped, smoothed her trembling accent. "As the days pass, she is requiring more and more oxygen. If her blood oxygen levels are too low, she is not going to be able to breathe on her own. At that point, only the respirator will be keeping her alive. Mr. and Mrs. Vandiver, I have to ask you what you would like us to do at that point?"

Daddy's graying eyebrows lifted with emphasis. His hooded blue eyes sagged wide. "If that happens," Daddy said, the words descending like a creek over rocks at night, the searchlights casting low ovals across the surface of his baritone, "we'll let her go."

"You don't wish artificial life support," said the beautiful doctor, her low inflection tinged with disbelief at the ease of choice.

"No," Daddy said, shaking his head.

"We've talked about it," Mama explained. She rested her pale hand lightly on the doctor's upper arm, as if to pet her. "We've known we might need to make that decision," Mama said slowly, gently. "If it comes to that, that's what we want. Doctor, it's all right. We're all right with it."

The beautiful doctor gazed at Mama as though Mama were a perfect newborn, a rare jewel, an almost-extinct songbird. A black tendril swished against the rounded cheekbone. "There are papers here for you both to sign, to the effect of your decision."

"Thank you," Mama said, her voice bending on the words. Daddy turned his head toward the window. He stared into the quadrangle of blue sky as though he were waiting for a train, late to arrive. "I know this wasn't easy," Mama said. "We know you have to ask all this; it's your procedure. We appreciate your taking time with us. We truly do." With the doctor's offered ink pen, she and Daddy reviewed, initialed, and signed away the chance of lingering reliance.

The beautiful doctor and I stood in the hallway. I had forgotten her name already. I left it forgotten, fallen to brutal futility. "How long?" I asked, my mouth contorting. The beautiful doctor curved her dark hands around the edges of her clipboard. Her eyes were like dark liniment, their kind glow spreading.

"There is no way to know," she said, tiptoeing through the phrases. "But she is fighting so many ailments at this point that it is almost certain she will not be able to hold out against all of them. The surgical wound is not healing. Medicine is pouring into her for the infection and for the pain, and it clogs her kidneys. We're giving her higher and higher levels of PEEP." The beautiful doctor sighed, groped for summary. "We do not think it is today, or tomorrow," she said. "But if it is several days or a few weeks, we cannot say."

She thinks of her sister. What would she want for her sister now? For the morbidly obese, she thinks, as was my sister, I wish for you a safe and loving environment—an honest one—in which to confront pain, behavior, and desires. I wish for you a successful first step toward a healthier body. Then a successful second step. And someone to cheer you on.

I wish for you firsthand knowledge of what good nutrition and healthy eating feel like. I wish for you help in sorting through conflicting advice and weight loss plans and remedies. I wish for you a person to whom you can be honest. I wish for you relief from judgment.

I wish for you eye contact and casual conversation with strangers, clothing in which you are not afraid or embarrassed to move or be seen, events that make happy memories. I wish for you pursuits that are more important than food, more important than an obsession with diet. And I wish you are never a doctor's nightmare.

"You should go home and get some rest," Mama suggested, patting my knee. "Go be with your husband and get some rest. She's just sleeping now. I don't even know for sure she knows we're here. When she starts recovering from the surgery, she'll be ready for visits again."

Joyce slept. Through the changing of bags and bottles, through the steady beeps and flashes of entrenched monitor statistics, through our gowned visits, she slept. I held her limp, leaden hand and watched TV, or studied her immobile face while minutes built brick walls of hours. I thought back to the previous winter. A short-lived sinus infection had planted itself then like a flag near my right ear. My head had felt swollen, the fine muscles around my eyes tight and tender, my throat choked as if I'd swallowed concrete. My mind had dulled, a chill had swirled under my skin, and the spongy stuff protected by my ribs had groaned for rest. And that was a single, small disorder, quickly cured. How many months, how many years had she carried her body's aquarium of infections? How long had pain robbed her of her smile? Had her body cheated her also of this, that she thought the pain was normal?

"I have to tell you goodbye now," I said. "I'll be back soon, though. I'll be back to see you." I leaned close to her cheek. The night-sky eye, the wary animal deep within its cave, edged toward me. Her face was like an empty beach, its fine, expressive muscles thick and still. "I know you're awake," I whispered. "Joyce. I know you won't stop fighting. I know. But listen. It's okay to win however you need to. Okay?" I brushed her hairline with cold, gloved fingers. "I'm coming back to see you," I said. "You'll be here."

I gave myself back to Kansas, first to the prairie drive, then to the corporate cubicle routine. I let work swallow me, Jonah in the big fish's dark belly. I sank to the unlit sea floor, where I paperclipped photocopies, circled passive verbs, made coffee when the central coffeepot ran low, all to the rhythm of slowly circling questions: Where is the line between believing someone is going to die and knowing she is going to die? Where is the line between knowing someone is going to die and wishing that she dies quickly rather than slowly?

Kerri, lithe and quietly buoyant, paused in my doorway every day. She manufactured professional inquiries, errands harmless as blunt scissors. She took my wan, apologetic smile from me like a used paper plate. Her own smile was diffused, the safe glow of the flashlight hidden for reading under covers. I was too tired to tell her how I felt. I was too tired to tell her how I'd ripped out the fat notebook pages one by one, fed Joyce's cryptic numbers and graphs to the kitchen trash bag. I was too tired to tell her about the morning's conversation with the stolid, pumpkin-haired ICU nurse.

"It may be a comfort to you," the nurse had said. "I worked at a military renal hospital for a number of years. The doctors there told me that when a patient has a heavy drug load, like your sister, something happens. The drug overload on the kidneys, it forces the kidneys to produce a substance that puts the patient in a state of euphoria."

"That's true?" I felt my voice crumbling like dried cheese in my throat. It came out trembling and crusty.

"It's what the doctors always told me, so, yes," she said. "When your sister's conscious, she's not in pain. On the contrary. All she feels is blissful and happy."

"Thank you," I said, thinking ahead to how I might forward the gift of euphoria, how I would hear on the phone lines Harry's solid comprehension and Mama's triumphant relief and Daddy's awed gratefulness. "Thank you so much."

Euphoria. The word fizzed, hydrogen peroxide on a soiled wound. Euphoria—the word echoed up from the belly of the whale, allowed me to nod and smile when colleagues greeted me. And when a senior colleague, alone with me in a quiet conference room, asked how things were going in Joyce's illness, I told him all but that word, euphoria. I kept euphoria to myself and told him instead of the barrage of disease, of the likelihood of her death. "You know," he said, attempting to comfort with reason, "sometimes it's better this way. Sometimes it's better for them to go quickly."

I clutched the word, euphoria, and kept my balance. In principle, I didn't disagree. But Joyce's death didn't feel quick; the past five weeks had stretched beyond time. Was he right? Should I want her to go quickly, when I could not want her to go at all? Maybe he knew. Maybe he had escorted someone he loved through an illness of years, like Uncle Troy's. Five hundred and fifty pounds—a doubt flashed, an abrupt horror—could she have eaten enough calories daily to sustain that weight? From Mama's kitchen, from her wallet, was it possible? What could it mean? How badly could her body have betrayed her?

The senior colleague sorted stapled papers on the conference table. I stared at him sidelong, from lowered eyes, pretending to study my notepad. Why does the butcher put so much meat on the sandwich? I wanted to ask him.

Maybe he'd know that one.

❖   2001   ❖

"So what is it about your sister?" Kerri asks. "Tell me." Our tiny office is a quiet alcove off a busy hallway. It's July, and after seven months as co-workers, we've learned to dedicate time in the day to talk, or our aimless, protracted conversation would weave us tight as flies in a web, unable to work. Kerri's laugh is like the fizz in the air above champagne; her laugh is like clean teeth. People want to talk to her. When she looks you in the eye, she means what her gaze implies: you are obviously an important person, somewhere to someone, I can tell it about you.

"My sister—see—has problems. She's about five feet tall. She weighs at least four hundred pounds. She refuses to go to a doctor. She refuses any help at all. It's going to kill her. She's gigantic. She can hardly move."

"Wow. That's hard," Kerri says softly. She sits back in her chair, surprised. "Do you think she'll ever go to a doctor?"

"I don't know. She says it's too expensive. I don't know how much money she has anymore. She lives with my parents. She hasn't worked in a year." Truth waits like a ghost for visibility. I describe the haunting. "Every conversation with Joyce has this urgency. If I'll find a way to get through to her. If she'll ever be ready to open up and get help. I think of her every day, and when I think of her I panic and my stomach knots up and I want to cry." Joyce lingers in my mind, her squashed, anguished eyes and stubborn silence. It's like falling in love with a prisoner. "The worst part is, I can't remember her happy. I can't remember what she looked like before. I can't remember her face when we were kids. I can't remember what her laugh sounds like. Sometimes she reaches out but when I reach back she slams the door. She hasn't let me love her, not in so, so long." Kerri's leaning forward, her hands clasped around a knee, her slow blue blink moist with sympathy. "Are you sure you want to hear all this?" I say.

"Do you want to talk about it?" she says.

"Yeah. I don't talk about my sister. I haven't told this to anybody."

"It's okay, then. I like learning about people's families. And too, I could tell. I mean, the look on your face. You can't mention her without this, you know, distress. I knew it was something." She shakes her head without taking her eyes off me. "You're grieving her."

Grief: a word for death, an opposite for denial. "To love her," I think out loud, "I have to grieve her or forget her. I can't forget her."

"How old is she?"

"She's thirty-eight. She's four and a half years older than me. She'll be thirty-nine in December."

"What do your parents say?"

"They won't talk about it. My mother told me to not to butt into it, that it's Joyce's life and that I don't know what's best for everybody." Not everybody can be like you, Ann. Not everybody wants the same things you do. "I kind of have a bossy reputation in my family."

"Huh."

"Yeah. So I'm not supposed to give any advice. It's really frustrating. Joyce starts talking to me about food and diet, but as soon as I say anything she clams up. You can almost hear the door slam shut."

"But wouldn't your parents support her if she tried to lose weight?"

"It's not like they'd ridicule her. But they don't know how to support her. I think their best idea of support is just not to interfere. So in one way they're in denial, but I know they're also constantly worried. I know it can't be off their minds. It's just so hard to face."

"I can see that. How hard, to look at your child in pain. And then having all the weight loss issues on top of it."

"Yeah. Who's to blame and what's the right solution. You know, I don't know whether they'd get it, that to lose two hundred pounds, a person has to change nearly everything. How she thinks about herself, how she lives her daily life." Joyce is the best natural cook in the family, says Mama. It's sure good having her here to cook. There's never any food in the house, says Joyce. "I don't know whether Joyce gets that, either. She lies to herself about her eating. She lies to herself about losing weight."

"How do you know?"

"She lies to me. She says in one breath that she's sticking to her diet and then ten minutes later tells me about the greasy fast food she ate last night because there was no salad in the house."

I buckled my seatbelt today, Joyce says. All the way around. You're kidding, I say. That's great. Yeah, she says, I don't want to tell you how long it's been since I could do that. I don't have any other way to know that this diet is working. What do you mean, no other way, I say, what about the scale? I think I'm too heavy for it, she says. When I get on it flashes all zeros and then it goes black. Is it broken? I ask, remembering it goes up to three hundred and fifty pounds. We can get you another one. She pauses. It's not broken, she says. Are you sure, because—It's not broken, she says, don't worry. It's okay. I think I've lost maybe ten pounds so far. My clothes are feeling a little looser.

Ten pounds? Nitin yanks me down to earth. She sounded so happy, I tell him. Honey, ten pounds—there's no way she can tell if she's lost ten pounds. At her size, she would have to lose fifty pounds before she could feel a difference. Think about it. Can you tell when you've lost a half a pound without getting on a scale? There's no way she knows she's lost ten pounds. It's in her head, honey. If she's not exercising she's not going to lose weight, seriously. I know you're right, I say, but—

It's not real, he says. I know you're right but the seatbelt thing is good, I say. She was so happy about it. Isn't it good that she can feel happy about that? Maybe, he says. It's good she's buckling her seat belt when she drives.

"Wow. You said she was a teacher, right?"

"Yeah."

"Do you think she'll ever teach again?"

"I don't know who would hire her. Parents won't want her in with kids. I can't—it's hard to describe her. It just sounds so ugly. She's so big, she looks unreal." She had returned this past spring to Dallas for her teaching position. No one seemed to remember a promise of re-employment. So she misted herself in perfumed body spray to follow her resume to interviews in Oklahoma. No one would hire her, even as a substitute. She's really depressed about it, says Daddy. You know why no one will hire her, I tell him. She's not healthy. She is healthy, Daddy insists. She's just big, and slow.

"I'm not sure what she spends her time doing," I tell Kerri, ashamed of my judgmental frustration. "I asked her if she would get out and volunteer or something, but she thought I was preaching at her. She does these needlepoint projects, family trees in needlepoint. She makes gift books—she's made us all these big scrapbooks of things that happened in the world on our birthdays. Last Christmas she gave me a recipe book, handwritten—she has beautiful handwriting—with little inspirational quotes between the recipes.

"She researches stuff online," I continue. "The family genealogy and stuff about her favorite celebrities." Mama finds Joyce one day crying in front of the computer. I can't reach the keyboard, Joyce cries. My arms aren't long enough to reach over my stomach.

"So, yeah, my parents, it's a hard time for them. They just got past my Grandma's death and being her primary caretakers. And my uncle, my Dad has a strong feeling for him, he has ALS. It's fatal, a wasting disease. So his health is up and down as he gradually gets worse. They're trying experimental medicines—once, he even straightened his fingers again—but it's not a good long-term prognosis. Nobody even knows how long the long term is."

"Does your aunt take care of your uncle?"

"I just love my aunt. She's been by his side and done everything a person could. She approached me about Joyce, you know, after Grandma's funeral. She said, 'Ann, look at your sister's eyes. In her eyes she looks just miserable.'

"When my Grandma died," I tell Kerri, "Joyce picked out all the music and the scriptures. She stayed nights with my Grandma when nobody else would." With an unsentimental thoroughness, Joyce cared for Grandma as for a colicky baby. Joyce brought coloring books for Grandma, and colored with her.

"She sends me funny e-mail greeting cards all the time," I say. Hello! Joyce has just sent you a greeting card. Happy World Sauntering Day!

"Like what?" Kerri's smile pulses encouragement; my sister's summation includes more than pain. It includes Oatmeal Month and Bathtub Party Day.

"Oh, for holidays nobody ever heard of. Everything she sends me is all about celebration. She never sends me anything that sounds sad or depressed. Ever." Take Your Houseplant for a Walk Day. International No Diet Day. Ice Cream Cone Day. My Sister Is . . . "She visited last year. It wasn't a fun visit. She stayed mad the whole time and wouldn't talk to me. But when she said goodbye, she hugged me really hard and said, 'I love you.' And there was more there, something, you know, just huge—in her eyes, I couldn't recognize it, she couldn't say it. I wanted to pull her back in the house and make her stay. If I could just see her happy, I could get it! But we said goodbye."

Search term: death.

Our body dies three deaths. It dies the continual death of cells; it dies the death of function; it dies the death of tissues.

The first kind of death is happening right now. Bits of us are dying and being born all the time. Old cells die, new cells form. We don't feel it; we don't know it's happening.

The second kind of death is when the vital functions of the body stop and cannot be restarted. The brain's electrical connections cease to fire and sizzle. The nerve endings stop feeling, the eyes stop seeing. The blood grows sluggish and inert in the arteries and veins. The heart's beat slows and disappears. The lungs relax. A last breath leaves, a gift, a final change upon the planet. When these things happen, we are dead.

Yet our bodies live on a while. The sheet is pulled over our faces, but below it our tissues have not died. The cells live on, unaware of grief or change. Like factory workers who haven't yet heard the plant's gone broke, they bustle on in their specialized jobs, repair and manufacture and fueling. Then, slowly, as blood no longer flows and oxygen no longer rushes in and electrical charges no longer burst, the cells lapse too. No longer part of you, a living thing, your cells transform: they become matter, and nothing more—matter, which decays, but not around you; matter, which disintegrates, but not around you; matter, to be embalmed and buried, a husk, without meaning, which you left behind.

She thinks of herself and the women in her weight loss support group. For those learning to manage their bodies, she thinks, I wish for us health and the ability to adventure physically. I wish that our lives are not about our weight. I wish for us to be told and believe that we are beautiful, desirable. That we find things to care about more than our weight. That we are free from jealousy of the thin.

I wish for us to be free from the need to disassociate from fat people. I wish for us that others' apprehensions don't stop our activity or pleasure. I wish for us to find comfort in our bodies, and utility. I wish for us to be free from obsession. And I wish us every chance to give love.

Mama and Daddy wouldn't be at St. John. The leather-trimmed bag was almost empty, a single change of clothes and shoes trifled over the rumpled black knits. Through the prairie hours, I tried to blot out the single song that hammered the mind's ear. I sang Christmas carols. I surfed fuzzy radio channels, argued back to talk show panelists bickering over our enemies' psyches. But the song threaded through the noise, infuriating, the words persistent, indelible from youth. *Just as I am, poor, wretched, blind—*

sight, riches, healing of the mind, Yea, all I need, in thee I find, O Lamb of God,
I come, I come . . .

The weekend nurses had unfamiliar faces, fresh and rested manners. I didn't ask them for statistics. The black tower of monitors loomed, defeated me with a vertigo of data. I didn't remember what the numbers meant. I gathered that the ventilator supplied most of her oxygen, most of her breath. Joyce, mothballed in antibiotic and palliative fog, fought for a flickering recognition. She blinked, moistened her darkened eyes. In her face, a tension of intent—Joyce tried to turn her head and was immobilized by the hose of the breathing tube. In her arm, a shift—she tried to raise her hand, but failed. I wiggled a cracked ice chip behind her swollen lip. It was too much work; she fell asleep. I tissue-blotted the meltwater dribbling down her neck. I poured the tiny cup of crystalline cylinders down the sink.

Just as I am! Thou wilt receive, wilt welcome, pardon, cleanse, relieve;
Because thy promise I believe, O Lamb of God, I come, I come . . .

"I'm going to see Lanette," I told her. "I'll be back before visiting hours end tonight. Then I'll come see you in the morning." In the squashed-moon face, the darkened eyes drifted back and forth as if in dreaming slumber.

She thinks of the pain she once felt, thinking of her sister; she thinks of her father trying to understand his obese daughters. For you who have never been fat but are trying to love a fat person, she thinks, I wish for you that weight is not the central fact of your relationships. I wish for you that you are loved. I wish for you to be free of revulsion and fear. I wish you are free of the need to judge and give unasked counsel. I wish for you to know how it feels to be treasured friends and champions of love. I wish that you never forget life's pain. I wish that you never forget life's joy.

"So how are your mom and dad doing?" In jeans and light jackets, Lanette and I sat on her front porch steps. The residential autumn night smelled like dry leaves and old asphalt, like wood smoke and a neighbor's fresh house paint. Lanette's cigarette lighter spouted a flame teardrop inside her cupped hand. Under the soft gold porch light, Lanette's short hair was the color of butter floating in cream. It spiked and fluffed around the broad, fair cheekbones, the sharp-eyed, impassive face.

"I don't know. I can't believe they don't know what's happening. Mama talks as though it weren't happening. And Daddy doesn't talk at all. He's there, but his eyes don't, you know, land on anything."

"Mom said they were in denial."

"Yeah, they worry about your mom being in denial."

Lanette exhaled fiercely, almost a laugh, and sipped another taste from the cigarette. "Yeah, that's something, isn't it."

"You know I watched them change the stoma bag today." The surgical wound had been clean and sensible, the exposed wheel of intestine pink as healthy gums. The nurse had stripped away the soiled bag, swabbed the white skin with cleansing wipes, pressed the clean bag's adhesive disk. I'd forced myself to see Joyce's naked belly. Her pale, tapioca skin stretched on a quivering expanse that could not have been identified, alone, as a torso. Her abdomen looked like a parachute falling as the skydiver touches ground. I couldn't look at Joyce's body and think of Joyce. They didn't seem to belong to each other. But I could grasp the surgical site, the stoma bag, as hers. Strained trusses of gauze and tape fought to splice the split skin together around the opening.

"Yeah?" Lanette says. "How was that?"

"Not so bad. But the reason I say it, see, Mama knows about stoma bags. She wants to learn about it, how to take care of Joyce. And it wasn't bad. If Mama had to, she could have done that for Joyce."

"People can do a lot of things when they need to."

"It makes me wish she needed to," I said. "I wish Mama could have gotten that chance. I feel a little crazy for what I wish." I planted my sneakers on the step below me, hugged my knees toward my chest.

Lanette stretched, tapped her cigarette against the step. "Yeah? What's up?"

"I feel crazy for wanting things to stay like this. Just like this. I want Joyce to stay in the hospital."

Lanette looked up into the bruised ambient haze of Tulsa night. "Yeah. That's not as crazy as you think."

"I want her to stay alive and in the hospital so I can keep visiting her. She's not in pain there. Lanette, see, in the hospital Joyce smiled at me for the first time in I don't know when. She lets me take care of her. She lets me touch her. Love her."

"She didn't before."

"No." I pictured the scowl, the shrug of spite. I pictured the steely smile below the oxygen mask. "I thought it would be hard to see her totally sedated, you know, cut off, unable to open her eyes. But it's strange. It's not hard. I feel closer to her now than I have in a long time. I wish I hadn't ever blamed her the way I did."

"Blamed her? You mean for the shape she was in?"

Calories in, calories out, I thought. Are the equations really so simple and equal for everyone, for the drastically overweight body? Does science even know? "I was so mad at her for being fat and miserable. But maybe it wasn't so simple for her. Maybe it wasn't something she could fix by herself. I know she tried. I could have listened more, instead of always trying to, you know, reform her, improve her. I held her accountable, constantly. I could have been a better sister."

"Whoa," Lanette said. The cola-rum voice deepened, the words rapid and sharp like the teeth of a hand saw. "Before you load all that guilt on yourself, you really need to think about this. Did she go to a doctor? Did she try to get help?"

"No."

"Did she actively resist help when it was offered to her?"

"People begged her."

"Look, okay. You can't feel guilty for her choices. Because maybe it's just not up to you to figure out what her choices were, right or wrong.

Maybe her health wasn't her fault, and maybe it was all her fault. But maybe it's not up to you to figure out whose fault anything is. Maybe it's just up to you to love your sister." Lanette glanced over at me. "Maybe that's all you get to do."

I don't feel guilty, I thought, the way she thinks I do. I don't think I was a bad sister. But I see now how to do better, and I wish I'd figured it out sooner. Lanette's glance raked over my face, compassionate. Her incisive calm was like painkiller. A rusted gear shifted deep in my ribs, love transferring, regenerating, multiplying. I hadn't known I'd loved my cousin. So this happens again, I thought.

"So how do you do it?" I asked her.

"What's that?"

"With your dad. I can't imagine how strong you would have to be. How have you done it, lasting so long?"

"Well." A pencil of white smoke streamed toward the lawn. She stubbed the cigarette on the concrete step. "We've been so close, so many times. He's almost gone, and then—yeah. You can't just grieve over and over again, without end. A lot of our grieving for him, we've already been through. Look," she said. "Nothing about grief is easy. None of this is easy. None of it's pretty. But you need to remember that you'll get through it. Do you hear me? You'll get through it."

A street away, a car horn honked twice; a dog barked; a door slammed. Tulsa floated around us, simple and sleepy. Stars blurred in the autumn night sky. I cleared my throat, my voice husky with tobacco smoke and cooling air.

"Knowing they're going isn't the same as wanting it to be over."

"No," Lanette said. "No, it's not."

She only has to make it through one day, she tells herself. One day of restraint, one day of diverting herself from food into activities, conversations. One day of drinking enough water. One day with a long walk.

On the second day, she tells herself she only has to make it through one day. She doesn't have to win it all today. She only has to keep going.

On the third day she feels it, an edge of emptiness in her stomach, a rush of thought not about food, a curiosity about her day. I'm doing it, she thinks. She's waking up. But this time, she remembers the dream. She remembers the truth and can acknowledge the danger without letting it frighten her. If her habits slip or if her positive attitude fails, the want will swell like a river behind a crumbling dam.

Don't worry on it, she tells herself. Live this hour well.

On Sunday morning, white sunlight illuminated ICU's glass rooms, even through closed blind slats. In the doctorless quiet, the door slid open behind me, and I jumped. Recognition sidled into my nerves, matching man to memory: the surgeon's long frame, the deep lines from cheek to jaw. I almost said it aloud: I'm so used to never seeing the doctors again.

"It's good to see you," I said.

He smiled a thin, flexible smile, the only curled line in his stance of angles. "I'm here to inspect the stoma," he said, hinting with a blink toward the door, toward an escape from graphic exposure.

"May I stay?" I asked. "I'll be all right."

He nodded. I backed against the wall. When his slow waltz of fingers on her skin was done, I followed him to the outer room. He peeled his gloves and dropped them in the waste bin. He waited for my hesitant, uneven breathing to cross into speech. His dark eyes glinted with warning.

"Please tell me," I said. "No one else in my family is asking. Please tell me how she is."

"The wound is clean," he said, "but it's not healing. Gravity's working against it."

I maneuvered the next question slowly, a canoe down a rocky river. Please know, I thought, I don't mean to be airy, callous. "Can you tell me her odds of survival?"

Irritation flashed up the surgeon's face like an accordion crunching. Humbled, I saw the stupidity of odds; I saw he'd saved her life. He hadn't treated the surgery as a gamble. "Well, the situation isn't good," he finally said. "She would have a great deal to overcome."

Joyce slept, immobile, immune to light, to sound. She slept inside the cradle of her soft body, inside the net of tubes. The machines puffed breath into her chest, past the pouted lips, the closed eyes. Don't make her fight like this, I thought. God, let her go if she can't fight. God, love her. I wanted just to love her. Can you make her know?

Just as I am! I'll have to turn my back now. I'll have to strip off the gloves and the gown, and soap my arms, all without looking back. *Just as I am! Thy love unknown has broken every barrier down.* I'll have to walk out of ICU, wait for an elevator, get in my car, drive out of Tulsa. *Now to be thine, yea, thine alone—O Lamb of God, I come! I come.* I could wait. But I'll still have to go. I touch her hair, her hand, the soft crook of her elbow. I smile, a toothy, eye-wrinkling smile. "Goodbye," I say.

Who is this woman? She is, among so many other things, an overeater, a binge eater, and obese. But though she is always her weight, she has decided she's not primarily her weight. Though she'll never be cured of obesity or her potential to self-destruct, she can manage her body's tendencies. She doesn't have to live in pain.

She knows this now. Watch how her knowledge saves her. None of us knows what she will do tomorrow. But today, she reaches toward life. Watch with me. Watch her when she crosses through your life, in your family, in your workplace, in your heart. Cheer her on.

Time was like a woven fabric I spooled tightly around myself, a magician's curtain. If time conformed to my body, surely I would disappear, and time would float free, harmless again. I dragged myself upstairs one night and lay down on the bed and cried. I cried and cried and cried. I wanted to be alone, not even together with my own body. There is something deeper than crying. There is crying that comes from your nerves and crying that comes from your heart and crying that comes from your eyes and crying that comes from your throat. This crying came from my small intestine. It heaved against my ribs. It pressed like frozen metal outward in every organ. This crying came from the pit of my belly, from my liver. It heaved up like bags of leaves raked. It heaved up like a split water pipe. Lying on the bed and hating its solidity, I sobbed so that wails came out gasps, as though I were punched, as though I were repeatedly falling on my ribs and head. Crying obliterated words. It was stronger than song. It was harder than sleep. I could not feel the tears. My face was aching, deformed, a melting candle. Nitin turned off the TV and came upstairs and lay down with me and held me without hushing me. He held me, and at first I stopped crying, and then I realized I didn't need to be alone and the crying came again, like vomiting more the second time though you thought the first time you would faint. I don't want her to die, I cried. I don't want her to die.

Tuesday, October 23. Morning turned Kansas lawns pale brown, streets gray. My empty cereal bowl garnished the dining table. The white cat leaned against my leg while I drummed my fingers and listened to the ICU phone ringing. The nurse answered, a sugary voice through the cordless handset. A flash of pumpkin hair, lacquered fingernails. I smiled. "How is Joyce this morning?"

"She's stable," the nurse said. "But then she would be, as she's fully dependent on the respirator now. It's all that's keeping her alive."

Detachment, a slow and gentle uprooting. Ice in the pit of my stomach. Mechanical response in my limbs, my voice. "Has anyone told my parents?"

"No, not yet. They haven't been in this morning."

"Oh, this is important. Someone has to tell my parents. They don't want to keep Joyce alive on the respirator. They've already decided. The doctor's talked to them. They know it's time."

"I see."

Ice churning in my stomach, grinding. The white cat rubbed his head on the toe of my boot. "Could you—please tell them that you talked to me. Please tell them that I know."

I sat at the table, in the big, quiet house, alone. I should be leaving for work right now, I thought. I won't call Nitin yet. I won't call work. I picked the white cat up, my hands under his slender haunches and fluffy belly. I scratched his head. He cossetted himself in the soft pit of my skirt and closed his eyes. The phone rang.

Mama greeted me, her voice even, gentle as a bend in a calm creek under the pines. "Thank you for telling them to find us," she said. "It's what we wanted."

"I'm going straight on to your house," I told her.

"That's probably best," she said. "Don't come here."

I pictured her silvered fluff of hair, her perfectly ironed, colorful rayon blouse, her straightened shoulders. I pictured Daddy's lost eyes, his chin in his hand. Don't be alone, I thought. "Have you called Harry?"

"He came this morning," she said. "He was here. Ann, I'm going to be in the room with her," Mama said. Her slow voice swung and creaked, a song to a baby. "I told your daddy he doesn't have to go. He doesn't want to be there." She sighed. The ice inside me melted under my mother's breath. "I think that's best, don't you?"

"I love you," I said.

"I love you, too," Mama told me.

Where is the line between belief and knowing? Where did my mother cross that line? As she walked down the hallway to hold my sister's hand, or while the doctors and nurses suctioned Joyce's mouth, inched the tubes out of her throat? Where is the line between knowing and surrendering? Did Joyce cross that line?

I wanted to turn the car toward Tulsa. I wanted the doctors, the nurses to be part of our lives. I wanted people back, people I had let go. I drove, my mind a blank granite wall, until I drove past the old river road, past the turn to the little brick house. I drove through Muskogee. I drove down the long, tree-lined hill into the green lap of Honor Heights park. The last summer roses clung to their stems. Christmas lights hung small and dark, high in the trees. I walked to the back of the small, shrub-circled pond, to a clearing under a pin oak, where grief knocked me down. Grief shredded the lungs, opened them as if for the cold, pure air of some planet humans were not fit enough for. Was she dead already? Had she gone by now? Where is the line between hope and knowing? Where did my father cross the line? Daddy, did you sit alone? Did you look out the window and wait?

They had finally put a chair for Mama in Joyce's room, only a week before. It wasn't needed now. Joyce lay in the quiet mansion of her body with her eyes closed, not a flutter of eyelash, not a gleam of blue. Her breath was not her own. Mama watched her daughter's smooth and child-like face slip from life to death. Mama watched the last breath fall, then collapse. Mama watched the pulse line flatten, watched the monitors fall dark. Mama was with Joyce when she died. Nurse Carol stood beside Mama, and held her.

Joyce died of complications from morbid obesity. She weighed five hundred and fifty pounds when she went in the hospital, and a hundred pounds less when she died six weeks later. Those numbers were important once. But now I have remembered her.

Joyce is buried between Grandma Hester and Great-Grandma Roberts, in a casket, in the earth, under a marker that bears her name over the single word, "Teacher." I love her still. My grief and love are separate.

I do not have to grieve her to love her now.

ACKNOWLEDGMENTS

My parents' generosity and trust made this book possible. I remain humbled and tutored by their quiet and honest hearts. I'm thankful also to my brother for his acceptance of this project and for the sureness of his own memories, separate from mine.

Kris Stockmyer, one of the world's marvelous readers and most steadfast of friends, read the pages as I wrote them. Her comments, questions, enthusiasm, and solace kept me writing during difficult days.

Early readers—Katie Rose, Elise Rippee, Karen Emery, Peggy Rabbit, Laura Filla, and Caroline O'Brien—helped me remember the power in words. A true friend, Kerri displayed special courage and generosity reading about herself without censorship or hesitancy. Robert K. Erwin, dear friend and unstinting critic, with us no longer, heartened me with his insistence that I make something of this project.

A host of friends, neighbors, and family, including the amazing Pai family in India, provided continual support. Cyndi Robidoux comforted me throughout my sister's illness and through the writing of this book. Linda Kerby, medical editor par excellence, and Dr. Gregory Curry kindly lent their services looking over text related to medical conditions. I was thrilled to work with a terrific copyeditor, Lori Kozey, who approached and improved the text with delicate precision and admirable, alert logic.

My oldest friends, Tracy Riley, Larry Van Meter, and Kara Van Meter have fed me with a love of books, words, and ideas for two decades. Kara responded to the early draft with love and compassion, healing a measure of grief and helping to open my heart.

Finally—no acknowledgment is sufficient for Nitin, who is everything to me: my universe without words, my universe of all the words, partner and dearest friend, husband and most wonderful traveling companion. May our love always be larger than the incidents of our lives.